# tools for cooks

# tools for cooks

Christine McFadden

foreword by Anne Willan
photography by Mark Williams and David Munns

jacqui
small

*This book is dedicated to the late Alan Fletcher, the designer whose work continues to inspire.*

First published in 2000 by Jacqui Small LLP
an imprint of Aurum Press Ltd
7 Greenland Street
London NW1 0ND

This revised and updated edition published 2007

| | |
|---|---|
| Publisher | Jacqui Small |
| Consultant editor | Nicola Graimes |
| Contributor | Roz Denny |
| Editor | Judith Hannam |
| Designer | Janet James |
| Food stylist | Alice Hart |
| Props stylist | Victoria Allen |
| Production | Peter Colley |

All photography by Mark Williams and David Munns except for the following pages: 67 Gus Filgate, from *Burgers* by Paul Gayler; 71 Peter Cassidy, from *Steak* by Paul Gayler; 94–5 Janine Hosegood, from *Spectacular Cakes* by Mich Turner; 117 and 248 Peter Cassidy, from *For Chocolate Lovers* by The Tanner Brothers; 258 Janine Hosegood, from *Fantastic Party Cakes* by Mich Turner; 290 Richard Jung, from *World Breads* by Paul Gayler.

ISBN-10: 1 903221 85 4
ISBN-13: 978 1 903221 85 3

2010 2009 2008 2007

10 9 8 7 6 5 4 3 2 1

Printed in Singapore

## RECIPE NOTES

The recipes use both metric and/or imperial or cup measurements. Follow the same units of measurement throughout – do not mix the two.

Where possible, use the size and shape of pan specified in the recipe, otherwise the cooking time or the amount of liquid may need adjusting. In the recipe tools lists, the terms 'small', 'medium' and 'large' refer to the following sizes:

### Frying pans
small 18–20 cm/7–8 inches
medium 2–3 litres/2–3 quarts
large 4–5 litres/4–5 quarts

### Saucepans
small 1.3–1.8 litres/1–2 quarts
medium 2–3 litres/2–3 quarts
large 4–5 litres/4–5 quarts

### Spoon measurements
These refer to measuring spoons rather than table cutlery, which varies in capacity. All spoon measurements are level.

### Herbs and spices
All are fresh unless dried are specified.

### Oils
If a recipe requires vegetable oil, use a light oil with a neutral taste, such as sunflower, grapeseed, safflower or groundnut. Blended oils and corn oil are not recommended. If 'olive oil' is indicated, use plain olive oil – a blend of refined and extra-virgin oils. Use 'extra virgin' oil only when specified.

### Other ingredients
Vegetables and fruit are medium-sized unless otherwise indicated. Eggs are large.

# contents

# foreword

A fine tool is a treasure. It curves to the hand, balanced, ready for action. With the right tool, egg whites are whisked in a matter of moments and stones pop from olives. Zest curls crisply from the rind of an orange, with a titillating puff of citrus to the nose. Where would a genoise be without its cake tin, or a fine sauce without a conical strainer? Thanks to the classic black frying pan, an omelette cooks and rolls almost effortlessly onto the plate, so carefully are the sides angled and the handle designed. My own favourite is the mandoline slicer – even the name is an inspiration – which whittles potatoes and other roots so effortlessly into perfect slices, julienne strips, latticed waffles, even dice if you make the right manoeuvre.

Don't get me wrong. I'm not talking about gadgets. Like any serious cook I hate those cheap cutters and plastic gizmos that are touted with such dexterity on the supermarket aisles. They clutter up the kitchen drawer and, as often as not, break the first time you use them. No, what I have in mind are those robust, timeless tools that simplify the cook's life and are built to last – the heavy copper pans, the sturdy rolling pins. My balance scales, for instance, are at least 100 years old and must once have belonged to a shopkeeper as the brass pans are stamped with the yearly assay to prove their accuracy. They weigh 5 kg of merchandise or more to the nearest 5 grams – what electronic marvel does the same?

Treasures do not always come cheap, though one of my most useful implements is a simple metal skewer that I use as a primitive meat thermometer. Most of all, I think of knives, the fundamental tool of any cook. A good knife knows its owner – the grip is polished and worn to accommodate an individual hand. The blade, kept sharp with loving care, performs tasks almost instinctively under its master's guidance. Both work in harmony to achieve miracles of precision and speed.

All these and many other implements are presented in this informative, accurate and well thought-out book. *Tools for Cooks* demonstrates that a fine tool is one of the great pleasures of life, both inside and outside the kitchen.

# introduction

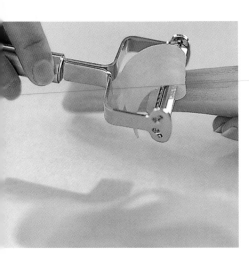

Since writing the first version of *Tools for Cooks* the choice of kitchen tools and cookware has continued to proliferate – hard to believe when the time most people actually spend cooking appears to be less and less.

The most noticeable change has been the increase in the number of websites offering anything and everything the home cook and the professional chef might need – a reflection of our increasingly relaxed attitude to buying online. Alongside the websites, awe-inspiring catering shops continue to supply the professionals and there are numerous high street cook shops for the amateur. Sadly, we have seen the demise of most of the old-fashioned dusty hardware shops that used to offer a surprising selection if you rummaged thoroughly enough.

Along with quantity, quality has continued to improve. Knives, pots and pans come in sleek ergonomic designs and state-of-the-art materials. That said, changes in design are sometimes no more than superficial styling – basic tools have been remodelled, traditional shapes have been smoothed and rounded, and colours range from retro pastels to flamboyant primaries.

No matter how design-conscious a tool is, I find function invariably wins out over style – if the shape is determined by its use, the tool tends to be more credible than one that bows to the short-term dictates of fashion. The criteria for inclusion in this book, therefore, are efficiency and comfort in use, durability in relation to cost and, finally, appearance. I have nevertheless included some 'designer' items simply because they appeal. You will also find some ugly ducklings included for the same reason.

With the choice of tools greater than ever, consumers have an increasing need for information on how and what to tools to choose. For example, how do you find out which type of knife should be used for a particular job? Should the blade be straight or curved, rigid or flexible, long or short? Why do some frying pans have lids and others not? Is stainless steel a better material than cast iron?

*Tools for Cooks* answers all these questions and many more. The book provides essential information for evaluating and choosing new tools and cookware, whether it's a humble potato peeler or a magnificent standing mixer. You'll find explanations of how tools work, if not immediately obvious, and how to use them in the most efficient way. There is also a guide to the pros and cons of different materials and how to care for them.

What you have in your kitchen is very much a personal choice. If you are new to cooking, build your *batterie de cuisine* gradually, allowing it to evolve as your cooking style develops. I tend to use the same trusty tools and pans for years, but when my cooking changes in some way – perhaps as a result of foreign travel, or reading something inspiring, or discovering a new ingredient – I indulge in a new piece of equipment, and what a pleasure that is.

Whether you are a novice or a proficient cook, I hope this new version of *Tools for Cooks* will inspire and inform, as well as open up the path to new and exciting culinary experiences.

Christine
McFadden

# materials choice

This list explains briefly the pros and cons of the principal materials from which cooking equipment is made, and provides guidance on care and cleaning.

## ALUMINIUM

**Uses** Pots, pans, bakeware, roasting pans, kettles, wrapping foil.
**Pros** Cheap, lightweight, conducts heat well and evenly as long as the gauge is heavy enough.
**Cons** Reacts with substances in food and therefore will discolour certain foods or impart a metallic taste. The metal itself tends to discolour and pit. Thin-gauge aluminium warps easily and heats unevenly.
**Care** Wash with hot soapy water, using a scouring pad if necessary. Remove stains by boiling in a weak solution of vinegar or cream of tartar.

## ANODISED ALUMINIUM

**Uses** As for aluminium.
**Pros** Anodising is an electro-chemical process that gives aluminium a hard, dense oxide coating that resists corrosion. Hard-anodizing does not just produce a coating – it changes the molecular structure of aluminium, making it harder than steel while maintaining excellent heat distribution.
**Cons** Dishwasher detergents cause coloured anodised aluminium pans to fade.
**Care** Wash with hot, soapy water. Do not use scouring pads.

## CAST IRON

**Uses** Pots, pans, griddles, grill pans, casseroles, baking dishes.
**Pros** Durable, strong, does not warp, conducts heat evenly and retains it well. Marvellous for long, slow cooking.
**Cons** Very heavy, so best for a pan that remains fairly static during cooking, e.g. a casserole. Its density makes it slow to heat. If dropped on a hard floor, it may break. If uncoated (with enamel or a non-stick surface), it needs seasoning with oil to prevent sticking and rusting.
**Care** Avoid washing uncoated cast iron; wipe with paper towels. Remove stuck-on food by lightly scouring under hot running water. Dry well and coat with oil before storing. Brush the cooking surface with oil before each use, then wipe off before adding oil for cooking. Wash coated cast iron with hot, soapy water but do not scour. To remove stubborn residue, leave the pan to soak for an hour or two.

## COPPER

**Uses** Pots, pans, gratin dishes, roasting pans, egg bowls, moulds.
**Pros** The traditional choice of chefs as it is unbeaten for rapid and uniform heat conduction. Lasts for ever.

**Cons** Pricey and needs cosseting. If unlined, reacts with most foods, causing discolouration and mild toxicity if contact is prolonged. Unlined copper does not retain heat well. The traditional tin lining blisters or melts if overheated. Silver lining blackens on contact with the air and sulphurous compounds in some foods. Needs re-lining periodically.
**Care** Wash with hot, soapy water. Never use scouring pads. Soak to remove stuck-on food. Dry with soft cloth to bring up the shine. Use a proprietary cleaner for the outside, or rub with salt and vinegar or salt and lemon juice. Buff up the inside of silver-lined pans with a proprietary cleaner.

## EARTHENWARE

**Uses** Casseroles, mixing bowls, gratin dishes, baking stones.
**Pros** Non-reactive, cheap, retains heat well and, as it is porous, moisture. Excellent for slow, moist cooking in the oven, or for use in a microwave oven.
**Cons** Dislikes sudden or extreme temperature changes. Not flameproof, but good-quality earthenware can be used on a heat diffuser over a low flame. Large rectangular and oval oven dishes are more prone to heat fracture than round ones.
**Care** Wash glazed, or partially glazed, pots with hot, soapy water without scouring. Completely unglazed pots such as a chicken brick or potato baker should be scrubbed clean with salty water. Don't use detergent as this will taint the food.

## POLYTETRAFLUOROETHYLENE (non-stick coatings)

Trade names include Probon, Silverstone, Tefal, Teflon, Xylan.
**Uses** Pots, pans, roasting pans, grill pans, griddles, casseroles, bakeware, utensils.
**Pros** Modern non-stick coatings are tough and long-lasting. Non-reactive and easy to clean, they are a boon for pans used for foods that stick, such as milk, and vital for low-fat cooking.
**Cons** The coating eventually wears off. Use utensils made of materials that are softer than the coating to prolong its life (e.g. wood, rubber or plastic). Not usually dishwasher-proof.
**Care** According to instructions. Avoid scouring and abrasive powders. Soak in warm water to remove stuck-on food.

## PORCELAIN

**Uses** Soufflé dishes, ramekins, gratin dishes, tart pans.
**Pros** Looks fragile but can withstand heat so makes excellent oven-to-tableware. Retains heat and conducts it evenly. Can be used briefly under the grill. Non-porous and non-reactive.
**Cons** Extreme temperature changes will cause cracking. Needs heat-diffuser if used on the hob. Can be hard to clean.
**Care** Wash in hot, soapy water. Soak to remove stuck-on food. If scouring is needed use a plastic pad.

## STAINLESS STEEL

**Uses** Pots, pans, roasting pans and racks, bowls, kettles, knives, utensils.

**Pros** Long-lasting and hygienic. Contains chrome, which is what makes it stainless, rustproof and non-reactive. Stainless-steel pots and pans also contain nickel. They may be described as 18/10, which means the ratio of chrome to nickel is 18% and 10% respectively. It is virtually immune to corrosion or pitting. Stainless steel used for most kitchen knives contains a lower level of chrome – at least 12% – and 0.15–0.80% carbon. Because of the reduction in chrome, it is more prone to staining, but the carbon provides strength.

**Cons** Poor and uneven conductor of heat. Manufacturers overcome this by giving pans a three- or five-layer sandwich base containing highly conductive metals such as aluminium or copper. Good stainless-steel pans have a base containing at least 5mm of aluminium or 3mm of copper. In the best-quality pans, the sandwiched layer continues up the sides, which prevents hot food from sizzling and sticking.

Stainless steel is not entirely stainless – it will discolour, stain or spot if left in contact with hard water, salt water, lemon, vinegar or even some detergents if not rinsed and dried carefully after washing. Small pits may form.

**Care** Clean with hot, soapy water, using a nylon scourer if necessary. Avoid bleach or harsh abrasives. Soak burnt-on foods. Remove stubborn stains with a stainless-steel cleaner.

## STONEWARE

**Uses** Casseroles, storage jars, bowls.

**Pros** Stronger than earthenware as it's fired at a higher temperature. Non-porous so does not need glazing. Ideal for dishes that need long, slow cooking in the oven.

**Cons** Does not take kindly to radical temperature changes.

**Care** As for glazed earthenware.

## TEMPERED GLASS

Flameproof glass (Pyroflam), and ovenproof glass (Duralex, Pyrex)

**Uses** Flameproof: saucepans, casseroles, baking dishes. Ovenproof: casseroles, baking dishes, bowls, measuring jugs.

**Pros** Both types retain heat well, are non-reactive and are ideal for the microwave. Flameproof glass can be used on the hob and in the oven, and can be taken from freezer to oven.

**Cons** Flameproof glass is expensive. It conducts heat unevenly, so develops hot spots when used on the hob, causing food to stick. Ovenproof glass may crack at extreme temperature changes. It must be used with a heat diffuser on the hob.

**Care** Soak in hot soapy water to remove burnt-on food. Avoid metal scourers or harsh abrasives.

## TITANIUM

**Uses** Casseroles, frying pans, sauté pans, grill pans.

**Pros** A rock-hard, light-weight metal that is naturally non-stick and virtually corrosion-resistant. It is great for low-fat cooking – the food sizzles round the pan with no oil. You can use metal utensils without causing damage.

**Cons** Expensive. Cannot be used on induction hobs.

**Care** Wash with warm, soapy water; do not scour.

## VITREOUS ENAMEL

**Uses** Pots, pans, casseroles, pie dishes, bowls, roasting pans.

**Pros** Used to coat cast iron, aluminium or steel. Gives an easy-to-clean, non-porous coating that is taint- and scratch-proof.

**Cons** May chip if used with sharp-edged metal utensils.

**Care** Wash with hot, soapy water. Do not scrub with harsh abrasives. Leave to soak if necessary.

cutting,
grating and
peeling

Next to your hands, the knife is probably the most important tool in the kitchen – it is certainly one of the most basic and ancient. Even though knives, like many cook's tools, have undergone changes in design and superficial styling, the same basic principles still hold true: sharpness, balance and comfort in use. If your chosen knives meet these criteria, and you treat them with care and respect, they should last your entire cooking life.

# cook's knives and accessories

## basic blades

All knife blades are made of steel, which is why, traditionally, they have been manufactured in metal-working towns such as Solingen in Germany and Sheffield in England. The composition of steel varies, the amount of carbon present determining the blade's ability to hold its edge. Traditional carbon-steel blades are sharper but the metal stains and corrodes so other agents must be added. 'Stainless' steel contains chromium, which is rustproof but also more difficult to sharpen. Today, good-quality knives are made of high-carbon, no-stain steel, which is not quite stainless. Despite the carbon element, these knives neither rust nor corrode.

Blades are either forged or stamped, and the difference in quality is obvious. Forged blades are evenly balanced and beautifully tapered at the cutting edge, which results in greater flexibility. A stamped-bladed knife is thin and flat, and feels handle-heavy. You'll need to grip it more tightly and exert more pressure towards the front to compensate.

## choosing knives

Choose knives individually – don't be tempted to buy sets. Hold a knife to assess it. It should feel heavy for its size and evenly weighted, neither front- nor back-heavy. Do not be put off by weight – a heavy knife is more effective than a light one, and requires less effort to use.

The handle of the knife should be comfortable to hold. If it has rivets, the tops should be smooth and flush. Make sure the bolster (see 'Knife speak', page 19) fuses smoothly with the handle.

Each knife is designed for a specific purpose, so think about the types of food you regularly prepare before making a choice. Ideally, you should try to use the correct knife for the job. If funds are short, though, opt for the best quality and have fewer knives. It is possible to manage with one decent cook's knife and a paring knife. However, the six basic knives shown will give you more scope.

### 1 BREAD KNIFE

The long, serrated blade cuts through bread or any other softish food with a tough crust or skin. Don't use serrated blades for cutting meat or dense-fleshed fruit and vegetables – you'll end up with a jagged mess.

### 2 COOK'S KNIFE

The undisputed workhorse of the kitchen, the cook's knife has a characteristically wide blade and a graceful curve along the entire length of the cutting edge – designed to cope with repeated impact against a chopping board. Use it for chopping or dicing anything from hefty lumps of meat to the finest of herbs. Cook's knives come in a variety of lengths; a 20–25 cm/8–10 inch blade is the most useful.

### 3 UTILITY KNIFE

As its name suggests, this knife can be used for a variety of cutting jobs, including slicing, peeling, paring and, depending on the length of the blade, carving. Although it is not designed for impact (the blade is narrower and less curved than the cook's knife), it can cope with chopping small amounts of not-too-tough food such as mushrooms or prawns. Look for a knife with a 13–18 cm/ 5–7 inch blade.

### 4 TOMATO/SANDWICH KNIFE

Invaluable for tasks for which a bread knife would be too big. The serrated edge is useful for slicing food with a tough exterior and a soft centre, such as salami.

### 5 PARING KNIFE

Basically a miniature version of the cook's knife, a paring knife is used for peeling, scraping and slicing small fruits and vegetables. It is perhaps easier to use than a cook's knife when finely chopping garlic and ginger. The blade must be short – about 8–10 cm/3–4 inches.

### 6 VEGETABLE KNIFE

With its slightly upturned tip and short, curved blade, this knife comes in handy for peeling small, round vegetables, and for gouging eyes from potatoes and seeds from courgettes (zucchini).

# beyond basics

As you become more experienced, you will undoubtedly want to add to your knife collection. The knives shown here are for specialist tasks or for dealing with specific foods. Some of them are expensive, but good knives are good to have, and once you've got them you can easily justify their existence. Buy oysters, eat grapefruit, or fillet your own fish . . .

## knife safety

Knives are dangerous tools. That said, if they are treated with respect rather than with presumption, they will be less likely to cause accidents.

• Never test for sharpness by running your finger along the cutting edge. If you cannot resist touching the blade, brush your finger lightly across it.

• A sharp knife is safer than a blunt one. A blunt knife needs more pressure to cut and could slip.

• If you use a magnetic rack for storage, make sure it is out of reach of children and pets.

• Don't leave knives hidden under soapy water in the sink.

• Don't use a knife with a greasy handle.

• If you leave a knife on the work surface, ensure that neither the handle nor the blade protrude over the edge. The knife could easily be grabbed by a child or knocked onto the floor or, worse still, onto someone's foot.

## 1 HAM/SMOKED SALMON SLICER

This is used for carving thin, elongated slices. The blade is narrow and reasonably flexible, and must be at least 25 cm/10 inches in length. It has a very slight taper through its thickness, enabling you to produce impressively straight slices, rather than veering diagonally off-course – an effect caused by a more pronounced taper.

## 2 FREEZER KNIFE

A freezer knife is not wholeheartedly recommended, as food texture and appearance may suffer if you hack at it while still frozen – it is better to let food defrost before cutting. If you do buy one, a strong, deeply toothed blade is a must. The blade should be longer than the largest item you are likely to cut.

## 3 FILLETING KNIFE

This elegant knife has a thin, gently curved blade, which is sufficiently pliable to remain in close contact with the contours of fish or poultry. The blade needs to be at least 18 cm/7 inches long, and should be kept scrupulously sharp in order to do its job.

## 4 BONING KNIFE

A boning knife has a tapered blade with a sharp point. Blades are flexible or rigid, and 1.5–2.5 cm/$^5/_8$–1 inch in width. A wide, rigid blade is good for a large cut of meat with simple bones, while a narrow, flexible blade copes with poultry or fish.

1    2    3    4

### 5 'UNIVERSAL' CHEESE KNIFE

The blade of this knife has holes that prevent cheese from sticking to it, while the serrated cutting edge copes with hard cheese. The forked tip assists with transferring cheese to a plate.

### 6 PARMESAN KNIFE

The rigid, leaf-shaped blade of this dumpy little knife prizes chunks from hard cheeses such as Parmesan. Embed it in the cheese and twist.

### 7 GRAPEFRUIT KNIFE

The long, thin, serrated blade, with a curved tip, neatly cuts between the pith and flesh, following the contours of the fruit.

### 8 OYSTER KNIFE

Two short, arrow-shaped cutting edges prize open the shell, breaking its vacuum. The guard at the hilt protects the hand and also prevents the knife from thrusting into the shell and out the other side. The pointed tip is used to sever the oyster meat from the shell.

5

6

7

8

9

### 9 CARVING KNIFE AND FORK

A carving knife glides cleanly through meat as if it were butter, while the fork enables you to anchor the meat in place without piercing it. Choose a knife with a blade that is at least 20 cm/8 inches long. This one has a beautifully subtle taper along the back, creating a narrow tip for assiduous probing of meat and bone. The generous curve on the underside effectively extends the cutting edge. The fork has bayonet prongs, rather than the curved type that follow more closely the contours of the meat. Press the sides of the prongs firmly down on the meat to hold it while you carve.

## knife speak

**BUTT** The downward-curving tip of the handle. This cushions your hand against the impact of chopping.
**HANDLE** The part attached to the tang. Make sure it feels comfortable and is neither too large nor too small for you to grip firmly.
**TANG** The unsharpened part of the knife blade that extends into the handle. The longer the tang, the better balanced will be the knife.
**BOLSTER** This is the splayed metal section on a forged knife blade that butts up flush to the handle. The bolster strengthens the blade and keeps your hand away from the cutting area.
**BLADE** The flattish part of the knife that forms the cutting edge.

# japanese knives

When it comes to knife making, the Japanese have turned science into an art. Artisan blacksmiths in Japan have become hallowed knife masters whose handcrafted knives can cost a great deal of money. It is no surprise, therefore, that many of the world's leading chefs cherish their Japanese kitchen knives because, with care and regular sharpening, they can last for decades. The reasons they do so are multiple.

First, the choice of material is paramount. Most Japanese knives are made with home-produced rather than imported steel combined with other elements for hardness, durability, rust-proofing and so on.

Steel is an alloy of iron and carbon. Carbon hardens the steel and a good knife will have a high carbon central core. Tempering the alloy (heating and cooling between extremes of temperature) also increases the strength of the steel. The addition of some chromium prevents the steel from chipping and rusting, but if too much is added, the blade becomes too hard to sharpen.

High-quality knives use the elements molybdenum and vanadium instead of chromium to toughen the steel. The steel is then laminated, layered or folded during the blade-making process for extra strength.

A good knife blade will be given a Rockwell rating; this is the degree of hardness of the steel alloy. Look for a rating of at least 56–58; the higher the rating (up to 66) the better the quality. A top-quality knife described as 'triple layer' will have a hard central carbon core for a sharp cutting edge with softer outer layers for efficient sharpening.

## choosing a japanese knife

Although all Japanese knives are a joy to the eye, make your choice according to need and how you cook, rather than looks. The best blades are designed to glide through flesh or a texture in one smooth action. Long blades are perfect for slicing through soft raw flesh, tomatoes, vegetables and meat. The name of the blade (not the brand name) gives a clue for its intended use. Blades sharpened on one side (bevelled edge) are easier to re-sharpen. Wider blades are best for chopping.

1

2

### 1 YANAGIBA (WILLOW LEAF)
The blade looks like a slender leaf. The bevelled, single-edge blade is perfect for slicing wafer-thin fish for sashimi and sushi. Also useful for cutting raw carpaccio meats, but, being long and slender, it is not a knife for chopping.

### 2 BRIETO PRO
A breathtakingly elegant long knife that is as light as a feather. Designed for slicing through both raw and cooked fish and meat, the scalloped, heat-treated blade makes for cleaner cut slices that neither stick nor compress.

### 3 USUBA
A high carbon steel cleaver perfect for dicing onions or cutting fine julienne strips. The large comfortable handle and rounded blade makes it perfect for rocking during chopping and the wide blade can then scoop up the finely chopped vegetables.

### 4 SANTOKU
This blade shape is perfect for slicing, dicing and mincing. Created by Takeo Murata, one of Japan's great knife masters, this blade (made of carbon-hardened steel with added tungsten) has a distinctive black coating caused by the oxidising process which produces a protective layer yet is still very easy to sharpen. It is regarded by many as one of the best knives in the world.

### 5 PETTY
A smaller utility knife with a blade made from a 49 layer of nickel steel (called Damascus steel in the trade) encasing a central core of exceptional high carbon steel. The combination of softer outer layers and a hard core means this blade is as sharp as a surgical scalpel and holds this sharpness for a long time. The distinctive wavy pattern (or metal wood) is typical of this very high-quality steel and gives the metal an almost non-stick surface.

## 8 CLEAVER

Used throughout the Orient, the cleaver is equally useful for demolishing bones or shredding spring onions. The blade is thick and rigid throughout most of its width, before tapering abruptly to a sharp bevel. The greater the weight, the less effort required, so buy the heaviest cleaver you can use with comfort. A 15 cm/6 inch blade is about the right length. This modern-style cleaver has a seamless blade and handle, which makes it easy to clean. Use the hole to hang it on the wall out of harm's way.

## 9 DEBA

Somewhat surprisingly, the medium-length, wide-bladed deba is used for the delicate task of boning and filleting fish. This is made possible by Japanese-style grinding, in which the blade is bevelled over a wide area on one side and the opposite side is left flat. This creates a razor-sharp, acutely angled cutting edge that slips effortlessly between flesh and bone.

## 10 LONG YANAGI

Sometimes called a sashimi knife, the long yanagi is single-bevelled like the deba (see above). The blade glides through raw fish, producing immaculately straight, paper-thin slices for sushi. The knife is also used to slice and chop vegetables, and to produce intricate oriental garnishes.

## 6 ZIRCONIUM CERAMIC KNIFE

Ceramic is second only to diamond in the scale of degrees of hardness. Hard to imagine, perhaps, but this utility knife has been fire-hardened with extreme heat and glides effortlessly through meat, fish, fruits and delicate salad leaves without staining or bruising. It cannot, however, be used as a chopping knife since, being brittle, it could snap. It won't rust or discolour and is best used on a wooden board. You can only sharpen it (occasionally) on a diamond steel.

## 7 KODEBA

This short-bladed 'brother' of the traditional Japanese deba knife (9) is perfect for filleting fish, chopping heads and gutting bellies. It also makes quick work of shredding greens and herbs. In fact, it is a safer alternative to the Western narrow paring knife. Although only one side is sharpened, the other has a slight concave finish so food won't stick to it.

'A good knife knows its owner – the blade, kept sharp with loving care, performs tasks almost instinctively.'

**ANNE WILLAN**

# knife storage

Store your knives in a knife block so the blades are protected and the knives are easily accessible. A wall-mounted magnetic rack is another option, though some people question the safety of these. Don't store knives loose in a drawer, as the cutting edges can be damaged by impact with other knives and utensils. Damage will be caused, too, by dumping knives in the sink. Some of the better-quality knives are dishwasher-proof, but if yours are not, wash, rinse and dry them individually immediately after use.

**3** **KNIFE BLOCK**
Instead of the usual slots, which can be fiddly, this block has tightly packed nylon filaments that hold knives without scratching them.

**4** **MAGNETIC KNIFE BLOCK**
A slim, freestanding knife block made by a reputable, long-established Sheffield knife manufacturer. It has a large magnetic surface and a steel holding bar for extra safety. The block is supplied with five useful classic knives (of which three are shown here), from a small paring knife and standard cook's knife to a serrated bread knife.

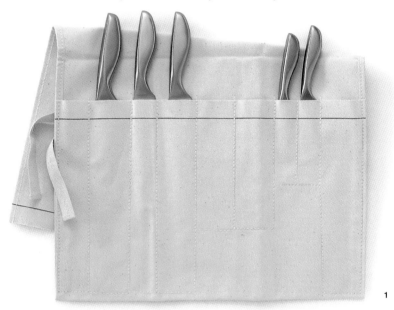

**1** **FABRIC ROLL**
For cooks on move, the old-fashioned heavy canvas pocketed roll keeps favourite knives in their own special pouches, whatever the length. You slip them in, fold over the flap, roll and tie. The fabric is strong enough not to let any sharp ends poke out and accidentally stab you en route. Even better, you can sew on a name tab and, when the outside gets a little grubby, pop the roll (*sans* knives) into the washing machine for a good clean.

**2** **MAGNETIC KNIFE RACK**
The simplest way to store knives. You simply press the metal blades onto the double magnetic strip, heavy handle uppermost, and gravity does the rest, keeping the knives at the ready.

# knife sharpeners

To keep your knives in prime condition, give each one a few strokes on a steel whenever you use it. Fast, flamboyant sharpening is not essential. More important is maintaining a 20° angle and sharpening the full length of the blade (see 'Using a Steel', opposite).

Treat the blade with care by using a wooden or polyethylene board to chop on. Don't use a plate or the work surface, as hard materials such as glass, granite or metal will harm the cutting edge.

## 2  WHETSTONE

A professional quality carborundum sharpening stone must first be soaked in cold water then placed flat on a work surface. Then the blade of a knife (fitted with a small metal guide clipped on top) is drawn several times down it at a shallow angle of 10–15°. Knives sharpened on one side only (mainly Japanese) should be ground on only the cutting side, otherwise grind both sides. Traditional whetstones are a once-in-a-lifetime purchase. They come in different grit finishes – for general use, aim for a brown, medium 1000 grit finish. This model comes fixed inside a plastic holder with non-slip feet.

2

## 1  V-SHAPED SHARPENER

The outer casing houses cunningly arranged, crossed pairs of steel rods set on springs and positioned at the 20° sharpening angle. The rods mimic the action of a conventional steel as the blade is drawn across them. This is a good tool for those who have difficulty using a steel.

1

## 3  SHARPENING STEEL

Somewhat surprisingly, a steel works not by sharpening, but by realigning the molecules that form the cutting edge. They are knocked out of alignment by repeated chopping.

A steel needs to be made of a substance that is harder than the tool to be sharpened. Ceramic or diamond-coated steels are hardest of all. Traditional steels are cylindrical with grooves running along the length of the rod, but some are oval or flat and others still have smoother surfaces. The finer the surface, the keener will be the finish. Choose a steel with a shaft that is longer than the blade of your biggest knife.

This superb steel is diamond-coated and has a flat, relatively smooth surface, providing greater contact than a cylindrical steel.

3

## 4 WATER WHEEL SHARPENER

For those who find the technique of using a traditional whetstone a tad tricky to master, a quick and easy way of keeping those blades at the cutting edge is to use a hand-held wheel sharpener placed flat on a work top. Looking like the small metal sharpener your grandma may have used, this sharpener contains two small stone wheels set at differing angles and is kept wet by pouring water through a small opening. Push the blade through the no.1 groove 8–15 times, depending on the knife quality, then through the no. 2 groove a few times more. Perfect for the keen cook.

5

4

## 5 KNIFE SHARPENER

This easy-to-hold hand-sharpening tool has two modules: one for coarse sharpening, another for fine sharpening and smoothing, without the need to wet it first. Suitable for uncoated knives with a straight edge, it suits both right- and left-handed cooks. Keep it out on the work top and draw your knives through it a few times every time you use them for that razor sharp chef's cutting edge.

## USING A STEEL: METHOD 1

Hold the steel vertically on a firm surface. Grasp the knife low on the handle, with the blade at a 20° angle to the steel. Bring the knife down and across the steel, drawing it to you so the tip meets the steel at the base. Reverse the action, holding the other side of the blade against the other side of the steel and pushing away from you. Repeat both actions until the blade is sharp.

## USING A STEEL: METHOD 2

Grasp the steel in one hand and the knife in the other. Place the handle ends of each together, with the blade at a 20° angle to the steel. Raise the elbows and part your hands so the blade travels up the steel, finishing with the tip of the blade against the steel. Repeat, holding the other side of the blade against the other side of the steel. Repeat both movements until the blade is sharp.

# chopping boards

Chopping boards not only protect worktops from scarring, they also prevent knife blades from becoming blunt. As they are used for both raw and cooked foods, they also need to be hygienic enough to cut down on cross-contamination. Professional chefs must conform to strict hygiene regulations and home cooks would do well to copy the same guidelines. To this end the catering industry uses coloured polypropylene boards according to meat, poultry, fish, vegetables and dairy, which are best stored propped upright in a rack. Even if you do not have space for a selection of coloured boards, it still helps to have at least two for raw and cooked foods. Wooden boards, once considered unhygienic because they could not be sterilised are now being reconsidered because they contain natural anti-bacterial qualities. Whatever your choice, always scrub boards with a good detergent (in the direction of the grain) between different foods. Rinse in very hot running water and dry well.

2

## 1 CHOPPING BOARD

Wood is the preferred material for most chopping boards, but is not usually recommended for raw poultry as it cannot be sterilised. It is attractive, easy to care for and least damaging to knife blades. Choose the sturdiest board you can find, preferably 4½ cm/1 inch thick. This one has cleated ends to prevent warping and cracking.

Polypropylene boards, though less pleasing visually, have an advantage over wood in that they can be sterilised with bleach or boiling water – essential after preparing raw poultry. They are also dishwasher safe. The rough-textured surface prevents both the food and the board from slipping, while a groove around the perimeter helps to stop any liquid from overflowing.

1

## 2 ENDGRAIN CHOPPING BOARD

This board is made of of long small pieces of wood (often sustainable bamboo) bonded tightly together with edible glue and then cut horizontally into a thick block. The result is a tough wooden board that won't warp when scrubbed in soapy water. Kinder to knives, being wood, the boards have a natural anti-bacterial quality and can last for years.

## 3 SILICONE FLEXIBLE BOARDS

Lightweight and as slim as a piece of card, these boards come in four colours so you can follow the correct hygiene colour guidelines – green for vegetables and onions, red for meats, blue for fish and yellow for dairy. Perfect for slipping into your luggage when travelling on self-catering trips and easy to scrub well and towel dry for maximum hygiene. They can also be bent into funnels to shoot chopped vegetables straight into a pan.

## 4 DUAL CHOPPING BOARD

Get the best of both worlds with this double layer wood/polypropylene board. The two separate boards are held together by strong magnets but slide apart when pushed sideways. One board is made of beech (the wood used for old country kitchen table tops) and the other of moulded polypropylene. Both boards are easy to scrub with soapy water and heat resistant up to 80°C/170°F. Use the polypropylene board for onion chopping, fish and meats and the wooden board for bread cutting and cheeses. This will help minimise possible cross contamination.

4

3

## filleting flat fish

**1** Place the fish on a chopping board. With the point of a filleting knife, cut the fish to the bone behind the gills, across the tail and round the edge of the flesh. This defines the shape of the fillets. Slice along the backbone from head to tail, down to the bone.

**2** Holding the knife almost flat, slide it under the flesh, beginning at the backbone. Keeping the knife flat, use a gentle sawing motion to ease away the first fillet from the bones. Repeat on the other side of the backbone for the second fillet.

**3** Turn the fish over. Use the knife point to define the shape of the third and fourth fillets, and cut down the backbone as described in step 1. Ease the fillets gently away from the bones as described in step 2.

## boning a whole chicken breast

 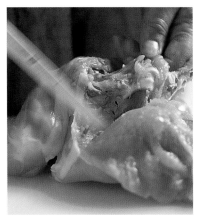 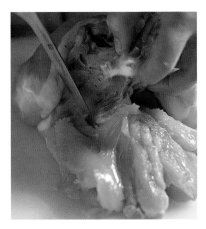

**1** Place skin-side down on a polypropylene chopping board. Grip the breast at either end and twist backwards to separate the breast- and collarbones. Poke your fingers into the flesh to locate the wishbone and remove it with the tip of a boning knife.

**2** With the skin-side facing down, use a gentle scraping motion with the tip end of the blade to carefully cut away the chicken flesh from either side of the breastbone. Once the flesh is cut free, remove the breast-bone.

**3** Cut the flesh away from the ribs, following the contours of the bones and cutting as close to them as possible. Remove the ribs and cut out the remaining cartilage. Trim the breasts neatly according to your chosen recipe.

# carving a leg of lamb

**1** Place the leg of lamb on a carving board with the meatier side uppermost. Wrap the shank end in a napkin. Carve thin slices from the rounded side of the leg, cutting away from you and almost parallel with the bone.

**2** Turn the leg over and carve about the same number of slices from the opposite side, slicing along the length of the leg and almost parallel with the bone.

**3** Insert the carving knife at the shank end of the leg and carve small, thin slices of meat from the bone. Try to carve an equal number of slices from each part of the leg.

# cutting vegetables

Vegetables cut into pieces of a uniform shape and size cook more evenly and improve the appearance of the finished dish. Most vegetables need to be cut in a particular way to suit the cooking method. With its wide, rigid blade and gently curved cutting edge, the cook's knife is the best one to use for chopping, slicing and dicing. A vegetable knife is better for peeling and slicing small vegetables and for gouging the eyes from potatoes. When cutting vegetables, always use a chopping board to protect your knife's blade.

### CHOPPING ONIONS

Peel the onion, leaving the root on, then slice in half from top to bottom with a cook's knife. Lay each half cut-side down on a chopping board. Slice thinly lengthways, stopping short at the root (to hold the slices together), then slice thinly crossways. Discard the piece with the root. This method causes fewer tears than haphazard chopping – the onion is held together during chopping, so tear-inducing chemicals have less chance of escaping.

### SLICING CHINESE CABBAGE

Remove any damaged outer leaves, then use a cook's knife to quarter or halve the cabbage from top to bottom. Place on a chopping board, cut-side down, and slice diagonally, beginning from the stalk end. Angled slices not only look attractive, they also increase the area of cut edges exposed to the fat or liquid, thus reducing the time needed for cooking.

### DICING CELERY

Using a cook's knife, trim the root and leaves from the stems. Remove any tough strings with a swivel peeler. Lay the stems on a board and slice them lengthways into three or four pieces of even width. Slice the wide part of the stems near the root into shorter strips that are the same width as the other pieces. Lay all the strips flat and then slice them crossways to produce small squares.

### JULIENNING CARROTS

Use a vegetable knife or cook's knife to trim the carrots. Peel with a vegetable knife or peeler. With a cook's knife, slice a thin strip off one side so the carrot lies flat. Slice crossways into 5 cm/2 inch pieces. Cut these lengthways into vertical slices about as thin as a matchstick. Stack the slices and slice again into thin strips, keeping the tip of the knife on the board as you rock the blade to and fro.

### CUTTING ROUND VEGETABLES INTO SEGMENTS

Depending on the vegetable's size, use a cook's knife or a vegetable knife. If cutting tomatoes, as shown here, use a very sharp vegetable knife or a serrated knife. Slice the vegetable in half from top to bottom. Place the halves cut-side down on a chopping board and slice in half again. Slice each quarter.

### RIBBON-CUTTING LEAFY VEGETABLES

To make the leaves easier to roll, remove any thick stems by cutting through the ribs with a cook's knife, close to either side of the stem. If the leaves are very wide, cut them in half lengthways. Stack the leaves and roll them into a tight wad. Slice the roll crossways into strips of the required width.

# Hong Kong-style broccoli and baby corn
## KEN HOM

Contributed by Ken Hom, a leading authority on Asian cooking, this easy-to-prepare stir-fry puts the cleaver to good use. As Ken says, 'Once you gain facility with a cleaver, you will see how it can be used on all types of food to slice, dice, chop, fillet, shred, crush or whatever.'

SERVES 4–6 AS A SIDE DISH OR LIGHT MEAL

**TOOLS**
preparation bowls
strainer
cleaver
vegetable peeler
large saucepan
wok or large frying pan
wok ladle or long-handled
   wooden spoon

**INGREDIENTS**
50 g/1¾ oz Chinese dried
   black mushrooms
450 g/1 lb broccoli
225 g/8 oz baby corn
1 tsp salt
½ tsp freshly ground black
   pepper
1 tsp sugar
1 tbsp Shaoxing rice wine or
   pale dry sherry
1 tbsp light soy sauce
3 tbsp oyster sauce or dark
   soy sauce
1½ tbsp groundnut oil
2 tsp dark sesame oil

**1** Soak the black mushrooms in warm water for 20 minutes. Drain them and squeeze out the excess liquid. Remove and discard the stems and finely shred the caps into thin strips. Set aside.

**2** Separate the broccoli heads into small florets, then peel and slice the stems. Blanch the broccoli pieces and baby corn in a large pot of boiling salted water for 3 minutes, then immerse them in cold water. Drain thoroughly.

**3** Combine the salt, pepper, sugar, rice wine, soy sauce and oyster sauce in a small bowl.

**4** Heat a wok or large frying pan over a high heat. Add the groundnut oil and when it is very hot and slightly smoking, add the broccoli, corn and mushrooms. Stir-fry the vegetables for 3 minutes.

**5** Add the seasoning and sauce mixture and continue stir-frying at a moderate-to-high heat for 2 minutes, until the vegetables are heated through.

**6** Add the sesame oil, stir-fry for a further 30 seconds, then serve.

**USING A CLEAVER** Hold the food with your fingertips curled under so your middle knuckles act as a guide for the blade. Don't raise the cleaver higher than your knuckles. Position the blade about 3 mm/⅛ inch from the edge of the food and slice downwards. Control the thickness of the slices by moving your fingers either away from or towards the edge being cut. To slice diagonally, position your fingers at a slant and use this to guide the blade.

# modern tuna nigiri
## EMI KAZUKO

Sushi was Japan's answer to the sandwich. This modern take on an old favourite was contributed by Emi Kazuko, a leading Japanese cookery writer and broadcaster based in London. The key to success in making nigiri, according to Emi, is to mould the sushi rice to an equal size and shape.

MAKES 12 PIECES

**TOOLS**
strainer
large lidded saucepan
wooden spatula
cup
handai or non-metallic mixing
  bowl
pastry brush
metal skewer

**INGREDIENTS**
*FOR THE SUSHI RICE*
225 g/1 cup sushi rice
250–300 ml/1–1¼ cups
  water
2⅔–3 tbsp ready-made sushi
  vinegar or 2 tbsp Japanese
  rice vinegar or white wine
  vinegar
1½ tsp sugar (2 tsp if using
  wine vinegar)

½ tsp salt
450 g/1 lb fresh tuna or
  salmon fillet, skinned
balsamic vinegar
salt and freshly ground black
  pepper
1 spring onion, finely shredded
2 tsp mayonnaise
½ clove garlic, grated
a few drops shoyu (soy sauce)
½ red onion, finely shredded

2 lemon slices, cut into pieces
parsley, to garnish

*FOR THE SAUCE*
1 tbsp lemon juice
1 tbsp extra virgin olive oil
1 tsp shoyu (soy sauce)

**1** Wash the sushi rice thoroughly, changing the water several times until it is clear, then leave to drain in a strainer for at least 30 minutes, ideally 1 hour. Absorbing water slowly makes the rice evenly milky white in colour.

**2** Place the rice in a large, deep saucepan and add the water; the water should not come higher than a third of the depth. Cover and bring to the boil on a medium heat – about 5 minutes. Lower the heat to minimum and, using a wooden spatula, quickly stir the rice from top to bottom. Cover and slowly simmer on a very low heat for 9–10 minutes until the water has been absorbed but bubbles are still forming on top of the rice. Lightly turn the rice over from top to bottom with the spatula and continue to simmer, covered, for another 1 minute. Remove from the heat, and leave to stand, covered, for 10 minutes.

**3** If not using the ready-mixed sushi vinegar, mix the rice vinegar, sugar and salt in a cup and stir until dissolved.

**4** Transfer the hot rice to a handai (wooden sumeshi tub) or non-metallic mixing bowl. Sprinkle the vinegar dressing over and, using the spatula, fold the vinegar mixture into the rice – do not stir. Quickly cool the rice using a fan while folding.

**5** Slice the tuna neatly into 12 sashimi pieces, measuring 7 x 3 x 5 cm/2½ x 1¼ x 2½ inches. Make crisscross slits on one side of 4 pieces, and very lightly grill on the side with the slits under a high heat for a few seconds, then remove and brush with some balsamic vinegar.

**6** Grill another 4 pieces on one side only, and, using a hot metal skewer, make a crisscross burned pattern on the grilled side.

**7** To make the balsamic flavoured tuna nigiri, take a tablespoonful of the sushi rice in one hand and mould into a 1.5 x 1.5 x 3 cm/ ¾ x ¾ x 1¼ inch rectangular finger sushi. Holding the tuna in your other hand, place the rice carefully on top and press gently together. Turn it over and shape into a neat nigiri with the topping uppermost. Brush with some more balsamic vinegar, sprinkle with salt and pepper and garnish with finely shredded spring onion. Make three more in the same way.

**8** For the grilled tuna with the burnt pattern, mix the mayonnaise, grated garlic and a few drops of shoyu, and put a dot of the mixture on top.

**9** For the raw tuna, mix the red onion shreds and the lemon pieces, and put a quarter of the mixture on top of each. Mix the sauce ingredients, season with salt and pepper, and sprinkle over the onion mixture.

**10** Arrange all the nigiri on a serving plate and garnish with a sprig of parsley on the side.

These specialised cutting tools ease fiddly or time-consuming food preparation tasks such as slicing, chopping, shredding and peeling. Sometimes oddly shaped, they are designed to perform a specific task, and the end result is therefore usually neater than it would be if you had not used the tool. These are sound investments rather than fly-by-night gadgets; most have been around for years and have proved their worth.

# more cutting tools

### 1 MEZZALUNA

Used mainly for cutting herbs, the mezzaluna ('half-moon' in Italian) works on the same principle as a cook's knife – a curved blade rocks back and forth over the material to be chopped. The two handles enable you to exert an even downward pressure, while the crescent-shaped blade increases the length of the cutting edge. Some types have two, or even three, blades. Though this speeds up chopping, more time needs to be spent scraping off herbs from the blades.

1

### 3 HACHOIR

The half-moon cutting blade and identically shaped bowl are ideal for chopping ginger, garlic or small amounts of herbs.

### 2 MANDOLIN

This stainless steel and black fibreglass model zips through vegetables with the utmost precision. Depending on the shape and position of the blade, you can quickly cut any firm vegetable into slices, matchsticks, waffles or ripples. Just hold the piece of vegetable firmly and pass it across the blades. There are alternative blades, and an adjustable gauge determines thickness of cut. Rubber feet hold it safely in place, and a guard protects your fingers. However, it is expensive.

2

3

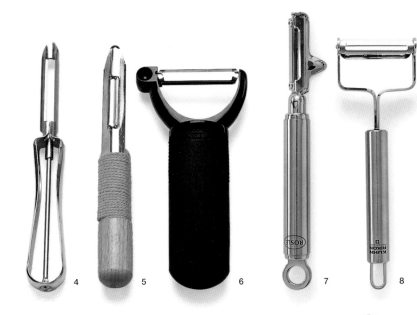

### 4 SWIVEL VEGETABLE PEELER

Practical and economical, the all-metal swivel vegetable peeler has a central slot that is wide and long enough not to trap peelings. The slot is sharpened on both sides, so it suits both left- and right-handed users. The swivel action enables the tool to follow more accurately the contours of the item being peeled, reducing wastage.

### 5 V-SHAPED PEELER

Instantly recognisable by its string-wrapped handle, this traditional British vegetable peeler has a V-shaped blade with a narrow slot, which can become clogged. The sharpened tip digs out blemishes.

### 6 Y-SHAPED PEELER

This smart Y-shaped peeler was originally designed for the manually disabled. It has a swivel blade and the handle is made of a non-slip rubber and polypropylene composite. The extra thickness makes it easier to grip.

### 7 PEELER WITH POTATO EYE GAUGER

Some cooks like vegetable peelers that strip off skins with a side action, others a model that pulls downwards – it's personal preference. This side-swivel peeler has an extra sharp blade on both sides and is ideal for right- or left-handed cooks. Plus in the centre is a little metal tongue to gauge out any lurking potato eyes. The robust contemporary design means it could see you through a lifetime of spud bashing.

### 8 DUAL PEELER

For keen cooks who want to imitate their chef heroes with thin julienne vegetable strands without resorting to using a cooks' knife, this stainless steel peeler with one deep serrated edge does the job reasonably well, although the vegetables need to be placed flat on a board first. Also, it is only suitable for carrots and root vegetables, not leeks or spring onions. The plain-sided blade on the peeler will make wafer thin vegetable slices.

### 9 CERAMIC PEELER

The Japanese have perfected the art of razor sharp ceramic blades which can be experienced in miniature with this amazing peeler. Not only does it glide effortlessly through vegetable and fruit skins, the easy-hold handle and twisting dial makes it ideal for right- or left-handed cooks so you can peel straight down or from the side.

### 10 SOFT FRUIT PEELER

Until now, if you wanted peeled peaches, plums or tomatoes you had to dunk them into a bowl of boiling water then strip off the peel from the squashy fruits. Now, you can peel them like apples or pears using this serrated edge peeler. There is also a 'Y' shape peeler if you prefer. Good, too, for those hairy little kiwi fruits at breakfast time.

### 11 MANGO SLICER

A mango has a large flat central stone with fibrous flesh that can prove quite baffling to prepare. Many a new cook has been caught out cutting it the wrong way. This nifty tool removes the central stone and slices the fruit in half with one firm push on the comfortable cushioned handles.

## 1 CANELLE KNIFE OR LEMON STRIPPER

A protruding, V-shaped tooth gouges out thin lengths of peel from citrus fruits. The knife can also be used to cut narrow grooves from unpeeled cucumbers or mushrooms, creating a scalloped edge when the vegetables are sliced. The tool shown is for right-handed use only, though left-handed models are available.

## 2 CITRUS ZESTER

Five sharp-edged holes set into an angled blade tip produce flavoursome wisps of citrus zest to use for decorating cakes and desserts. The blade's shallow angle ensures that it cuts only into the zest, or outer surface of the peel, rather than into the bitter pith.

## BEAN SLICERS

3 This sturdy, cast-iron slicer is useful for processing large quantities of any type of bean. Beans are fed through slots into the path of three very sharp blades set into a disc that revolves as you turn the crank handle. They emerge as paper-thin, diagonally cut slices with no evidence of stringiness. One possible drawback is that the clamp cannot be attached to a work surface that is thicker than 3 cm/1¼ inches.

4 The small plastic slicer works like magic on runner beans, simultaneously removing the strings and slicing the bean into spaghetti-like strands. Simply insert a bean into the hole and push it through the four blades. When it emerges, grasp the end and pull. Beans need to be crisp and firm, and the tool is practical for small amounts only.

## 5 PIZZA WHEEL

When it comes to dividing up pizza, the pizza wheel outclasses even the sharpest knife. The wobble-free, circular blade carves cleanly through topping and crust, giving neat, manageable slices. The guard protects your fingers from slipping onto the blade.

## 6 CHEESE PLANE

This efficient tool was originally designed for shaving wafer-thin slices from Scandinavian cheeses too pungent to be eaten in larger amounts. The angled cutting edge guides slices through a slot and onto the spade-shaped blade. The blade supports the cheese and stops it from splitting as it is transported to your plate.

### 7 FISH TWEEZERS

These tweezers alleviate the anxiety that sometimes accompanies eating fish. The 15.5 cm/6 inch shafts terminate in rounded tips that are ridged on the inner sides. When clamped together, there is enough surface area to grasp and tweeze out lurking bones.

7

### 8 FISH SCALER

The underside of this solid aluminium tool is covered with close-set, sharp-edged studs that catch on the scales, lifting and ripping them out as you pass the scaler over the fish. If possible, descale your fish before gutting it – the fish will be firmer and rounder, and therefore easier to manipulate.

8

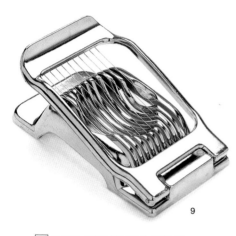

9

### 9 HARD-BOILED EGG SLICER

Ten taut wires attached to a frame cut cleanly and evenly through white and yolk. Since the wires do not drag, the yolk does not crumble.

### 10 FRENCH-FRY CUTTER

This is the tool for those who prefer regimented chips to homely hand-cut ones. Push down the handle to force a peeled potato through a cutting grid. Alternative grids provide a choice of chip sizes, ranging from fat to thin.

10

### 11 MEAT SLICER

For a large family or small caterer where thinly sliced meats are popular, an electric meat slicer makes quick work of whole salami or a boned, home-cooked joint. Good, too, for slicing baker's loaves of bread when you want thin slices for dainty sandwiches. The slicing wheel is operated electrically, leaving you to guide the meat through with a hand press. But take care whilst the wheel is in motion and make sure your fingers are nowhere near the razor-sharp disc.

11

# cutting vegetable ribbons

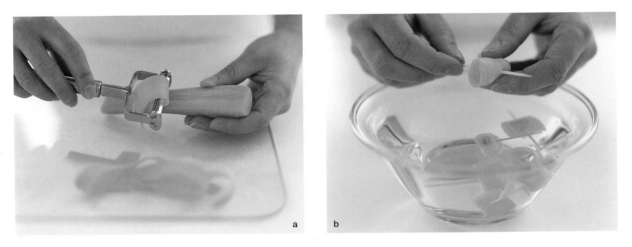

a b

**TOOLS** peeler, chopping board, small/medium glass bowl, cocktail stick (toothpick)

**1** Choose even-sized carrots, cucumbers or courgettes (zucchini) at least 2–3 cm/³⁄₄–1¹⁄₄ inches in diameter. Top and tail, then carefully pull a wide peeler down the length of the vegetable to remove long slices 3–5 mm/¹⁄₈–¹⁄₄ inch thick. Toss into salads or stir-fries.

**2** Carrots can be curled into rounds, secured with a cocktail stick (toothpick) and soaked in cold water for 1–2 hours.

# pinboning fish

**TOOLS** tweezers

When a fish has been filleted, check for any stray pinbones by running your fingertips along the flesh from the tail end to the head. Grip the tip of each bone with tweezers and pull firmly, tilting the tweezers slightly backwards. Check for pinbones around the fins on the side and cut out.

# scaling fish

**TOOLS** fish scaler, large plastic bag

Place the unscaled fish in a large plastic bag to catch the scales and rub the scaler along the fish, starting from the tail. Whole fish are best scaled ungutted, to keep them firm. Fish with soft scales, such as red mullet, can be scaled with your fingers. Sharp scaled fish, such as wrasse, can cut your skin, so take care.

With its two handles and gentle rocking motion, the mezzaluna creates an even downward pressure that speedily reduces a mountain of fresh herbs to a mound, cutting cleanly through the leaves without bruising them.

# pasta with fresh herbs, lemon zest and broad beans

Requiring a range of cutting tools, this recipe combines fragrant herbs such as thyme, savory and oregano with a generous amount of lemon zest to produce a bright, fresh-flavoured dish. Savory goes particularly well with broad (fava) beans, and the toasted breadcrumbs add a pleasing crunch. Prepare the herbs, lemon zest and Parmesan shavings just before you start to cook.

SERVES 4

**TOOLS**
mezzaluna
small cook's knife
chopping board
citrus zester
swivel peeler
small roasting pan for
   toasting breadcrumbs
pasta pot
medium-sized frying pan

**INGREDIENTS**
250 g/9 oz dried flat, long
   pasta, such as linguine or
   fettuccine
200 g/1½ cups podded baby
   broad (fava) beans, fresh or
   frozen
8 tbsp olive oil

1 garlic clove, thinly sliced
1 small bunch flat-leaf parsley,
   finely chopped
good handful mixed fresh
   herbs, such as basil,
   oregano, thyme or savory,
   finely chopped
finely shredded zest of 1½
   lemons

4 tbsp stale breadcrumbs,
   toasted in the oven
sea salt flakes
coarsely ground black pepper
fresh Parmesan shavings, to
   garnish

**1** Cook the pasta in plenty of boiling, salted water until 'al dente' – tender but still with some bite. Drain thoroughly and tip into a warmed serving dish.

**2** Meanwhile, plunge the beans into a pan of boiling water. Bring back to the boil, boil for 1 minute, then drain.

**3** Heat the oil in a frying pan until it is very hot but not smoking. Toss in the garlic, cook for a few seconds, then remove the pan from the heat the moment the garlic starts to colour. Immediately stir in the herbs and lemon zest.

**4** Toss the entire contents of the pan over the pasta. Add a generous seasoning of sea salt and black pepper, and toss thoroughly to mix. Now add the beans and breadcrumbs. Toss again briefly – don't let the beans disappear to the bottom of the dish – and scatter over a few Parmesan shavings.

**USING A MEZZALUNA** Working from one end to the other, and using a rocking motion, chop the sprigs crossways into very thin shreds about 2–3 mm/⅛ inch wide. For even thinner shreds, turn and chop in the opposite direction.

**USING A CITRUS ZESTER** To cut away the outer layer of lemon zest without removing the bitter pith, drag the zester across the peel, exerting firm pressure to produce thin, short shreds. Cutting longer shreds needs more practice.

**TO MAKE PARMESAN SHAVINGS** Hold a lump of Parmesan in one hand and a swivel peeler in the other. Drag the peeler over the surface to shave away thin wafers.

'A Matfer mandolin zips through the squash, cutting them into thin julienne sticks.'

**ANNE WILLAN**

# summer squash salad
## ANNE WILLAN

The recipe for this colourful summer salad was contributed by Anne Willan, founder of the famous La Varenne cookery school at Château du Feÿ in Burgundy, France, and one of the world's most trusted teachers. The salad can be served at once, or after an hour or so, when the vegetables have wilted and softened slightly, though remaining crisp.

SERVES 6–8 AS A STARTER

**TOOLS**
cook's knife
mandolin
bowl
citrus juicer
small flat whisk

**INGREDIENTS**
4 small green courgettes (zucchini), weighing about 450 g/1 lb
4 small yellow courgettes (zucchini) or other yellow squash, weighing about 450 g/1 lb
juice of 2 lemons or limes
2 shallots, finely chopped

salt and freshly ground black pepper
8 tbsp vegetable oil, such as grapeseed or sunflower
2 tbsp chopped fresh dill (or your favourite fresh herb)
fresh dill or other herb sprigs, to garnish

**1** Trim the ends from the courgettes and cut them into 5 cm/2 inch lengths.

**2** Slice the pieces of courgette lengthways on the julienne blade of a mandolin, rotating them as you slice, so that you come up with a julienne of the colourful outer peel and some of the flesh, but discarding the seeds and central core. Tip into a bowl.

**3** Make a vinaigrette dressing by whisking the lemon or lime juice with the shallots, salt and pepper. Then whisk in the oil and add the herbs.

**4** Toss the vegetable julienne with the dressing, taste, and adjust the seasoning. Divide between individual serving plates and garnish with a small sprig of dill or your chosen herb.

**USING A MANDOLIN** To slice vegetables or dense-fleshed fruit, insert the smooth or waffle-edged side of the reversible blade into its slot, then turn the knob under the bearing plate to bring the edge closer to the slicing blade. Once you've adjusted the distance between the two, tighten the knob under the bearing plate. To make sticks, slide the chosen cutting blade into place and adjust the cutting thickness as before. For greater stability, cut the vegetable in half to create a flat surface to rest on the bearing plate. Place the pusher on top, press down firmly, then use the pusher to slide the vegetable towards the blade. Unless you want neatly sliced fingertips, do not be tempted to work without the pusher as a guard.

# black bean mango salsa
## BOBBY FLAY

Contributed by Bobby Flay, one of America's most critically acclaimed chefs, this salsa can be prepared and refrigerated up to a day ahead. The often tricky task of preparing a mango is made much easier with the use of a mango slicer.

SERVES 4

**TOOLS**
mango slicer
large bowl

**INGREDIENTS**
200 g/1 cup cooked or canned black beans, drained
1 mango, peeled, pitted and finely diced
1/2 small red onion finely diced
1 jalapeño or serrano chilli, deseeded and finely diced
4 tbsp fresh lime juice

1–2 tablespoons honey (depending on the sweetness of the mango)
4 tbsp olive oil
4 tbsp coarsely chopped fresh coriander (cilantro)
salt and freshly ground black pepper

Combine all the ingredients except for the salt and pepper in a large bowl.
Season to taste and serve.

**NOTE** If making ahead, bring to room temperature 1 hour before serving.

'The OXO mango slicer blows me away – it gets the job done quickly, safely and perfectly every time.' **BOBBY FLAY**

Scissors and shears cut cleanly, leaving no jagged edges. Many people prefer to use scissors instead of a knife, as more muscular control can be exercised when cutting, and fingers are kept safely out of the way of the blades. A strong pair of kitchen scissors can be used for a range of tasks, such as cutting paper and string, trimming fins from fish and tips from artichokes, snipping herbs and bacon rind, and cutting dried fruit into bite-size chunks.

# tools for shearing and piercing

There are numerous occasions when food or certain types of container need to be pierced, and there are a variety of tools designed to do the job. Basic piercing tools such as skewers and corkscrews are essential kitchen kit. However, some tools are so specialist they border on mirth-provoking; others still are so flimsily made they aren't worth kitchen drawer space. But there are surprises – you'll often find you get attached to a tool and it becomes indispensable.

## 1 KITCHEN SHEARS

The blades of these neat, all-purpose shears have a notch for cutting through poultry joints, while various parts of the handle can be used for opening jars and bottles, prizing off lids, and as a screwdriver. The shears can be taken apart for washing and are dishwasher-proof.

## 2 KITCHEN SCISSORS

These differ from household scissors in having longer blades, and one is usually serrated, making it easier to cut chicken or fish. The best scissors have forged blades and are made of stainless steel, which will not rust. Choose a pair with a screw rather than a rivet, so you can take the blades apart for cleaning or sharpening. Check handles for comfort.

## 3 POULTRY SHEARS

These shears easily sever bones, sinew and flesh. The blades are curved and pointed for intricate cutting, and a notch holds bones firmly during cracking. The strong spring kicks the handles apart, but it is a trap for raw poultry juices and needs thorough cleaning after use. A hook holds the handles together during storage.

## CORERS

To use a corer, push the circular cutting edge vertically through the middle of a fruit or vegetable, then withdraw it, bringing the core out in the cylinder. If you veer from the vertical, remnants of pip and core will be left embedded in the flesh, as they will if the core's diameter is greater than the cylinder's.

4 The shorter apple corer works reasonably well on apples and pears but it is not suitable for anything longer.

5 To core courgettes (zucchini), aubergines (eggplants) and other elongated vegetables, you will need the longer vegetable corer.

2

1          3

## deseeding a cucumber

**TOOLS** melon baller, chopping board

Halve the cucumber lengthways and place seed-side up. Draw a melon baller down the centre pulling out the central seeds in a long sweep. (You can also use the tip of a teaspoon for this task, although it does not result in such a neat job.)

## coring an apple

**TOOLS** corer, chopping board

This works best on apples that are the same length as the corers. Place the apple base-side down on a board and push the corer firmly through the stalk end, ensuring the corer is straight and encloses the whole of the core. When the corer reaches the board, twist it firmly 2–3 times then, holding the apple steady, pull out sharply removing the core. Push this out from the metal tube of the corer. You may have to reinsert the corer again to remove any remaining core.

### 6 | MELON BALLER

The melon baller is useful for occasions when neat spheres of melon are preferable to rough-cut chunks. To use the baller, press it deep into the flesh until juice flows from the hole in the base of the bowl. Then twist and remove. Some ballers have a smaller scoop at the other end, for removing shallow flesh close to the rind.

### 7 | PINEAPPLE CORER/SLICER

This tool does work, but it is probably worth buying only if you eat pineapples on a regular basis. Slice the top off the pineapple, then wind the slicer down over the core. When it reaches the bottom, pull upwards and out will come a continuous spiral of pineapple flesh, devoid of unwelcome brown spots. The shell remains intact, ready for retro dishes such as pineapple boats.

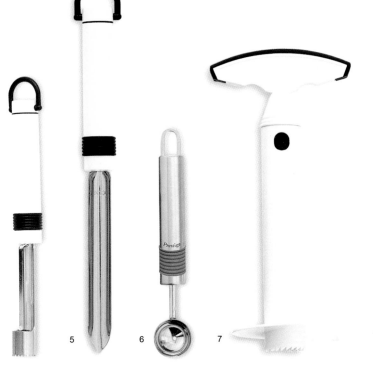

4    5    6    7

8

### 8 | CHERRY/OLIVE STONER

The juiciest olives are sold unstoned (unpitted), so make light work of removing the stones (pits) with a neat, all-in-one action stoner. Good, too, for fresh cherries – simply put a fruit in the middle of the small cup, stalk end uppermost, and press down on the spear to push out the stone (pit) in one easy action.

## SKEWERS

Skewers conduct heat through food, close flaps and hold things in place. They are also used for testing cakes and poultry for doneness, and for piercing small citrus fruits and the skin of fatty birds to allow juice or fat to flow during cooking.

### 1 BAMBOO SKEWERS

These do not conduct heat as well as metal skewers, but they are fine for small kebabs such as chicken satay. Though some cooks advise soaking bamboo skewers in water before use, I never do, and so far have not had to deal with a serious conflagration.

### 4 SMALL ROUND SKEWERS

Sometimes called poultry lacers, these come in a range of sizes and are ideal for sealing poultry orifices and closing flaps. String can be threaded through the eye and used to close cavities more securely. The skewers are also useful for securing small parcels of food. Butcher's skewers are used in much the same way.

### 2 KEBAB SKEWERS

These are made of flat metal to prevent impaled food from spinning round when you turn the skewer over. The most useful size is 25–30 cm/10–12 inches, though there are longer and more flamboyant models for gaucho-style barbecues. Stainless-steel skewers are rust-proof and easiest to keep clean.

### 3 POTATO BAKING SPIKE

Four metal spikes speed up baking by conducting heat to the centre of the potato. There are drawbacks: baked-on starch is very difficult to remove from the spikes, the tool takes up a fair amount of oven space, and if you cook less than four potatoes it becomes unbalanced. The spike is worth having, however, if you regularly bake potatoes for four people.

### 7 'UNIVERSAL' OPENER/JAR WRENCH

Not strictly for piercing, this tool forces open unwilling lids and can cope with several sizes. Serrated inner edges create enough traction to grip and loosen the lid as you twist, while the sturdy non-slip handles allow you to use plenty of force. Various protuberances act as vacuum releasers, crown cap removers and can piercers. The tool saves time, reduces frustration and more than justifies its existence.

## CAN OPENERS

A good can opener should work cleanly and continuously without coming to a halt halfway round the can. It should be effortless to use and feel comfortable in the hand.

### 5

The blue opener is easy to operate and is suitable for both right- and left-handed people. It is marginally less safe than some types, though, as it removes the entire rim of the can, leaving a clean but exposed sharp edge.

### 6

The chrome opener has an easy-to-grip butterfly handle and rounded black plastic inserts that protect the palms. The steel blade hooks over the rim of the can, leaving it in place once cutting is complete.

### 8 BOTTLE JAR OPENER

Even the strongest wrist needs some help when faced with a determined screw-top lid. Slip the larger opening of this stainless steel tool over the neck of a metal bottle or jar top and twist to release it. For a more traditional beer bottle top, use the smaller rectangular opening at the other end.

## CORKSCREWS

Being a firm believer in 'cook's nips', I see the corkscrew as an essential tool. Even if you rarely imbibe, you will need wine for sauces and gravies.

9

### 9  WAITER'S FRIEND™

The original and iconic waiter's friend has been acknowledged world wide for over sixty years. Available in a range of designs and colours, the basic principle remains the same, and most sommeliers would agree that nothing else compares when removing a cork from a bottle.

### 10  WINGED CORKSKREW

Easy to use and reliable, this winged, stainless steel corkscrew has a self-centring frame that sits on the bottle rim, guiding the solid-shafted spiral through the cork. Turn the handle until the wings are fully raised, then press them down to remove the cork.

### 11  SCREWPULL®

The Screwpull® corkscrew by Le Creuset has a comfortable handle and an 'endless', Teflon®-coated, spiral shaft that turns until the cork emerges. The shaft is open, with a well-rounded profile, enabling it to grip corks firmly (solid-shafted spirals do not grip as well).

### 12  LEVER CORKSKREW

This state-of-the-art, lever-based model may look fearsome, but it's easy to use. With the lever fully open and the pincers gripping the bottle, swing the lever up and over to the closed position. This drives the screw into the cork. Swing the lever back to the open position and the cork will emerge.

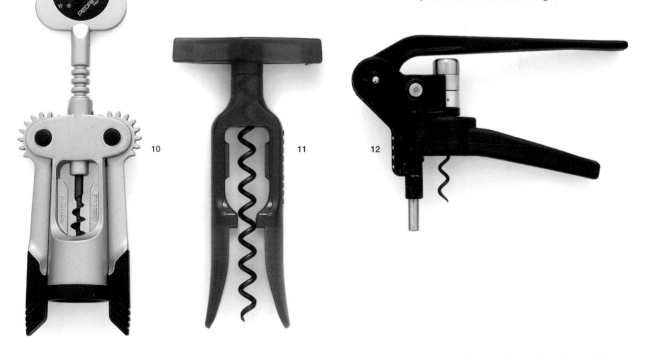

10          11          12

'It is vital to have a
corkscrew around the
kitchen as almost every
recipe has a splash of
wine in it, not to forget
the needs of the cook.'

**FERGUS HENDERSON**

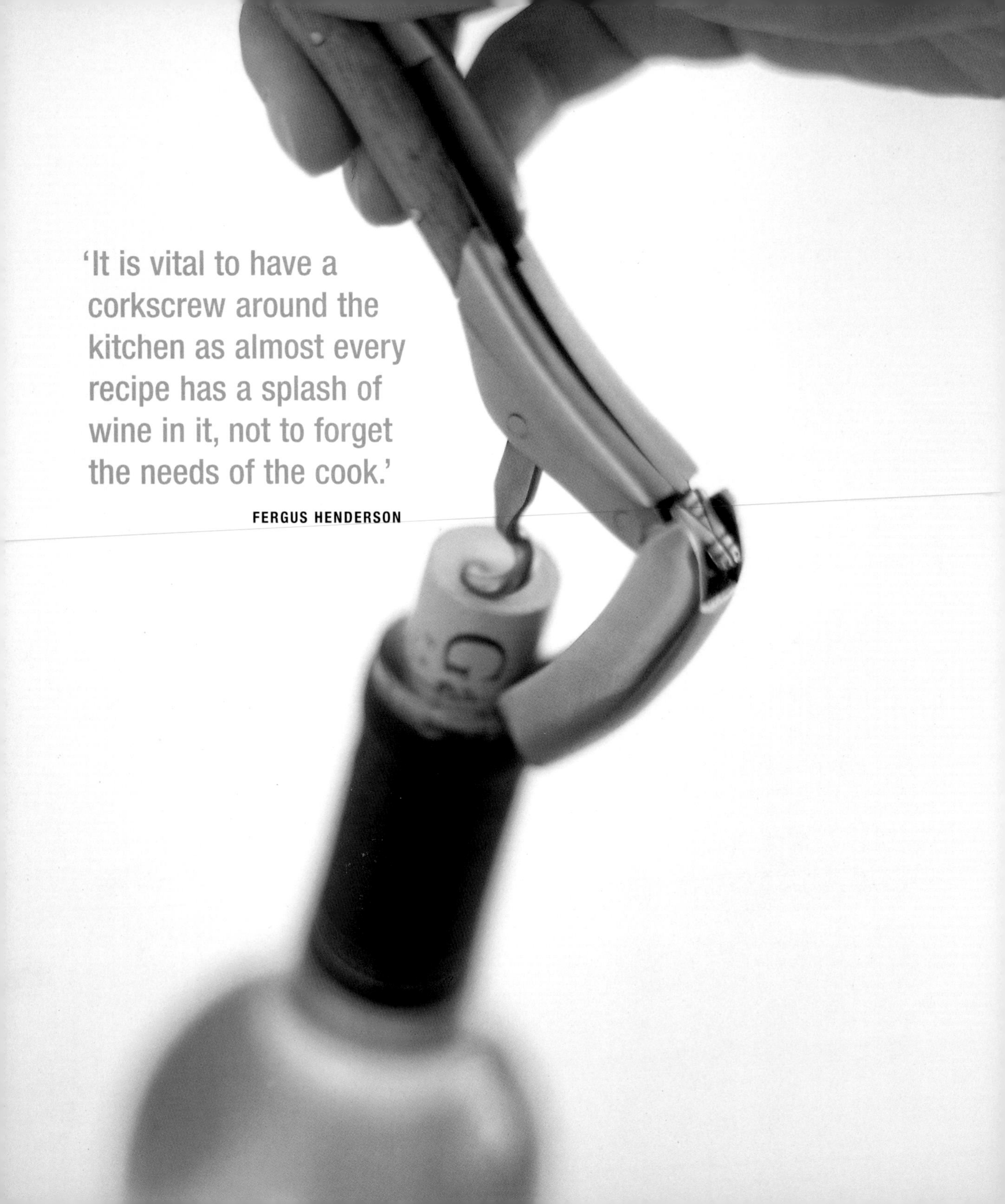

a  b

c

## using a waiter's friend™

Always keep the bottle resting on a table. To remove the foil, rest the blade on top of the bottle flange (a). Exerting slight pressure on the blade, turn the bottle with one hand, and turn the blade in the opposite direction until the foil is severed all round. Close the blade and remove the foil to expose the cork.

Fold out the spiral and lever. With the bottle still resting on the table, position the tip of the spiral in the centre of the cork. Push the spiral into the cork as you rotate the bottle a quarter turn at a time (b). Be sure to keep the spiral vertically centralised in the cork.

Continue turning the bottle until the spiral is embedded far enough for the end of the lever to rest securely on the rim of the bottle. Gripping the neck of the bottle with one hand, and making sure the lever remains in place on the rim (c), pull the blade-end upwards. The cork should slide smoothly out of the bottle with a pleasing pop.

The effort needed to extract the cork depends on the angle of the lever in relation to the spiral in the cork. Synthetic corks are more stubborn than genuine corks, and therefore need more pulling power.

a

b

c

d

# spatchcocked poussins with rosemary-and-orange butter

The best way to grill whole birds is to cut out the backbones with poultry shears and press the carcasses flat. They form neat, flat shapes that cook evenly and quickly. Skewers keep the birds rigid when you turn them and help to conduct heat through to the thickest part of the thigh. Pushing herb butter under the skin keeps the flesh deliciously juicy.

SERVES 4

| TOOLS | INGREDIENTS |
|---|---|
| mezzaluna or cook's knife | 100 g/1 stick unsalted butter, softened to room |
| garlic press | temperature |
| citrus grater | 2 tbsp finely chopped rosemary |
| pestle and mortar | 1 large garlic clove, crushed |
| small bowl | finely grated zest of 1 small orange |
| fork | 1/2 tsp black peppercorns, crushed |
| polypropylene chopping board | generous pinch of sea salt flakes |
| poultry shears or strong | 2 poussins, each weighing about 450 g/1 lb |
| kitchen scissors | a few small rosemary sprigs, to garnish |
| 4 flat metal skewers | |
| grill pan with rack | |

**1** Combine the butter, rosemary, garlic, orange zest, peppercorns and sea salt flakes, mixing well with a fork.

**2** Put the birds on a polypropylene board, breast-side down. Using poultry shears or strong kitchen scissors, cut off the wing tips and lumpy joints at the end of the legs. Remove the backbone and parson's nose (the stubby tail protruberance) by cutting along the entire length of the bird, either side of the backbone (a).

**3** Open out the birds and turn them breast-side up. Press down sharply with the heel of your hand to break and flatten the breastbone (b).

**4** Separate the skin from the meat on the breasts, thighs and drumsticks by carefully inserting your fingers between the skin and the flesh. Push knobs of the seasoned butter under the skin, spreading it as evenly as possible and moulding it to the shape of the birds (c). Cover and leave in the fridge for at least 2 hours, or up to 24 hours.

**5** When ready to grill, arrange the flattened birds so the drumsticks are turned inwards, nestling close to the rib cage. Insert a metal skewer diagonally through the thigh, drumstick and breast on one side and out through the wing on the other side (d). Insert a second skewer in the same way from the opposite side.

**6** Heat the grill until very hot. Place the poussins breast-side down on a rack in a clean grill pan and position the pan 15 cm/6 inches from the heat source. Grill for 15 minutes, then turn over and grill for another 15 minutes, or until the juices are no longer pink when you pierce the thickest part of the thigh.

**7** Pull out the skewers – use oven gloves as they will be hot. Using clean poultry shears or kitchen scissors, cut each poussin into quarters, and pile up in a warmed serving dish. Pour the buttery juices over, scraping up the sticky, tasty sediment from the bottom of the pan. Garnish with a sprig or two of rosemary and serve at once.

'The microplane makes such light work of grating ginger and garlic, zesting lemons and limes and producing feather-light shavings of parmesan that it has become as essential as a sharp knife in my kitchen.' **BILL GRANGER**

A grater is essentially a surface covered with rows of small, sharp, cutting edges and, as such, it accomplishes the work of a knife in far less time and often with more uniformity. Some graters work in two directions, others in one only. When choosing a metal grater, make sure it is made of stainless steel, otherwise it will rust. To clean stubborn debris from the cutting edges, rinse the grater under running water, then scrub with a nailbrush.

# graters

### 1 CITRUS GRATER

Made of acid resistant stainless steel, the lemon grater has very fine perforations. This enables you to grate the zest, or outer surface of the rind, without taking up any of the bitter pith.

1

### 2 PORCELAIN GRATER

This thick, flat porcelain grater (oroshigane) from Japan is a pleasure to use. Instead of perforations, it has rows of pyramid-like teeth angled in two directions. Used for ginger root and daikon radish, the resulting pulp is moist, flavourful and not at all fibrous. The grater can also be used for nutmeg.

2

### 3 CARD

This flexible friendly credit card-style grater has raised rough ridges on one side like a dolly's wash board, When you rub a peeled clove of garlic against them they mince it to a juicy pulp. There are no fiddly holes to clean out afterwards. You simply wash the card under running water.

**GarlicCard**
www.garliccard.com

3

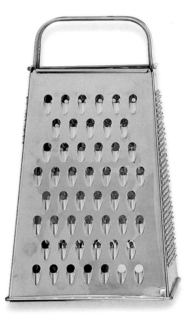

4

### 4 BOX GRATER

A box grater provides the greatest choice of cutting surfaces, ranging from very fine to coarse. It also has a slot for slicing cucumbers or shaving Parmesan. The rectangular base makes the grater self-supporting, which allows you to exert downward pressure more easily. The disadvantage is that the boxy shape makes it awkward to remove the raspings from the inside. This grater is also bulky to store and may not fit easily into a drawer.

### 5 NUTMEG GRATER

Freshly grated nutmeg has a much better taste and aroma than the pre-ground sort, so it is worth investing in a special grater or mill. The nutmeg grater has very fine perforations and a curved surface, both of which reduce the risk of grated fingertips.

### 6 ROTARY GRATER

Ideal for thrifty cooks and for children, the rotary grater deals with scraps of cheese and can also be used for carrots, nuts and chocolate. There is no risk of grating your fingertips as the food is pressed against the rotating drum by a wide covering plate at the end of the upper handle. Extra cylinders provide a choice of perforation sizes.

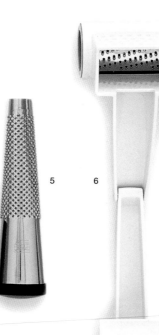

5   6

### 7 MICROPLANE® GRATER

This state-of-the-art grater has rows of ultra-sharp blades in various sizes that cut food precisely and cleanly with no shredding, tearing or clogging. No pressure is required from the user. It has two drawbacks: the price, and the fact that you have to buy more than one grater if you want a choice of fine and coarse perforations.

7

## grating vegetables

Coarsely grating vegetables such as courgettes (zucchini) is an excellent way of ensuring they cook evenly and fast, whether boiled, steamed, braised or stir-fried. To stir-fry, tip the grated vegetables into a pan in which you have melted a knob of butter with a little olive oil. Stir-fry for 2–3 minutes, seasoning to taste.

## grating nutmeg

Nutmeg is at its most aromatic when freshly grated. Use a small fine-holed grater and grate directly over the food. Here a creamy rice pudding is prepared for the oven prior to baking. Cooked spinach, pasta tossed in cream, hot toddies and cappuccino are also enhanced with freshly grated nutmeg.

## grating chocolate

Chocolate is messy to grate so the job is more easily done by remote control. Pop a small square into a rotary grater and grate directly over desserts such as ice-cream sundaes. A little goes a long way and the tool is particularly useful for those who enjoy chocolate but need to watch their weight.

# cannellini bean soup with fontina gremolata
## PAUL GAYLER

A heart warming, lightly spiced soup topped with stringy fontina cheese and spiked with lemon contributed by Paul Gayler, executive chef at the pestigious Lanesborough hotel near London's Hyde Park. Paul was one of the first chefs to create dishes on his à la carte menu specifically catering for vegetarians. Serve with chunks of good bread.

SERVES 4

**TOOLS**
chef's knife
fine microplane
large saucepan
blender
sieve

**INGREDIENTS**
50 g/$1/2$ stick unsalted butter
75 g/$1/2$ cup diced onions
1 garlic clove, crushed
200 g/1 generous cup
  cannellini beans, soaked
  overnight then drained
50 g/$1/3$ cup diced carrot
$1/2$ red chilli, deseeded and
  finely chopped
2 ripe tomatoes, chopped
2 cardamom pods, crushed
1 tsp cumin seeds

1.3 litres/$51/3$ cups chicken or
  vegetable stock
salt and freshly ground black
  pepper

**FOR THE GREMOLATA**
75g/$3/4$ cup Fontina cheese,
  very finely grated
1 tbsp finely grated lemon zest
1 tbsp fresh thyme leaves
2 garlic cloves, crushed

**1** Melt the butter in a pan over a medium heat, add the onions and garlic and sauté for 4–5 minutes until softened. Add the cannellini beans, carrot, chilli and tomatoes then cover and cook gently for 5 minutes.

**2** Next, stir in the cardamom, cumin seeds and stock, and bring to the boil. Reduce the heat and simmer for 1–1$1/2$ hours or until the beans are tender.

**3** Pour the soup into a blender and blitz to a purée, then strain it through a fine sieve to give a creamy texture. Adjust the seasoning and reheat gently.

**4** For the gremolata, mix all the ingredients together in a bowl. Pour the soup into warm bowls, scatter with gremolata and serve straight away.

grinding,
mashing and
crushing

These tools change the size and texture of ingredients, usually by abrading or crushing them between two hard surfaces in a closely confined space. A manual or mechanised rotary movement causes friction, which in turn produces the desired grounds, powder or paste. Using tools of this sort will immeasurably improve the flavour of your cooking, as they allow you to use raw materials rather than processed travesties.

# mills, mortars and mincers

Once crushed or ground, hard-coated ingredients such as coffee beans, peppercorns and other spices release the volatile oils responsible for their distinctive flavours. When they are exposed to the atmosphere, the oils quickly oxidise and lose their pungency. Similarly, the fat in ground or grated Parmesan cheese will oxidise and become rancid before long, and a piece of meat will deteriorate rapidly once ground, because the much greater surface area increases its exposure to the atmosphere and to harmful organisms.

Tools for grinding and grating are therefore invaluable, enabling you to process ingredients at exactly the right moment for maximum flavour and minimum deterioration. Some tools not only grind but also act as storage containers, protecting the contents from the effects of light and air.

## choosing grinding tools

A pepper mill is a must. Choose one that holds at least three tablespoons of peppercorns, or you will be constantly refilling it. The best mills allow you to control the size of the grounds. Often sold as a pair with a pepper mill, a salt mill is useful in humid climates where caking is likely to be a problem.

No kitchen should be without a pestle and mortar. It performs a variety of tasks – grinding spices, making pesto, crushing garlic, for example – and so reduces the need for several different tools.

The other mills are a matter of personal choice. Whether you need them depends on how often you use an ingredient, and whether you prefer a mill or a grater. If you regularly use ground meat, it's worth buying a meat grinder. Yes, you have to clamp it to a table and wash the parts after use, but it repays the effort. You can choose a decent cut of meat, there is no risk of contamination from meat that has previously passed through the grinder, and you can add your own seasonings.

## mill maintenance

Use a pepper mill for pepper and a salt mill for salt. If you use salt in a pepper mill it will corrode the metal grinding mechanism. (A salt mill's mechanism is usually made from a non-corroding material such as nylon.)

• Lubricate the top of the spindle, where it meets the adjusting screw, with a drop of cooking oil. This will prevent rusting and keep the thread in good working order.

• Don't mill over open pans as steam causes rusting and dampens the grounds, which can clog up the mechanism. It's better to mill into a large spoon or over a plate or piece of paper, then tip the grounds into the pan.

• Keep mill bodies clean by wiping them with a damp cloth. Rub wooden mills with vegetable oil occasionally to prevent the wood from drying out.

The first steel peppercorn grinder was launched by the Peugeot family in France in the mid-nineteenth century, half a century before they started to make cars. It is still one of the most reliable grinders on the market. But around 150 years later, in 1998, UK company T&G Woodware launched a new grinding mechanism using ceramic grinders which work on a principle similar to that of old millstones. There is no central spindle and the grinders are not vulnerable to rust or corrosion. You can also grind whole dried spices and woody herbs in these ceramic grinders quicker than it takes to hand crush them with a pestle and mortar.

### 1 METAL MILLS

This stylish, polished metal mill has a pull-down 'laundry chute' refilling system that saves unscrewing and dismantling the top. The grinding mechanism, made from high-quality hardened steel, adjusts to produce a range of fine and coarse grounds.

### 2 WOODEN MILLS

Designed in a classic hourglass shape, these wooden mills have a chromed steel band for adjusting the grounds from fine to coarse. The stainless-steel grinding mechanism is constructed in such a way that there is no metal-to-metal contact, and it is therefore unlikely to wear out.

### 3 NUTMEG MILL

This chrome and acrylic nutmeg mill stores up to four additional nutmegs.

### 5 ELECTRIC SALT AND PEPPER MILL

It might seem like the ultimate in kitchen decadence, but pushing a button on a battery-operated mill with one hand whilst you stir with the other does make sense, especially when a small bulb lights up so you can see into the pan or bowl below as the machine whirls. The stainless steel grinder mechanism has a unique design of a double row of spiral teeth and Peugeot are so confident of its reliability they have guaranteed it for life.

### 6 SPICE MILL

There's no doubt grinding whole dried spices does give the best aroma and flavour to a dish. But grinding small amounts with a pestle and mortar can take time. It is much easier to keep your favourite blend in a mill at the ready. The T&G Spice Mill has the grinding mechanism (using the unique CrushGrind® system) on top, so no spicy dust is left behind on the worktop.

### 4 CRUSHGRIND® MILLS

These matching sea salt and peppercorn mills are made in stainless steel and acrylic capstan shapes. Not only do you get even ground grains from the unique CrushGrind® ceramic grinders at the base, it is much easier to refill the mills without a spindle mechanism in the way. So there are no more stray peppercorns bouncing around the worktop.

# meat grinders

Nearly all carnivores love mince in some form or other. Bolognese, cottage pies, homemade burgers and meat balls are more delicious if made with freshly ground meat from lean cuts. Not only that, but you can choose from lamb, veal, turkey and even game meats or liver for pâtés.

## 1 MEAT GRINDER

A true kitchen classic, this cast iron, hand-cranked grinder funnels meat into the spiral shaft of a revolving screw. From there, it is forced through rotating blades and finally through a perforated cutting disc. Alternative cutting discs can be fitted to regulate the fineness or coarseness of the end product.

## 2 ELECTRIC FOOD MINCING SYSTEM

Serious home cooks and small caterers will find an electric mincing machine takes them into new culinary realms. Not only does it effortlessly mince fresh meat, but it also makes short work of chopping onions, apples and celery, and you can experiment with other foods such as fish and breadcrumbs. The robust mincer comes with three grinding discs of varying thicknesses, and useful settings for making your own homemade sausages.

## 3 MEAT MINCERS

This updated modern meat grinder does not have to be clamped onto a kitchen table (not always possible in 21st century kitchens); it has a suction cup instead. There is a choice of two perforated cutting discs for thin or coarser mince. Plus you can choose a colour to suit your kitchen scheme: white, black or red.

'A hand-cranked mincer is surprisingly satisfying to use. For homemade burgers, meat should be coarsely minced; if it is too finely minced, the burger is likely to fall apart and the texture is less appealing.'

**PAUL GAYLER**

# coffee mills

A coffee mill is a must for connoisseurs. In the same way that freshly ground black pepper has an unbeatable flavour and aroma, coffee beans ground just before brewing make a superior cup of coffee. When choosing a coffee mill, bear in mind the brewing method – filter, espresso, cafetière – as the fineness or coarseness of the grind is dictated by this.

### 1 HAND-CRANKED COFFEE MILL
A leisurely way of grinding beans is with a hand-cranked coffee mill. As you turn the handle, the beans are fed into the hopper and through the metal grinding mechanism. The coffee grounds drop into the receiving drawer below. Based on a traditional design, this clear perspex mill allows you to see the beans being ground. It produces reasonable results, but the grounds are quite coarse.

1

2

### 2 ELECTRIC COFFEE MILL
Working on the same principle as a blender, the two-armed blade of this electric mill pulverises coffee beans in seconds. Though it is compact and easy to use, the grounds are uneven in size and you have to guess how long to whizz for. It is also noisy.

### 3 BURR GRINDER
Burr mills work on the same principle as old-fashioned millstones, grinding coarse foods (in this case coffee beans) between two stones or metal plates. This always gives a uniform size of ground beans no matter how much you put into the hopper above, unlike bladed coffee mills which give a more varied degree of grind. This machine has eighteen different grind settings to match whatever style of hot steaming coffee you want – fine for espresso, medium for filter or coarse for a cafetière jug. The clear view hopper at the top of the machine has a 225 g/8 oz capacity, enough for up to eighteen cups. You choose a setting for the degree of grind then press the number of cups you need to fill and the machine does it in a trice.

3

# pestles and mortars

## 1 SOLID METAL

This solid metal pestle and mortar is designed primarily for grinding seeds and spices. The interior of the mortar has a flat base and straight, outwardly sloping sides, instead of the usual rounded bowl shape. The flat-tipped pestle mirrors the shape of the mortar and so maximises the surface area available for grinding.

## 2 CERAMIC

The ceramic mortar has a slightly abrasive, unglazed surface that grinds both dry and moist ingredients. Smooth mortars made from marble or glazed ceramic should have a ground surface on the inside, otherwise dry foods will slide over the surface.

## 3 JAPANESE (SURIBACHI)

The Japanese mortar has a characteristically wide, shallow bowl, with an interior covered with unglazed ridges running in different directions. Used with the broad-tipped wooden pestle (surikogi), it efficiently grinds oily seeds and raw chopped fish or poultry to a coarse paste.

## 4 MARBLE

This neo-classic design mortar, made from Italian Carrara marble, is carved with four useful handles which you can hold as you crush whole dried or fresh spices with a wooden pestle. The roughened interior helps to hold loose spices in place whilst you pound and grind them with the pestle.

## 5 OLIVE WOOD

Smaller lighter pestle and mortars made from olive wood are found all over the Mediterranean. They are perhaps more suited to crushing softer fresh ingredients, such as garlic and ginger, or making pesto with basil, pinenuts and Parmesan moistened with olive oil, than grinding down hard whole spices or peppercorns. They are also perfect for crushing coarse sea or rock salt instead of using a salt mill.

## 6 GRANITE

Black granite is a solid heavy material frequently used for pestle and mortars, often in more rustic finishes and styles. This sophisticated and artistic design by John Julian is, however, carved to imitate a beautifully turned pot and the matching granite pestle is topped with an elegant stainless steel handle.

# rubs

Rubs are a dry, intensely flavourful alternative to marinades. They are a combination of herbs, usually dried, spices and seasonings blended together and applied to the exterior surface of meat just before grilling or roasting. They create an almost smoky aroma and, in forming a crusty coating on the outside, help retain the meat juices. For these rubs contributed by Paul Gaylor, simply mix all the ingredients together for each rub and use for your favourite steak.

### NORTH AFRICAN RUB
2 tsp ground cumin
2 tsp ground coriander
2 tsp paprika
2 tsp chilli powder
1 tsp garlic powder
pinch of turmeric
salt and freshly cracked black pepper

### FIVE-SPICE RUB
1 tbsp ground cumin
1 tsp ground allspice
1 tsp curry powder
1 tsp ground cinnamon
1 tsp garlic powder
salt and freshly cracked black pepper

### KITCHEN TABASCO RUB
20g/3⁄4 oz dried porcini mushrooms,
   ground to a powder
1 tsp dried thyme
1 tsp dried rosemary
1 tsp garlic powder

### MEDITERRANEAN RUB
1 tbsp ground cumin
1 tsp brown sugar
1 tsp dried tarragon
1 tsp dried oregano
1⁄4 tsp mustard powder
salt and freshly cracked black pepper
zest of 1 orange

### CUBAN RUB
2 tbsp finely ground light-roast coffee
2 tbsp brown sugar
1 tsp dried sage
1 tsp freshly cracked black pepper
1 tsp powdered garlic
pinch of cinnamon
pinch of ground ginger

## garam masala

Freshly ground garam masala (meaning 'heating spices') lifts a curry from the mundane to the magnificent. A basic mixture includes an equal weight of cinnamon sticks, cloves and black peppercorns, and a small amount of black cardamom seeds. Experiment with additional spices such as dried chillies, and fennel, cumin and coriander seeds. For the best flavour, lightly toast whole spices and grind them to a powder just before use.

## pesto alla genovese

Bruising and pounding fresh basil leaves with a pestle beats any other method. Put 2 good handfuls of torn-basil leaves, 2 mashed garlic cloves, 3 tablespoons of pinenuts and a generous pinch of sea salt in a mortar and grind to a paste, moving the pestle around the mortar and crushing the ingredients against the sides. Add 8 tablespoons of freshly grated Parmesan and 2 tablespoons freshly grated Pecorino Romano cheese, grinding until evenly mixed. Beat in 8 tablespoons extra-virgin olive oil. This makes about 120 ml/1⁄2 cup pesto.

# coconut vegetable stew
## DAS SREEDHARAN

Specialising in the light, home-style cooking of Kerala in south-western India, Das Sreedharan's London-based Rasa chain of restaurants have revealed a very different side to Indian food. This colourful mixture of vegetables, cooked in a subtle blend of freshly ground spices, grated fresh coconut and tangy yoghurt, is typical of Keralan cooking. Known as 'avial', it is a traditional festival dish, and no wedding or feast would be complete without it.

Drumsticks, or Indian asparagus, are podded seeds from a tropical tree. The pulp and seeds are sucked out of the cooked pods, rather like eating asparagus. To prepare drumsticks, string them like celery and cut into 2.5–5 cm/1–2 inch lengths. They have an assertive flavour and some cooks like to parboil them for 10 minutes before proceeding with the recipe.

Green mango has a sour, fruity taste. Both green mango and drumsticks are available from good Asian food stores. If you have difficulty finding them, increase the quantity of the other vegetables, or substitute different ones. Instead of green mango, use a firm ordinary mango tossed with a pinch of citric acid or amchoor powder, available from good supermarkets.

SERVES 4 AS A SIDE DISH

**TOOLS**
pestle and mortar
paring knife
vegetable peeler
large saucepan
wooden spoon
grater
colander

**INGREDIENTS**
1 tsp cumin seeds
2.5 cm/1 inch piece fresh
  ginger root, roughly
  chopped
1 green chilli, deseeded and
  roughly chopped

3 small carrots
2 potatoes
1 small green mango
100 g/3½ oz drumsticks,
  strings removed
100 g/3½ oz green beans
20 curry leaves (optional)

1 tsp ground turmeric
1 tsp salt, or to taste
8–10 tbsp thick plain yoghurt
3 tbsp coarsely grated fresh
  coconut
few shreds fresh coconut, to
  garnish

**1** Using a pestle and mortar, grind the cumin seeds, ginger root and chilli to a paste with 1 tablespoon water.

**2** Slice the carrots, potatoes and green mango into fingers about 1 cm/½ inch thick and 5 cm/2 inches long. Slice the drumsticks and beans into 5 cm/2 inch pieces.

**3** Put the carrots and drumsticks in a large, heavy-based saucepan with barely enough water to cover – about 300 ml/1¼ cups. Bring to the boil and simmer, uncovered, for 5 minutes, stirring occasionally to prevent sticking.

**4** Add the potatoes and simmer over a medium heat, stirring now and then until nearly cooked, about 5 minutes.

**5** Add the green beans, mango and curry leaves, if using, and stir in the turmeric, salt and spice paste. Reduce the heat and simmer for a further 5 minutes or so with the lid on, stirring occasionally, until the vegetables are cooked.

**6** Remove the vegetables from the heat and stir in the yoghurt and coconut. Reheat gently if necessary but do not allow to simmer or the yoghurt will curdle. Garnish with a few coconut shreds before serving.

'Indian cooking is based on the ability to layer flavours. It is important to measure spices correctly – too much can kill the taste of the main ingredient whereas too little will result in a flat, lifeless dish.'

**MONISHA BHARADWAJ**

These invaluable tools break down the texture of raw or cooked food so that it becomes more palatable. They tenderise tough fibres, pierce thick skins, smash impenetrable nuts and produce delectable mashes and purées. These tools are not mere gadgets. They have stood the test of time and do their job efficiently and well. Although their basic structure and function have not greatly altered, many of them are produced in stylish modern designs that complement today's kitchens.

# mashers, crushers and crackers

### 1 TOMATO PRESS

A good old-fashioned machine that conveniently separates juice and pulp from seeds and peel. As you turn the handle, the flanged drum catches and traps halved tomatoes, pressing them onto a perforated plate that funnels the liquid down a chute. A second flange sweeps the solids towards another chute. It is not very easy to clean, but well worth having if your garden produces a fair-sized tomato harvest.

### 2 FOOD MILL

Before the days of food processors and blenders cooks would rub cooked foods and soft fruits into purées through a perforated disc set in a colander-like frame. The French called them moulis and many cooks still use them. This mill comes with a handled press mounted on a thick spring that clips into a frame fitted a perforated ridged disc with hinged legs. These clip over the top of a bowl to hold the mill steady as the handle is worked round the disc rapidly pressing the food into a purée below.

### 3 GARLIC PRESS

This sleek, space-age garlic press works in exactly the same way as a traditional one. A flat-faced pusher forces peeled or unpeeled garlic through the holes in the bowl of the press. Some presses have an extra protuberance and bowl for stoning (pitting) olives or cherries, for example. Others have a spiked self-cleaning device that pushes out every bit of debris from the holes.

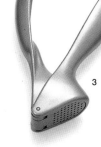

## 4 MEAT MALLET/TENDERISER

The short stubby handle of this tenderiser can either be gripped firmly with your fist so you can use the smooth round end for beating tender meat such as chicken breasts, or held at a right angle so you can use the ridged surface to soften denser meats such as steaks.

4

## 5 MEAT MALLET/TENDERISER

This hefty lump of cast aluminium is used for pounding and tenderising meat. The notches on one side break down the fibres; the smooth side bashes the meat flat.

5

## 7 POTATO MASHER

A traditional potato masher with a modern twist, this tool has a gridded base of stainless steel mesh and a thick, horizontal handle that is easy and comfortable to push down on firmly.

7

6

## 6 VEGETABLE PRESS

The wide, gently curved, perforated surface is rocked over soft-textured vegetables and fruit, reducing them to a rough pulp. The wooden handles on this one make the press comfortable to hold and help to exert downward pressure, but the receiving bowl needs to be wide and shallow so the handles do not hit the sides. Some models have a U-shaped handle, which is less comfortable to hold but perhaps more convenient.

8

## 8 POTATO RICER

Another traditional-style utensil that produces light textured potato for serving as mash or pomme purée. You spoon one or two medium-size cooked potatoes into the perforated drum and press a lever disc down on top, pushing the tender flesh into a bowl below. The flesh comes out in little rice-shaped squiggles and can be served as is, drizzled with some melted butter, or beaten into mash, enriched with butter, hot cream and seasoning.

## pumpkin purée

**TOOLS** chef's kife, steamer, food mill

Cut peeled pumpkin or winter squash into chunks and simmer or steam until tender. Drain well and push through a food mill. The purée can be used to make pumpkin pie. Alternatively, for a colourful soup, dilute to desired thickness with good chicken stock. Add cooked black beans and some roasted mashed chilli. Simmer gently to reheat. Pour into soup bowls and top with crumbled white cheese, pumpkin seeds and a slick of pumpkin-seed oil or extra-virgin sunflower oil.

## tenderising meat/flattening scaloppine

**TOOLS** meat mallet, board suitable for meat

By breaking up long meat fibres into shorter ones, using the notched or ribbed side of a heavy meat mallet, one can tenderise cheap cuts of lean meat for pan frying. The flat part of a meat mallet is used to beat out pork, veal or chicken escalopes between two sheets of non-stick baking parchment until very thin so they cook quickly. These can then either be egg-and-crumbed for scaloppini or schnitzels, or wrapped around a stuffing and cooked like beef olives.

# basic mashed potato

a

b

Though it seems simple, producing a mound of light, airy, lump-free mashed potato requires a little know-how. Variety of potato is important – use a floury type with a distinctive flavour (see Ingredients). Some cooks argue that it is better to boil potatoes unpeeled so water cannot penetrate and cause a waterlogged mash. I have tried boiling the same variety of potato with and without its skin, and cannot honestly detect any noticeable difference. When you are ready to mash, use a potato masher or, for a creamier result, a potato ricer or food mill. Never use a food processor – unless you want wallpaper paste.

SERVES 4

**TOOLS**
saucepan with a lid
colander
clean tea towel
potato masher, ricer or food mill
wooden spoon or balloon whisk

**INGREDIENTS**
1 kg/2¼ lb evenly-sized floury
    potatoes, such as Kerr's Pink,
    Yukon Gold or King Edward,
    peeled or unpeeled
salt
100 g/1 stick butter, softened and
    cut into pieces
150–300 ml/²/₃–1¼ cups hot milk

**1** Put the potatoes in a saucepan with enough water to just cover them. Add 1 tablespoon of salt and cover with a tight-fitting lid. Bring to the boil, then simmer gently, with the lid in place, until tender – about 20 minutes. Drain well, peel if necessary, and put back in the pan. Cover with a clean tea towel for a minute or two to get rid of excess moisture.

**2** For coarse-textured mash, bash the potatoes and butter with a masher (a). Season to taste with sea salt and freshly ground black pepper.

**3** For a smoother, fluffier mash, add some hot milk and, using a wooden spoon or balloon whisk, beat until you can beat no more (b). Add extra milk if needed.

## mashed potato using a potato ricer

**TOOLS** vegetable peeler, cook's knife, potato ricer, saucepan, mixing bowl, wooden spoon.

A traditional tool for making perfect, lump-free potato mash. Use floury potatoes, peel and cut them into equal size chunks, then boil until just tender, about 12–15 mins.

Drain and return to the stove in the pan set over a low heat to dry out. Then press a few lumps at a time through the ricer so the cooked flesh is extruded in little squiggles into a bowl. Beat in some hot milk and a little butter, and mix with a wooden spoon until creamy.

# sweet potato mash with chilli and sizzled ginger

This flavoursome variation on mashed potato is delicious served with spicy grilled chicken, lamb or fish. You can, of course, use ordinary potatoes, but sweet potato goes particularly well with ingredients such as ginger and chilli, which share its tropical origins.

SERVES 4 AS A SIDE DISH

**TOOLS**
vegetable peeler
cook's knife
saucepan with a lid
colander
clean tea towel
potato masher
wooden spoon
medium frying pan

**INGREDIENTS**
1.25 kg/2¾ lb orange-fleshed sweet potatoes, peeled and cut into even-sized pieces
sea salt and freshly ground black pepper
4 tbsp chopped fresh coriander (cilantro)
2 tbsp butter
40 g/1¼ oz fresh ginger root, sliced into 2.5 cm/1 inch matchsticks
½ red chilli, deseeded and very finely chopped

**1** Cook the sweet potatoes following the method given in step 1 of 'basic mashed potato' opposite. They may need a little less cooking time than ordinary potatoes.

**2** Bash the potatoes with a masher to break up the lumps. Season with sea salt and freshly ground black pepper and stir in the coriander (cilantro). Spoon into a warmed serving dish.

**3** Heat the butter in a frying pan. When it is sizzling, throw in the ginger and chilli and fry for a minute or two until the ginger is golden. Pour over the potato, stir to partially mix, and serve at once.

# crackers

Whether it's nut, lobster or crabmeat, extracting the choicest nuggets requires strength, patience and a certain amount of precision if the meat is to remain intact. Product designers are constantly coming up with new solutions when all that's needed is a tool with good leverage and a grip that can cope with different sizes and shapes. The material with which the tool is made needs to be sturdy and hinges should be strongly constructed.

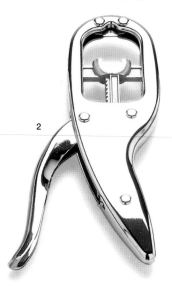

## 2 RACHET CRACKER

The ratchet cracker does all the work for you. Simply place the nut between the ratchet and the top of the crackers and work the ratchet up with the lever until the shell cracks and falls apart.

## 1 HINGED NUTCRACKERS

Pincer-style nutcrackers come in many designs but all work in the same way. You place a nut towards the top of the crackers and press the two handles firmly together until the shell cracks. Take care to squeeze firmly and slowly to avoid smashing the shell and fleshy nut inside. The knack is to crack the shell just enough to lift it off neatly. The long cracker can crack small nuts (hazels and almonds) and larger walnuts and Brazils.

1

2

## 4 LOBSTER PICK

Extracting the sweet flesh from a lobster or crab claw or leg is best done with a long-handled metal pick. It is generally presented alongside a lobster cracker, unless, of course, the claws and legs are already cracked for picking open.

## 3 LOBSTER/CRAB CRACKERS

Resembling lobster claws, these crackers work in the same way as hinged nutcrackers. The inside edges are ridged so you can grip unyielding lobster or crab claws firmly enough to crack them.

3

4

# cracking a lobster

**TOOLS** lobster crackers, lobster pick

**1** Pull off the claws from the main body (a). Grasp the larger lower claw in the crackers and press hard to just crack. Then, holding the upper, thinner claw, snap this back until it disjoints and push hard towards the lower claw (b). This should loosen the meat inside and push it out in one neat portion.

**2** You can then crack smaller claws with the crackers (c) and use a long thin lobster pick to extract the sweet meat inside like a skewer (d).

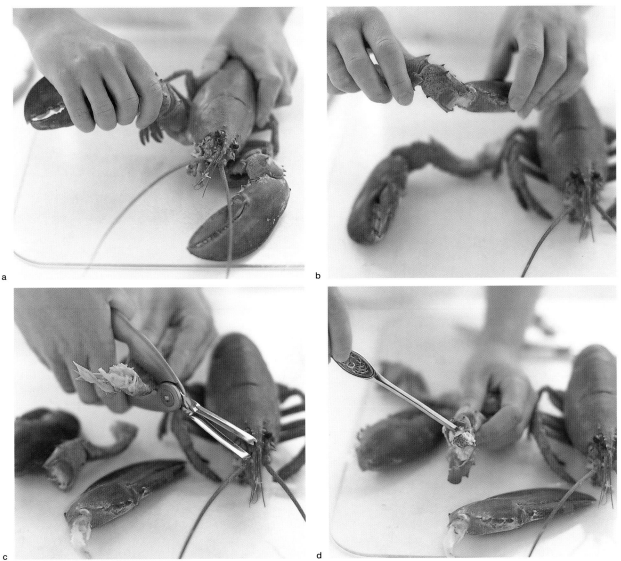

a

b

c

d

# citrus reamers, presses and squeezers

There's no need to resort to an electric juicer if you are extracting juice from a small amount of citrus fruit. All you need is a hand-held tool that gives maximum yield with ease and speed.

### 1 REAMER

The late great food writer Elizabeth David was said to be a great fan of the old-fashioned lemon squeezer known as a reamer. Like a traditional lemon squeezer, which is placed on a table, this style requires you to push the lemon into the grooves with one hand whilst you twist the handle in the opposite direction releasing the juice. A thick, brightly coloured painted handle gives a lively contemporary feel.

### 2 CITRUS PRESSES

These Mexican squeezers for oranges, lemons and limes (in matching orange, yellow and green colours) work on the reverse principle to the more familiar cone-shaped presses. Place the fruit half, cut-side down, over the perforated cup, then press down firmly with the solid cup, turning the fruit inside out to extract the juice.

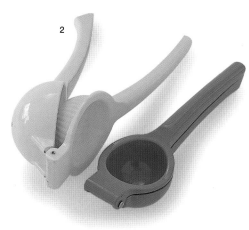

2

3

### 3 GLASS LEMON SQUEEZER

This glass lemon squeezer is of a traditional design. Place halved fruit over the dome and then press and twist to extract the juice. The pointed teeth arranged around the base of the dome prevent pips from trespassing into the juice-collecting gutter.

### 4 CITRUS PRESS

This magnificent, tall, chrome citrus press is for serious juicing. Place half an orange or a large lemon in the press, pull down the handle and the geared mechanism will extract every drop of juice from the fruit.

4

# mixing
# and
# whisking

Bowls are the nuts and bolts of kitchen utensils. After all, if you didn't have some sort of receptacle to mix, store or serve in, how would meals ever be prepared? Bowls come in a wide range of materials: glass, copper, stainless steel, aluminium, enamel, ceramic, earthenware, melamine and polyethylene. As with knives, you will need a variety of shapes and sizes for different tasks.

# bowls

Bowls are vital for orderly, well-organised meal preparation. Get in the habit of preparing all your ingredients before you start to cook, and have them ready and waiting in appropriate bowls. Your 'prep' bowls should include several small ones for ingredients such as chopped garlic and ginger. Equally vital are three or four 1–4 litre/1–4¼ quart bowls that can double up as serving bowls. If you regularly whisk egg whites or batters, you'll need a bowl that is deep enough to stop the mixture splattering your kitchen. You may want to treat yourself to a copper bowl for egg whites – your meringues will be unrivalled. Not absolutely essential, but useful nevertheless, is a big ceramic bowl for the occasional large mixing task such as making a Christmas cake.

### 1 BASIC GLASS BOWL

This plain glass bowl has a rolled rim for easy pouring. It comes with a plastic lid and is available in several sizes.

### 2 DURALEX 9-PIECE SET

A bowl for every occasion, made from heat-tempered, oven- and microwave-proof glass. Use them for preparation, cooking, serving and storing. This is a useful set to have if your storage space is limited.

### 3 STAINLESS-STEEL BOWLS

Stainless-steel is the ideal material for food preparation bowls as it is resistant to acid and is not tainted by smells. Pristine, shiny and indestructible, these bowls are so elegant you won't want to put them away. Use them for preparation, serving and storage.

### 4 COPPER BOWL

An essential piece of equipment for meringue makers, this bowl transforms egg whites into billowing clouds of stable foam like no other bowl, thanks to the alchemy that takes place between copper and egg whites (see 'miraculous meringue', page 101). The sloping sides and rounded base make for effortless whisking, while the bowl's generous diameter allows for rapid expansion of foam. The most useful size is about 30 cm/12 inches in diameter. Make sure your bowl has a rolled rim to keep its shape, and a hook so you can show it off on the wall.

4

5

### 6 MELAMINE BOWLS

There's a whiff of the 'swinging sixties' about these virtually unbreakable melamine bowls from Danish company Rösti, based on the original Margrethe bowl named in honour of the Queen of Denmark. But good designs never die, they just get tweaked and updated and acquire new generations of fans. The beautifully balanced pouring lip and elegance of these bowls brings them bang into the 21st century. Heatproof and dishwasher safe they have practical rubberised bases to hold them steady on the work top as you stir and mix.

### 5 CERAMIC BOWL

This traditional mixing bowl is made of glazed ceramic. The flattened area on the side keeps the bowl steady when it is tilted at an angle as you beat.

6

7

### 7 BATTER BOWL

This mixing bowl comes with a wide 3 litre/3 quart bowl that has a distinctive sloping notch on the base and a comfy handle on the side so you can tilt the bowl towards you as you whisk up a batter. The spout ensures easy pouring and because it is made from heavy duty polypropylene this capacious bowl is microwave and dishwasher safe.

Spoons are among the earliest and most basic of kitchen tools. They are essential for any job involving mixing, and in many ways are simply a replacement for the hand. They help the cook transfer food from one pan or container to another, and they stir, beat, scoop and scrape. They can also be used as a measuring tool.

# spoons, ladles and spatulas

## spoons

Wooden spoons are a must. They are strong, inflexible and poor conductors of heat. Though they may look somewhat crude, wooden spoons are subtly designed to perform a range of different tasks. Those made from hardwoods, such as beech or boxwood, are  strong and taint-free. Pine or other softwoods can impart a resinous smell to food, and they also have a tendency to splinter and crack. Always wash and dry wooden spoons thoroughly after you use them, and preferably allow them to air.

A long-handled, large metal spoon is another must. The thin edge delicately cuts through airy mixtures such as whisked egg whites so they don't collapse as you fold in other ingredients. Use a metal spoon also for basting meat – the long handle will protect you from the heat – and for serving rice – the thin edge will not break up delicate grains as you scoop them up. Buy a spoon that you can hang on a hook, ready for its thousand and one uses.

### WOODEN SPOONS

1 A spoon with a straight edge and angled point fits snugly into the corners of a flat-bottomed pan, while the curved side copes with rounded pans. The blunt end can be used to shunt food around a sauté pan and dislodge sticky sediment from the base. This is a good spoon for making gravy.

2 This traditional wooden spoon is an essential tool. It is made of beech and has a beautifully curved oval bowl with thick sides.

3 This smaller basic wooden spoon is made of closely grained golden boxwood. The bowl is a similar shape to the beech spoon (2).

4 A long-handled spoon (at least 40 cm/16 inches) is ideal for stirring continuously over furnace-like heat – when using a wok, for instance – or for stirring polenta.

1        2        3        4

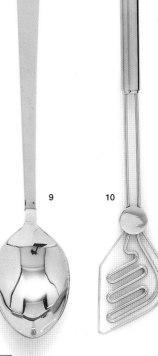

### 5 | BLACK PLASTIC SPOON

Heatproof black plastic spoons, either solid or perforated, are the best utensils to use with non-stick pans that might otherwise be scratched with metal ones. The designs are elegant enough to double as serving spoons and some designs feature a hanging hole for storage. Although heatproof it is advisable not to leave the spoons in a pan for more than a short time during cooking.

### 7 | ICE CREAM SCOOP

Making perfect rounded scoops of ice cream requires a spoon-shaped metal head and a wide slip-proof handle and thumb rest for a firm comfortable grip. Plunge the spoon into the centre of an ice cream tub, then twist and lift a neat perfect scoop. For firmer ice creams this sturdy scoop can be drawn across the top of the tub creating a neat rolled scoop.

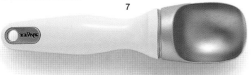

## folding whipped egg whites into chocolate mixture

**TOOLS** long-handled metal spoon, mixing bowl

A long-handled metal spoon is ideal for folding light whipped cream or egg whites gently into a heavier, more creamy cake mix, batter or soufflé sauce base. The idea is the metal spoon edges are thinner and so will not knock out the air.

First drop 2 spoonfuls of whisked egg or cream into the base mix and lightly beat to loosen the heavier mix (a). Then spoon in the remaining whisked mix and, using the big metal spoon, turn the two mixtures gently together in a figure of 8, making sure you spoon right down to the base of the bowl (b). Don't over mix, just enough to incorporate most of the whisked/whipped mix.

### 6 | FLEXIBLE SILICONE SCRAPER SPOON

These bendy scrapers can wipe a bowl almost completely clean because silicone is so flexible as it glides around curved bowls. The spoon-shaped head helps to hold mixture and because silicone is also heatproof this tool can be used to stir bubbling mixtures in a saucepan.

### 8 | SCOOP

Useful for shovelling up dry goods such as flour or grains, the scoop has a straight-sided, deep bowl that holds a generous amount without spilling. Traditionally made of tinned steel, scoops such as this will rust if used for moist foods.

### 9 | METAL MIXING SPOON

With its perfect oval bowl and long handle, this metal spoon is of a high quality. Made from a single piece of metal, the handle will not work loose from the bowl.

### 10 | WIRE MIXING SPOON

This stylish spoon is used with rounded pans. The outer wire skims over any crust that may have built up on the pan base without incorporating it into the mixture. The thicker inner wire is strong enough for mixing, lifting and turning. The spoon can also be used for whisking.

a    b

# risotto with red wine and sausages
## JILL DUPLEIX

Australian food writer Jill Dupleix cannot cook without a wooden spoon: 'It beats, it mashes, it stirs, it crushes garlic. It's a tasting spoon, a scraper, a risotto spoon, a porridge spoon, a salad server . . . Wooden spoons are like tea towels – no matter how many you have in the house, you will use them all.' She puts her spoon to good use in this recipe. Keep the stock simmering in a small saucepan so it is hot when you add it to the rice.

SERVES 4

| TOOLS | INGREDIENTS | |
|---|---|---|
| medium non-stick frying pan | 275 g/9½ oz Italian pork sausages, or coarse-grained pure pork sausages | 1.3 litres/5⅓ cups light chicken stock, preferably homemade, heated |
| cook's knife | 1 tbsp extra-virgin olive oil | 2 tbsp freshly grated Parmesan |
| large heavy-based sauté pan | 2 tbsp butter | sea salt |
| wooden spoon | 1 onion, finely chopped | freshly ground black pepper |
| small saucepan | 300 g/10½ oz arborio rice | Parmesan shavings and small rosemary sprig, to garnish |
| ladle | 200 ml/1 scant cup red wine | |
| grater | | |

**1** Take the skin off the sausages and pinch the meat into a heated non-stick frying pan. Fry the meat until crusty and golden, then drain off the oil and set the meat aside.

**2** Heat the olive oil and half the butter in a heavy-based sauté pan. Fry the onion gently until softened but not browned. Add the rice and, using a wooden spoon, toss well until the rice is coated in the buttery onions. Pour in the red wine and bring to the boil, stirring.

**3** Using a ladle, add 120 ml/½ cup of hot chicken stock to the rice. Stir carefully and calmly with a wooden spoon over a medium heat. When the stock has been absorbed by the rice, add another 120 ml/½ cup. From now on it is all in the timing. Add stock, a ladleful at a time, only when the previous stock has been absorbed by the rice. Keep the rice moving in the pan. If you go through a lot of stock quickly, the heat may be too high. If the rice doesn't absorb the stock easily, the heat may be too low.

**4** After 20 minutes or so, add the sausage meat and stir for another 10 minutes until the rice is cooked but not soft, and there is a general creaminess to the sauce; it should be neither soupy nor dry.

**5** Turn off the heat. Add the Parmesan, the remaining butter, and sea salt and freshly ground pepper to taste, and stir it through. Cover and leave to rest for 3–4 minutes before serving. Garnish with a rosemary sprig and a few Parmesan shavings. Serve with plenty of red wine on the side (to drink, naturally).

# ladles and spatulas

Ladles are needed for transferring measured amounts of liquid or semi-liquid food. They are invariably brought to the table, so buy a presentable one. To be avoided at all costs are ladles with painted wooden handles – they are guaranteed to flake or work loose. Make sure the bowl has a lip or continuous rolled edge for spill-free pouring. Hanging hooks are also useful.

Spatulas have virtually the same uses as spoons – they stir, mix, fold and scrape, push things through sieves and lift food from pans. Some cooks prefer a wooden spatula to a wooden spoon. One of the advantages of a spatula is that, being flat, it does not harbour clumps of unmixed food. You can also scrape it clean against the edge of the pan. Spatulas come in different materials and shapes. As with spoons, it's useful to have a selection for different tasks.

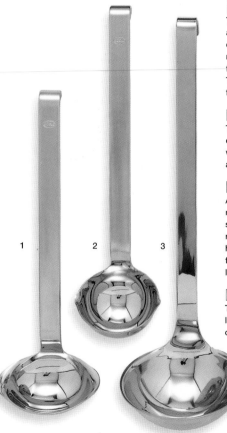

5     6

### 1  SALAD DRESSING LADLE
This ladle has a vertical handle that allows you to dip it into a tall, narrow container. The angle of the handle also makes it easier to pour with care over food that has been arranged on a plate. The bowl has a two-sided lip, designed for right- and left-handed use.

### 2  PORTIONING LADLE
The 6 cm/2½ inch bowl has a pouring lip on each side that enables you to pour with precision, and is designed for right- and left-handed use.

### 3  SOUP LADLE
A generous 9 cm/3½ inch bowl will hold nearly 150 ml/⅔ cup of liquid – ideal for serving soup. The bowl has a continuous rolled lip to prevent drips, and the handle has a hanging hook that stops the ladle from becoming submerged should you leave it sitting in a large pot of liquid.

### 4  CHINESE WOK LADLE
The wide, shallow bowl is perfect for lifting, tossing and turning the contents of a wok. The long handle distances you from the heat, and the 50° angle mirrors the contours of the wok, making the ladle more comfortable to use. Choose a stainless-steel ladle rather than rust-prone carbon steel.

### 5  RUBBER SPATULA
Shaped more like a spoon, this flexible spatula combines the benefits of a slightly concave bowl with straight edges and rounded corners. It will scrape clean a mixing bowl or pan without scratching.

### 6  PLASTIC SPATULA
Available in three sizes, the flexible, fine-edged blade cleanly removes the very last scrap of mixture from a bowl, jar or food processor goblet. One side deals with angled corners, the other with rounded.

1    2    3      4

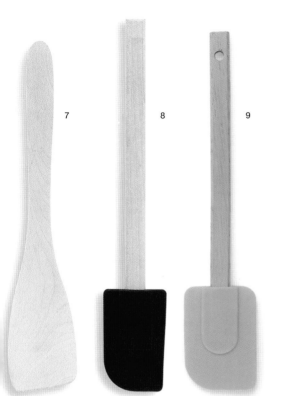

7        8        9

# poaching an egg using a ladle

**TOOLS** saucepan, large ladle, kitchen towel

To retain a perfect shaped oval when poaching a fresh egg, first bring a pan of water to the boil, add some salt to season and a tablespoon of wine vinegar (generally white vinegar, although eggs can be poached in red vinegar water also). Crack an egg into a large ladle (a) then, using a large spoon, whirl the water into a vortex whilst lowering the egg in the ladle into the centre (b). The vortex will help to set the egg into a neat shape.

Turn the water right down to a bare simmer. Have ready a wad of kitchen paper towel. When the egg is poached, after 2–3 minutes, remove it with the ladle, holding it at the pan edge slightly at an angle to drain off excess water, then lift out and slide briefly onto the paper towel (c). Immediately slide onto a piece of hot buttered toast or on top of a poached fillet of smoked haddock.

a                                    b

c

### 7 | WOODEN SPATULA
The slightly angled end is useful for scraping mixtures out of corners and shunting food around the pan. More importantly, the blunt edges will not scratch a non-stick surface, however firmly you scrape.

### 8 | COLOURED PLASTIC SPATULA
Similar in design and function, the coloured spatula has the added benefit of being heat resistant. It will not melt or discolour, even at very high temperatures, nor will it damage non-stick cookware. It is available in a range of colours and sizes.

### 9 | SILICONE SPATULA
Wiping a mixing bowl clean with a wooden or metal spoon always leaves behind mixture clinging to the bowl sides. This flexible spatula makes short work of scraping almost every trace of mixture in a thrice. A variety of fun colours livens up your storage pot of kitchen tools.

# moist carrot cake
## MICH TURNER

Contributed by Mich Turner of Little Venice Cake Company, London, this moist carrot cake – baked with walnuts, rum-soaked sultanas and coconut – is a delightfully light alternative to a rich fruit cake. Once baked, it is spiked with a fresh citrus syrup, which helps keep it moist and fruity. So, too, does the use of sunflower oil, and because the recipe uses no dairy products, it is suitable for those with a dairy intolerance. Although no filling is necessary for this moist cake, it tastes particularly good if split and layered with fresh orange buttercream. For best results, have all the ingredients at room temperature.

MAKES A 20 CM/8 INCH SQUARE CAKE

**TOOLS**
20 cm/8 inch square
    cake tin
non-stick baking parchment
small bowl
large mixing bowl
sieve
citrus zester
coarse grater
large metal spoon
citrus juicer
small jug

**INGREDIENTS**
50 ml/2fl oz dark rum
200 g/1⅓ cups sultanas
350 g/2⅔ cups plain (all-
    purpose) flour
4 tsp ground cinnamon
2 tsp ground nutmeg
2 tsp bicarbonate of soda
    (baking soda)
300 ml/1¼ cups sunflower oil
150 g/¾ cup golden caster
    (superfine) sugar

150 g/¾ cup light brown
    sugar
4 medium eggs, beaten
zest of 2 lemons
zest of 2 oranges
350 g/12 oz carrots, peeled
    and grated
100 g/3½ oz desiccated
    (shredded) coconut
100 g/3½ oz walnuts,
    chopped

2 tsp vanilla extract
1 tbsp chopped glacé ginger
    (optional)

**FOR THE CITRUS SYRUP**
115 g/generous ½ cup light
brown sugar
juice of 1½ lemons
juice of 1½ oranges

**1** Pour the rum over the sultanas and leave to infuse for 1 hour. Preheat the oven to 150°C/300°F/gas 1. Grease and line a 20 cm/8 inch cake tin with non-stick baking parchment.

**2** Sieve the flour together with the ground cinnamon, ground nutmeg and bicarbonate of soda. Beat together the sunflower oil, golden caster and light brown sugars, and eggs until smooth.

**3** Stir the flour mixture into the smooth batter. Add the lemon and orange zest, grated carrot, desiccated coconut, walnuts, vanilla extract, rum and chopped glacé ginger (if using) and stir well to combine. Spoon the mixture into the prepared tin and bake for 2 hours or until a skewer inserted into the centre of the cake comes out clean.

**4** Meanwhile, make the syrup. Place the sugar in a jug, then add the sieved lemon and orange juice. Stir well and continue to stir at intervals. Once the cake is baked, remove it from the oven and immediately pierce it with a skewer several times. Carefully spoon or pour over the citrus syrup then leave the cake to cool before removing it from the tin.

**TIP** When lining the tin, ensure the baking paper is at least 2 cm/½inch above the height of the tin. Once the cake is skewered and the citrus syrup is poured over, it will appear flooded. This is perfectly normal and all this delicious juice will be absorbed into the cake.

**TO STORE** This cake keeps fresh for up to 14 days if covered and decorated with icing or wrapped in greaseproof (waxed) paper and kept in an airtight container. It is also suitable for freezing. Allow to defrost overnight.

Air is the least recognised – but one of the most fundamental – ingredients in cooking and, as we need a means of incorporating it into food, the whisk could rightly be called the most fundamental of tools. A whisk works by cutting at high speed through egg whites, batters and sauces, not only incorporating air but also smoothing out lumps and uneven concentrations. It breaks down fat globules so they emulsify with non-fat liquids – oil and vinegar in a salad dressing, for example.

# whisks

A whisk 'denatures' proteins – think of egg whites and the way a viscous mess miraculously turns into a frothy cloud. In this case, the whisk cuts through interwoven strands of protein molecules in unbeaten egg white, effectively chopping them into tiny pieces and introducing air at the same time.

There are a number of shapes and sizes of whisk, designed for a variety of jobs. If choice is restricted, however, a balloon whisk and possibly a small flat whisk are the ones to go for. Choose those made of stainless steel rather than tin plate, which is likely to discolour and rust. The handle should be comfortably thick and sit well in the hand and, in the interests of hygiene, should be well sealed at both ends. The wires should be firmly welded in place.

### 1 BALLOON WHISK
The balloon whisk's slightly flexible wires will effectively aerate anything from egg whites to double (heavy) cream. Their bulbous shape increases the area that is in contact with the mixture, so the more wires the better.

### 2 EGG WHISK
The egg or sauce whisk is designed to mix, emulsify and aerate egg-based sauces. More elongated and rigid than a balloon whisk, the wires cut through egg proteins in a hollandaise sauce, for example, preventing coagulation and curdling.

### 3 TWIRL WHISK
Also called a whip, this is made from one piece of coiled wire, which gives it greater flexibility. Though the shape makes it useful for working into corners and round the entire base of a container, it is not as efficient as a balloon or egg whisk. It is good for whisking in slim containers, however.

### 4 SPIRAL WHISK
A spiral whisk is made from a coil of fine, springy wire, looped round a circular wire frame. It can be used in a small amount of liquid, so is invaluable for whisking sauces in shallow pans and also incorporates mixture from around the edge of the mixing bowl.

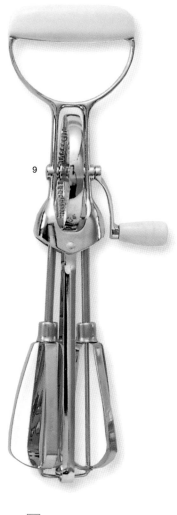

### 7 | SAUCEPAN WHISK

This is a balloon whisk with eight flattened spokes. The idea is it reaches right into the corner of a saucepan for thorough mixing of even the thickest sauce. But because it is metal it cannot be used in non-stick pans unless metal-proof.

### 8 | BALL-ENDED WHISK

The spokes of this whisk end in round metal balls making it look like an office desk toy. In fact the balls have a practical purpose in that they can whisk hot milk to a good froth, make well-emulsified vinaigrettes and beat lumpy sauces into smooth. Again, not for non-stick pans unless metal-proof.

### 9 | ROTARY WHISK

Good old designs never go out of fashion. The handles may get new colours but the function remains true. The basics of a rotary whisk go back well over a century: two whisks that whirl and whip in tandem when turned creating perfect whipped cream, egg whites for meringues, eggs for scrambling and light pancake batters.

### 5 | JUG WHISK

Not essential, but nevertheless useful, the long jug whisk comes in handy for whisking in narrow glasses, measuring jugs and cocktail shakers.

### 6 | FLAT WHISK

This whisk is excellent for mixing small amounts, or for beating a single egg yolk, stirring delicate items or mixing herbs into cream.

### 10 | AEROLATTE MILK FROTHER

This battery-operated frother looks like a whisk from a dolly's kitchen but in fact it performs brilliantly well in beating up hot milk in cups, mugs or jugs for hot chocolate, coffee lattes. It also makes short work of whisking.

## sabayon sauce

**TOOLS** large balloon whisk, bowl, saucepan or zabaglione pan

Use a large balloon whisk to make a light, sweet sauce to serve
with hot pies and puddings, or to spoon over summer berries.
Put 3 large free-range egg yolks, 50 g/¼ cup of caster (superfine)
sugar and 100 ml/scant ½ cup of sparkling white wine into a
large heatproof bowl. Set this over a saucepan or zabaglione pan
(see page 148) of gently simmering water. Beat the mixture steadily
until it increases in volume and becomes a firm but light and
creamy foam that forms a trail when the whisk is lifted.

Serves 4 ·

# mayonnaise

**TOOLS** egg or sauce whisk, glass bowl

Use an egg whisk or sauce whisk to make creamy mayonnaise for salads and dips. Put 2 organic egg yolks, 1/4 teaspoon sea salt, 1/4 teaspoon mustard powder, a little freshly ground black pepper and 1/2 teaspoon olive or sunflower oil into a medium-size bowl. Beat until smooth, then beat in another 1/2 teaspoon oil. Continue adding oil in tiny amounts, increasing the flow as the mixture thickens. You will need a total of 250 ml/1 cup oil. Finally, mix in 1 tablespoon white wine vinegar and 1 tablespoon warm water. Check the seasoning. To make aïoli, add 5–6 garlic cloves, pounded to a paste with sea salt, at the start and omit the vinegar.

Makes about 350 ml/1 1/2 cups.

Note: This contains raw eggs, which can be hazardous to young children, pregnant women and the elderly.

'Air and egg whites beaten together with sugar produce one of life's miracles – a snowy foam, which, when slowly baked in the oven, is transformed into utterly irresistible, melt-in-the-mouth meringue.'

# miraculous meringue

Making meringue is simple if you follow a few basic rules. Bowl and beaters must be scrupulously clean – if there is the slightest trace of grease or moisture the egg whites won't whisk properly. Egg whites even absorb moisture from the atmosphere, so don't make meringues on a humid or rainy day. Temperature is important, too. Egg whites at room temperature have a lower surface tension than those straight from the fridge. A relaxed gel allows air to be beaten in more easily, which results in a higher volume of foam. Separate the whites from the yolks an hour or so before whisking. Crack the eggs carefully as the yolk is 30 per cent fat and even a speck will contaminate the whites. Ideally, the base of your mixing bowl should be spherical so foam does not get trapped in a corner. Use a one made of glass, ceramic or stainless steel rather than plastic, which is hard to keep grease-free. Best of all is an unlined copper bowl. A chemical reaction between the metal and the egg whites strengthens the bubbles, producing a creamier, more stable foam. However, if you leave the whites in a copper bowl more than 15 minutes, they will turn an unappetising grey. To avoid this, clean the bowl before you use it with a tablespoon of salt and the juice of half a lemon or a tablespoon of vinegar. Rub the mixture round the bowl with your fingers. Rinse the bowl with hot water and dry with a clean cloth.

a

# basic meringue

MAKES 600 ml/20 fl oz

| TOOLS | INGREDIENTS |
|---|---|
| small bowl | 4 egg whites |
| large mixing bowl | pinch of salt |
| balloon whisk or hand-held | 200 g/scant 1 cup caster |
|    electric mixer |   (superfine) sugar |
| large metal spoon | |

**1** Separate the eggs, pour the whites into a large clean bowl and add a pinch of salt. This helps keep the foam stable. Using the whisk or hand-held mixer, beat gently until the whites begin to change into a frothy foam.

**2** Now beat rapidly with a circular motion that lifts the whites and incorporates air, until you have a uniformly foamy mass. When you lift some of the white with the whisk it should form a soft, droopy peak (a). At this stage the foam can be used for soufflés and mousses.

**3** For baked meringue, continue to beat until the foam forms stiff, pointy peaks. Do not overbeat at this stage or you will end up with dry lumps of foam. Add half the caster sugar, a spoonful at a time, beating well after each addition. The foam should now be smooth and shiny (b).

**4** Using a large metal spoon, lightly and evenly fold in the rest of the sugar (c). Use right away, as the mixture quickly starts to liquefy.

b

c

# passion fruit pavlova

The meringue mixture for a pavlova includes cornflour and vinegar, which produce the characteristic texture – crunchy on the outside and soft within. To balance the sweetness of meringue, I have added passion-fruit juice to the cream and topped the pavlova with a selection of luscious tart fruits. Shreds of caramelised orange peel make the pavlova sparkle and add texture. Allow several hours for making the base as it needs to dry thoroughly. Don't worry if it cracks – that's part of the pavlova's characteristic appearance. Serve the finished dish within an hour of assembling it, otherwise it will become soggy.

SERVES 8–10

**TOOLS**
baking parchment
25 cm/10 inch plate
baking (cookie) sheet
small bowl
copper bowl or large mixing bowl
balloon whisk or hand-held electric mixer
large metal spoon
fine sieve
palette knife (metal spatula)
mixing bowl
cook's knife
nylon sieve for straining passion-fruit pulp
wooden spoon
small saucepan
tongs
swivel peeler

**INGREDIENTS**
6 large egg whites
pinch of salt
300 g/1½ cups caster (superfine) sugar, plus 2 tbsp
1½ tsp cornflour (cornstarch), sifted
1½ tsp white wine vinegar
300 ml/1¼ cups double (heavy) cream
sieved juice from 6 passion fruit
peel from 1 small orange without any pith, sliced into thin shreds
4 tbsp grenadine syrup
1 small papaya
1 small star fruit
4 kumquats, thinly sliced
4 physalis, husks removed and fruits halved

**1** Preheat the oven to 150°C/300°F/gas 2. Draw a 25 cm/10 inch circle on a sheet of baking parchment, tracing round a plate. Place the paper on a baking sheet, marked side down, so no ink transfers to the base of the meringue.

**2** Make the meringue mixture following steps 1–4 for 'basic meringue' (see page 101), using the 300 g/1½ cups of sugar. Sprinkle the cornflour and vinegar over the foam and gently fold in.

**3** Spoon the meringue onto the traced circle, using a palette knife to level the top and smooth the sides.

**4** Place the baking sheet in the oven and immediately turn the heat down to 140°C/275°F/gas 1. Bake for 1¼ hours until the meringue is firm. Turn the oven off but leave the meringue inside with the door closed until the oven is completely cool.

**5** An hour before assembling, whip the cream, then fold in the passion-fruit juice and the 2 tablespoons of sugar. Cover and put in the fridge to chill.

**6** Blanch the orange-peel shreds in boiling water for 3 minutes. Drain and tip back into the pan. Add 150 ml/⅔ cup of fresh water and the grenadine syrup. Simmer briskly for 12–15 minutes until syrupy, but still with some liquid left in the pan. Fish out the shreds with tongs and place on a metal plate to cool, separating any clumps.

**7** Cut the papaya in half lengthways and scrape out the seeds, leaving a smooth cavity. Carefully remove the peel, then place each half on a board cut-side down and slice crossways into thin crescents. Cut the crescents into two or three neat pieces, depending on the size.

**8** Cut the star fruit in half and reserve one half for another use. Using a swivel peeler, shave off the dark stripe along the edge of the ribs. Slice the flesh thinly into about eight slices.

**9** Place the meringue base on a serving plate. Spoon the cream over the meringue, spreading it out with a palette knife. Arrange the fruits on top, scatter with the orange-peel shreds, and carry proudly to the table.

# spicy prawn crêpes with coriander sauce

For successful crêpes and pancakes, use a balloon whisk, which effectively mixes and aerates the batter, and smooths out lumps. Do not over-beat or your crêpes will be tough. Use a small, heavy pan that conducts heat evenly and does not stick. A crêpe pan or a well-seasoned omelette pan is ideal.

MAKES 8

**TOOLS**
sieve
mixing bowl
balloon whisk
small measuring jug
paring knife
cook's knife or mezzaluna
ladle
18 cm/7 inch non-stick
    crêpe pan
turner
greaseproof (waxed) paper
small frying pan

**INGREDIENTS**
100 g/³/₄ cup unbleached
    plain (all-purpose) flour
pinch of salt
1 egg, plus 1 egg yolk
300 ml/1¼ cups milk
1 tbsp vegetable oil or melted
    butter
1½ tsp ground turmeric
vegetable oil, for frying

**FOR THE SAUCE**
1 garlic clove, finely chopped
3 tbsp chopped fresh
    coriander
200 ml/1 scant cup wholemilk
    yoghurt
½ tsp freshly ground cumin
sea salt and freshly ground
    black pepper

**FOR THE FILLING**
1 tbsp vegetable oil
½ onion, finely chopped
2 tsp red Thai curry paste
225 g/1cup canned chopped
    tomatoes with juice
sea salt
24 large peeled tiger prawns
1 tbsp lemon juice
2 tbsp chopped fresh
    coriander (cilantro)

**1** Sift the flour and salt into a bowl. Make a well in the centre and add the egg and extra yolk (a). Add half the milk and whisk well (b). Continue to whisk, gradually adding the rest of the milk, until the batter is smooth. Pour into a small measuring jug and set aside.

**2** Mix together all the ingredients for the sauce. Leave to stand to allow the flavours to develop.

**3** Whisk the vegetable oil or melted butter into the batter along with the turmeric. Heat enough oil to lightly film an 18 cm/7 inch frying pan. When the oil is hot but not smoking, quickly add a small ladleful of batter, tilting and turning the pan as you do so (c). Fry quickly over a medium-high heat until set on top and brown underneath. Using a fish slice or quick flip of the pan, turn the pancake and cook until the underside is brown.

**4** Transfer the pancake to a plate and keep warm. Repeat, using the remaining batter, to make seven more pancakes. Stack the pancakes with a sheet of greaseproof paper between each one. Cover with foil and keep warm.

**5** To make the filling, heat the oil in a small frying pan and gently fry the onion until golden. Add the curry paste and stir-fry for 1 minute. Stir in the tomatoes and season with salt to taste. Simmer for 1–2 minutes. Add the prawns, lemon juice and coriander. Simmer for a few minutes until the prawns are thoroughly heated through.

**7** Fold the pancakes in half, and then in half again to make quadrant-shaped cones. Spoon the filling into the top pocket. Arrange in a warmed serving dish or on individual plates, and top with a spoonful of sauce.

a    b    c

# easy lime delicious
## BILL GRANGER

Australian chef Bill Granger is as famous for his sunny disposition as he is for his sweet dishes that have fans queuing round the block to indulge at his Sydney cafes. 'I like to cook the kind of food that people like to eat,' says Bill. He uses a balloon whisk to incorporate air into these delightfully light puddings, which are typical of his easy-going approach to food.

SERVES 2

| TOOLS | INGREDIENTS | TO SERVE |
|---|---|---|
| balloon whisk | 75 g/1/3 cup caster | double (heavy) |
| 2 x 250 ml/1 cup ovenproof | (superfine) sugar | cream |
| dishes | 1 1/2 tbsp plain (all-purpose) | |
| large bowl | flour, sifted | |
| | 2 tbsp lime juice | |
| | 1 tsp finely grated lime zest | |
| | 2 eggs, separated | |
| | 1 tbsp butter, melted | |
| | 100 ml/scant 1/2 cup | |

**1** Preheat the oven to 180°C/350°F/gas 4 and lightly grease two 250 ml/1 cup capacity ovenproof dishes.

**2** Place 2 tablespoons of the sugar, the flour, lime juice and zest and egg yolks into a large bowl and whisk to combine. Add the melted butter and milk, and whisk until well combined.

**3** In a separate bowl, whisk the egg whites and remaining sugar until firm peaks form. Gently fold the egg whites into the lime mixture. Divide the mixture between the two dishes. Place in the preheated oven and bake for 15 minutes or until golden and set. Serve with a dollop of thick cream.

These multi-purpose machines not only chop and slice, but shred, beat, juice, whisk and mix. They work at high speed, and are ideal for processing large quantities of ingredients quickly. Although they are convenient, these items deprive cooks of some of the pleasure of preparing food. They also make it difficult to detect subtle physical changes in food while it is being processed.

# electric mixers and processors

Electric mixers and processors are worth their weight in gold if used judiciously, though if you become reliant on a machine before you have learnt to perform the tasks manually, you are unlikely to develop a true understanding of how and why ingredients behave as they do.

Having made the financial outlay, make sure your mixer or processor earns its keep. You are more likely to use a machine if it is permanently within reach on the work surface, rather than hidden in a cupboard.

## 1 STANDING MIXER

A classic mixer for the serious home baker, this machine has a 4 litre/4¼ quart stainless-steel bowl that holds 2.25 kg/5 lb of ingredients. The rotary head 'moves like Elvis', gyrating from the inside to the outside of the bowl in a series of circles, drawing in every scrap of mixture from the sides and base, and mixing it quickly, evenly and thoroughly. The mixer has three basic attachments – a wire whip, a flat beater and a dough hook – as well as numerous optional extras for a wide variety of tasks.

1

## 2 FOOD PROCESSOR

The basic design of food processors hasn't changed for decades – that is razor sharp blades that whirl horizontally from a commercial grade motor, grinding everything in the bowl to a pulp almost instantaneously. The largest domestic size Magimix 5200 is perfect for the serial entertainer and comes with three tough polycarbonate bowls of varying size to cope with a range of quantities from small fistfuls of herbs right up to 1.6 kg/3½ lb of pastry. Separate attachments include blades for grating, slicing, juicing, whipping egg whites and beating bread doughs. A guarantee for a staggering 12 years is testament to their durability.

## 3 STICK BLENDER

From Michelin star chefs to new mothers, the stick blender has a place in many kitchens. A small scale horizontal blade operates at the end of a metal stick to make purées, baby food, mayonnaise, chop onions and herbs, mince (grind) meat, grind nuts, spices and even coffee within seconds. You can purée cooked vegetables or churn sauces into cappuccino froths by moving the blender up and down rapidly in a pan. Deluxe versions have a selection of attachments, and domestic Mono models come with a clear mixing beaker and meat-mincer.

2

3

## 5 BLENDER

A kitchen classic, this deco blender has a powerful two-speed motor and a large, heat-resistant goblet. It blends, mixes and juices, whizzing up the smoothest of smoothies, velvety sauces, soups, purées and crushed ice. With its small diameter, the goblet keeps food within reach of the short, straight blades, so you don't have to keep stopping and stirring. Though a blender copes with smaller amounts of food than a processor, there must be enough to cover the blades. You will also need to add liquid, otherwise the food at the top will not be blended.

## 6 MULTI-PURPOSE KITCHEN MACHINE

This revolutionary machine has a compact motorised base with a universal coupling device to which various attachments are easily fitted. The machine therefore combines several machines in one – the only drawback is its price. The basic model is supplied with a mixing bowl only, which has as accessories a lid, dough hook, double beater and bowl scraper. The more expensive model comes with a blender and food processor, as well as the mixing bowl. Optional extras for both models include a mincer (grinder), a continuous shredder and a grain mill.

## 4 JUICER

For those who enjoy their fresh fruit and vegetable intake in the form of vitamin-high smoothies or squeezed juices there is a selection of machines ranging from simple electric squeezers to those that crush other fruits and vegetables to juices. You feed the fruits in at the top and out comes fresh juice through a spout. The Magimix Le Duo Plus also makes baby purées and fruit coulis to serve with ice cream.

## 7 ICE CREAM MAKER

Hand-made ice creams churned in tabletop machines can make quick and simple desserts within 30 minutes. The best machines are those with a built-in freezer unit and a lift out metal bowl. You can start your fun experimenting with simple fruit and cream or thick yoghurt ices and simple sorbets then graduate to chef-style ones using crème Anglais custards, chocolate, caramels and ground nuts. These machines are heavy to lift because of the freezer units, but if you use one frequently there's no need to keep it in a cupboard. Not cheap, but perfect for the dedicated cook-hostess.

## 8 HAND-HELD MIXER

Keen home cooks like to count amongst their tools a good hand-held mixer to use in their own mixing bowls. The Dualit model comes at a good 300W power and with two flat beaters, two dough hooks for yeasty mixes and one balloon whisk for egg whites, all of which can operate at five speed settings. The power cord retracts for easy storage. It is perfect for domestic and light commercial use.

## 9 BREADMAKER

If you fancy the aroma of homemade bread wafting through your house each day then a breadmaker should be a popular machine in your kitchen. There are several models on the market but the brand that frequently reaches the 'best buy' categories is the Panasonic. You add bread flour (white, wholemeal), fast-action yeast and water, even nuts and raisins. But that's just the start. Well written recipe books (for a change) display a versatility of bread from Italian-style, to sweet breads, even simple cakes and jams (presumably to spread on your fresh, heavenly homemade bread). This range also gives you the option to use the machine as a dough prover only or an oven only.

# macadamia nut-crusted chicken breasts with lemon grass-coconut emulsion
## CHARLIE TROTTER

Contributed by award-winning American chef and restaurant owner Charlie Trotter, this dish is rich and delicious, with sensual flavours that harmonise perfectly. The slightly wilted watercress is essential for cutting the richness of the macadamia nuts and balancing all the flavours. Use a hand-held electric blender or mixer to froth up the sauce.

SERVES 4

**TOOLS**
preparation bowls
cook's knife
vegetable knife
small saucepan
sieve
citrus juicer
small roasting pan
small frying pan
large frying pan
perforated turner
hand-held electric blender
  or mixer

**INGREDIENTS**
400 g/1¾ cups canned
  coconut milk
250 ml/1 cup milk
8 stalks chopped lemon grass
1 tbsp rice vinegar
1 tbsp lemon juice
1 yellow (bell) pepper, halved
  and deseeded
50 g/1¾ oz leek, cut into
  julienne strips
3½ tbsp groundnut or
  sunflower oil
6 cm/2½ inch piece fresh

ginger root, peeled and cut
  into julienne strips
4 skinless, boneless chicken
  breasts, about 140 g/5 oz
  each
salt and freshly ground black
  pepper
4 tbsp chopped macadamia
  nuts
50 g/2 cups trimmed
  watercress
2 tbsp desiccated (shredded)
  coconut, lightly toasted
2 tbsp chopped chives

**1** Simmer the coconut milk, milk and lemon grass in a small saucepan for 15 minutes. Strain through a sieve and pour back into the pan. Add the vinegar and lemon juice, and set the pan aside.

**2** Meanwhile, grill the pepper until blackened. Peel off the skin, cut the flesh into julienne strips and keep warm.

3 Plunge the strips of leek into a pan of boiling water. Bring back to the boil and boil for a few seconds, then drain the leek strips and keep warm.

**4** Heat 1½ tablespoons of the oil in a small frying pan. Add the ginger and fry for a minute or so until just golden. Remove from the pan and keep warm.

**5** Season the chicken breasts with salt and pepper, and coat the tops with the nuts. Heat the remaining oil in a large, hot frying pan, add the chicken and cook for 3 minutes on each side or until cooked through. Transfer to a plate and keep warm.

**6** Add the watercress to the pan in which you cooked the chicken. Cook it gently for 1 minute or until wilted. Season to taste with salt and pepper.

**7** Gently reheat the coconut emulsion, whisking with a hand-held blender or mixer until frothy.

**8** To assemble the dish, place some yellow pepper and leek in the middle of each serving bowl. Arrange some of the watercress over the vegetables and top with a chicken breast. Pour the emulsion around each bowl and sprinkle with the fried ginger and toasted coconut. Sprinkle the chives around the emulsion.

# smoothies and juices
## NICOLA GRAIMES

An electric blender makes easy work of creamy, fruit-filled smoothies, milkshakes and cocktails. Food writer Nicola Graimes recommends a model with various speeds and functions. For juices, it is worth investing in a high-powered juicer with a strong motor.

## banana and cardamom smoothie

SERVES 2

**TOOLS**
chef's knife, pestle and mortar, blender

**INGREDIENTS**
3 cardamom pods, split
2 bananas
1 mango
200 ml/scant 1 cup coconut milk
200 ml/scant 1 cup thick natural (plain) yoghurt
ice, to serve

**1** Remove the seeds from the cardamom pods and crush them using a pestle and mortar.

**2** Chop the bananas and put them into a blender. Peel, stone (pit) and roughly chop the mango and add to the blender with the coconut milk and yoghurt. Blend until smooth and frothy.

**3** To serve, pour the smoothie into two tall glasses, stir in the cardamom and add ice.

## apple and carrot juice

SERVES 2

**TOOLS**
chef's knife, juicer

**INGREDIENTS**
2 large tart green apples
1 large raw beetroot
2 medium carrots
2.5 cm/1 inch piece fresh ginger root
freshly squeezed lemon juice, to taste

**1** Remove the stalks from the apples and cut into quarters. Peel and cut the beetroot into quarters, chop the carrots and peel the ginger.

**2** Juice the apples, beetroot, carrots and ginger and pour into two glasses. Add lemon juice to taste, stir and serve.

## strawberries and cream smoothie

SERVES 2

**TOOLS**
vegetable peeler, chef's knife, hand blender

**INGREDIENTS**
1/2 vanilla pod (bean), split
350 g/12 oz strawberries, hulled
150 ml/5 fl oz thick Greek yoghurt
350 ml/scant 11/2 cups milk
2 scoops real dairy vanilla ice cream

**1** Scrape the seeds from a quarter of the vanilla pod into the beaker that comes with the hand blender. Roughly chop the strawberries and add half to the beaker with half of the yoghurt and milk.

**2** Put the hand blender into the beaker and pulse until smooth and creamy. Pour into a tall glass and add a scoop of vanilla ice cream. Repeat to make another smoothie.

## orchard fruit juice

SERVES 2

**TOOLS**
vegetable knife, juicer

**INGREDIENTS**
2 pears
3 peaches
4 apricots
freshly squeezed lemon juice, to taste

**1** Core the pears and cut into quarters. Halve and remove the stones (pits) from the peaches and apricots.

**2** Juice the pears, peaches and apricots and pour into two glasses. Add lemon juice to taste, stir and serve.

# white chocolate and chilli ice cream

## CHRIS TANNER · JAMES TANNER

This unusual ice cream is contributed by top UK TV chefs and restauranteurs the Tanner Brothers. The mouth-tingling, clean flavour of the red chilli works well with the white chocolate and the dish has become a big favourite at their restaurant, Tanners, in Plymouth, Devon.

MAKES ABOUT 1 LITRE/4 CUPS

**TOOLS**
2 x medium saucepans
heatproof bowl
bowl
whisk
spatula
wooden spoon
ice cream maker
freezer-proof container

**INGREDIENTS**
60 ml/4 tbsp water
200 g/scant 1 cup caster (superfine) sugar
2 tsp deseeded and finely diced red chilli
400 ml/1¾ cups double (heavy) cream
400 ml/1¾ cups semi-skimmed milk
1 vanilla pod (bean), split
300 g/10½ oz white chocolate, broken into pieces
8 organic eggs

**1** Bring the water to the boil in a saucepan. Add 1 tablespoon of the caster sugar and chilli and then reduce the heat and simmer for 5 minutes until it becomes a light syrup. Remove from the heat and allow to cool.

**2** Put the cream, milk and vanilla pod in a saucepan and bring up to the boil. Remove from the heat and allow to infuse and cool.

**3** Melt the chocolate in a heatproof bowl placed over a saucepan of gently simmering water. Leave to cool.

**4** Whisk the eggs yolks with the rest of the sugar until light and fluffy. Pour the infused milk into the egg mixture and stir with a spatula. Pour the mixture into a clean pan and heat gently, stirring continuously, until it is thick enough to coat the back of a wooden spoon: do not allow it to boil or the mixture will curdle. Remove the vanilla pod and pass the mixture through a fine sieve into a bowl. Fold in the white chocolate.

**5** Pour the mixture into an ice cream maker, churn and, when the ice cream starts to freeze, add the chilli mixture, churn for a further 2 minutes and then freeze. If making by hand, pour the mixture into a freezer-proof container then freeze for 40 minutes. Remove from the freezer, whisk to break up any ice crystals, stir in the chilli mixture, then refreeze. Repeat this process for the next 2½ hours, then freeze until firm.

**6** Leave the ice cream to soften for 5–10 minutes, then serve in scoops.

# sieving
# and
# straining

These tools refine the texture of food. They smooth lumps and coarse particles from free-flowing powders; and they indirectly lighten mixtures, because the process of sieving or sifting helps to incorporate air as the powder floats down into the bowl. Sieves are additionally used to separate solids from liquids, as in draining peas, or to alter the texture of food. For example, hard-boiled egg yolk can be transformed into a mimosa-like garnish by pushing it through a fine-meshed sieve.

# sieves and dredgers

A sieve divests raspberries of their seeds and is also useful for rescuing lumpy gravy or a béchamel sauce that is not as smooth as it should be – place the sieve over a clean saucepan, pour the mixture into the sieve, and smooth out the lumps by pressing with the back of a wooden spoon.

A sieve should sit comfortably over the receiving container. Conical sieves work best with tall containers; bowl-shaped sieves are best used with bowls. The container needs to be large and deep enough to accommodate both the depth of the sieve and the depth of the ingredients once sieved. Don't sift dry powder in a damp sieve as you'll end up with paste. Nor is it advisable to sieve seedy or fibrous food through an ultra-fine sieve – it will be very difficult to clean. If you do need to clean fibrous material from a sieve, hold it under running water with the inside facing down and scrub the outside of the sieve with a nail brush. Turn the sieve bowl-side up, scrub the inside and rinse again.

## choosing sieves

Essential are two or three medium-to-large bowl-shaped sieves; then you will always have a dry one ready for use. A large sieve, measuring about 25 cm/10 inches in diameter, is worth having for sieving any reasonable quantity of flour or icing (confectioner's) sugar. If the sieve is too small, the powder tends to either spill over the edge of the sieve or float into the atmosphere; a sieve with a generous-sized bowl will keep it in place.

**BOWL-SHAPED SIEVES**
The very fine mesh of these attractive stainless steel sieves is ideal for sifting flour, icing (confectioner's) sugar and other fine powders.

1 The larger sieve can also be used to drain small amounts of vegetables.

2 The small sieve is useful for sprinkling icing (confectioner's) sugar over cakes, as it enables you to aim more accurately.

A couple of smaller sieves, about 10–12 cm/4–4½ inches in diameter, are useful for directing powder or liquid into a narrow-necked container such as a measuring jug. Essential for sieving soft fruits or removing pips from citrus juice is a fine-meshed sieve made of nylon, which, unlike metal, does not react with the acid in the fruit.

When buying, check the sieve has an ear or lip to rest on the edge of the container. Also, check the strength of the mesh, as this will take the brunt of the pressure when you work foods through it. The weakest point is the base of the bowl, which may eventually wear out

### 3 | CHINOIS SIEVE AND PESTLE

Also called a 'bouillon strainer', this conical sieve funnels liquids downwards into the tip for more accurate pouring. The ultra-fine, twill-like mesh clears stocks of every sediment, and strains sauces to velvety smoothness. The sieve is sturdily made with a wide top band to which are welded the handle, hook and frame. The frame protects the mesh from damage.

The pestle is tapered to fit into the bottom of the sieve. Use it to extract flavoursome juices from solid matter, and to produce a very thin purée from softened vegetables – great for thickening and flavouring sauces.

### 4 | NYLON SIEVE

A nylon sieve is non-corroding and therefore preferable for sieving acidic foods that might be tainted by metal. It is moulded from one piece of plastic, and therefore has no joints to break or work loose. This sieve will last a lifetime.

### 5 | DOUBLE-MESH SIEVE

This sieve is made of two metal meshes laid on top of each other at an angle. In effect you are giving flour and icing (confectioner's) sugar a double sifting at once. This particular sieve comes as part of a set of four, ranging from a small 14 cm/5½ inch drum size to a generous 20 cm/8 inch sieve that will sift a lot of flour at once.

## 6 DRUM SIEVE

Used in India and known as a 'tamis' in France, this sieve has a closely woven mesh stretched tightly over its circular frame. Frames come in wood, plastic or metal, and in a wide range of diameters. Meshes are made of nylon, silk or metal, and are usually interchangeable. Depending on the closeness of the weave, the sieve removes lumps from powders and coarse particles from spices and grains. A drum sieve is useful for sieving large amounts, as ingredients pass through a flat mesh more quickly than a concave one. However, dry ingredients tend to randomly sprinkle over a wide area, which may be a problem if you want to confine them to a small space.

6

8

## 7 DREDGERS

A dredger is used to store and dispense flour (large holes) or sugar (small). Turn the dredger upside down and shake it like a salt cellar. The top unscrews for filling. When refilling a sugar dredger, take care not to let the crystals stick to the thread. They will cause problems with screwing and unscrewing.

7

## 8 FLOUR SIFTER

This spring-set sifter aerates clumpy flour to a light, uniform consistency. It has a fine-meshed base with spokes set above it that agitate the flour as you press the trigger in the handle. The process is somewhat laborious, so the tool is suitable for sifting small quantities of flour only. Try to refrain from washing it, as a damp sifter turns flour to paste. It will remain clean enough if you store it in a plastic bag in a cupboard or drawer.

'The process of sieving helps to incorporate air as the powder floats down into the bowl.'

Though the terms 'sieve' and 'strain' may be used interchangeably, a strainer usually has a coarser mesh than a sieve, or holes as in a colander, perforated spoon or centrifugal salad spinner. Strainers are used mainly to separate solids from liquids, whereas skimmers remove sediment, fat and scum from the surface of liquids.

# strainers and skimmers

If you cook for crowds, make large amounts of stock, or regularly make pasta for four or more people, a colander is essential; you will need one at least 28 cm/11 inches in diameter. It should have feet or a solid base so both your hands are free for lifting the pan from which you are pouring the food. Smaller colanders do not need feet, but should have a sturdy lip and a handle for resting on the receiving utensil. The base should be fairly flat so food at the bottom is not crushed. To drain efficiently, a colander needs a generous number of holes that are reasonably-sized but not so large that peas slip through them. Check they are evenly distributed and come up the sides of the colander.

If you enjoy properly dressed salads, a spinner for drying leaves is another must. A collapsible wire basket is attractive, but does not do as good a job as an enclosed spinner that strains by centrifugal force. Some spinners have a perforated base – the idea being that you hold it over the sink, and spin and drain in one go. I usually end up showering my feet, so I prefer a spinner with a solid base. Other essential straining tools are a large perforated metal spoon (look for one that is made from a single piece of metal) and, if you make tea with loose leaves, a tea strainer.

1 **CHEESECLOTH**
A lightweight muslin cloth that filters out fine sediment from stocks or clarified butter. Place a large piece inside a sieve or colander and pour the liquid through. It is light-textured enough to wrap round soft food such as yoghurt cheese (see page 132) to mould it or hold it in shape.

2 **COLLAPSIBLE COLANDER**
This is a good piece of lateral kitchen thought that takes into account the fact that modern kitchens often have limited storage space. This clever collapsible colander is made in sections that you push out to form a stepped bowl with strainer at the base; then push together to squash back into a round disc.

1

2

## STAINLESS STEEL COLANDERS

3  This well-designed stainless steel colander has wide grips for lifting or for resting on a bowl, a solid stand, widely spaced holes and an eyelet for hanging. The flat base helps prevent food from being crushed. It is available in diameters ranging from 16–28 cm/6–11 inches. Buy the largest one possible.

4  Although you can set the long-handled colander down, you are more likely to hold it with one hand and the pan from which you are pouring in the other. It is therefore best used for straining manageable amounts rather than the contents of a vast and heavy pot. A diameter of 18–20 cm/7–8 inches is a useful size to have.

## 5  ENAMEL COLANDER

Old-fashioned enamelled colanders add timeless grace and style to country kitchens with their sturdy metal shape, evenly punctuated holes and simple metal handles. Now the style has been updated with contemporary bright colours and lozenge-shaped perforations. Still the same worthy job description.

## 6  SINK STRAINER

Who decrees colanders shall be round? Not Good Grips – they have a design that fits the shape of a large sink when you want to rinse large bulky leafy vegetables or a basket of apples under the tap. The foldable handles can also be pulled under the rectangular bowl so it can stand, literally on its own two feet. Handy when you want to use two hands for peeling directly into the bowl section.

## 2 PERFORATED SPOON

This vital utensil simultaneously strains and lifts small amounts of food from pans. Cooking juices, water or fat drains off through the perforations.

## 4 TEA STRAINER

Made of stainless steel, this smart little strainer has a very fine mesh for straining freshly brewed tea or coffee. The wire ear and handle allow you to rest it on your cup – useful if you need two hands to lift a large teapot.

1

2

3

4

5

6

## 1 PAN DRAINER

Shaped like a crescent moon, the stainless steel strainer drains small-to-medium amounts of pasta or vegetables directly from the pan. It is held in place by a rim that attaches to the pan edge, and will fit a range of pan sizes.

## 3 WIRE SCOOP

This is ideal for scooping up french fries, sauté potatoes and any deep-fried food. Oil quickly drains away through the coarse wire mesh. The scoop also makes a useful skimmer.

## 5 CONICAL STRAINER

This coarse-meshed strainer is handy for straining into a small or narrow container such as a gravy boat or sauce jug. It is available in four diameters ranging from 8–20 cm/3–8 inches.

## 6 DRAINER SCOOP

School cooks can often be seen brandishing these sturdy stainless steel basket scoops when they are serving peas or sweetcorn from hot bain maries. In fact they have other uses – such as you can use them to dunk tomatoes or peaches into boiling water, prior to peeling them. If you have the two different sizes you can make deep-fried potato baskets by lining the larger one with potato slices, pressing in the smaller one to shape, then deep-frying in oil. This style of strainer is popular with Chinese cooks too.

### 7 PERFORATED SKIMMER

The extra-wide, flat bowl skims froth and skin formed by impurities from the surface of stews and stocks. The skimmer can also be used for lifting and draining dumplings, gnocchi or quenelles from broth.

### 8 WIRE SKIMMER

This skimmer is designed for removing fried food from deep fat. The wires allow fat and small bits of sediment to drain quickly away.

### 9 NOODLE/PASTA SCOOP

This simply designed wire strainer has a pleasingly deep and generous bowl that is ideal for scooping up and straining gnocchi, dumplings and stuffed pasta or noodles such as ravioli, wontons or pot stickers.

### 11 SALAD SPINNER

Old-style cooks would dry wet salad leaves by tying them in a tea towel which they would whirl around their head. This was simple and effective but did rely on no one else being within spraying distance. Now the principle of centrifugal force has been turned ninety degrees and leaves are whirled horizontally in a special spinner with the leaves put into an inner perforated basket. You turn the handle on the top, slowly at first until it gains speed and the water is collected into a small bowl.

7

8

9

### 10 WIRE SHAKER

Charming though it may be, there is no avoiding the fact that water sprays everywhere when you whirl this shaker round. Shaking it gently over the sink does not do the job effectively, and it is best used in the garden.

10

11

# chicken stock

This gelatinous stock forms part of the 'pumpkin and girolle soup' recipe contributed by Alain Ducasse (see page 135). The stock differs from others in that the chicken carcasses are brought to the boil quickly, then boiled for 5 minutes, during which time the scum is removed – most recipes specify that this stage is carried out slowly. After rapid boiling, the carcasses are drained and returned to the pan with fresh water, and the usual slow simmering begins. This method certainly speeds things up, and the finished stock is delicious.

MAKES 2 LITRES/2 1/2 QUARTS

**TOOLS**
cook's knife
vegetable peeler
stockpot
skimmer or perforated
   spoon
strainer or colander
large piece cheesecloth or
   butter muslin
large bowl

**INGREDIENTS**
3 kg/6 1/2 lb raw chicken
   carcasses and/or parts
2 onions, quartered
1 large leek, green parts only,
   rinsed well and cut into
   5 cm/2 inch pieces
1 carrot, halved
2 celery stalks, cut into 5 cm/
   2 inch pieces
1 tomato, quartered
6 parsley stems
1 tbsp coarse sea salt
1 tsp black peppercorns

**1** Place the chicken in a large stockpot. Cover with cold water and bring to the boil over a high heat. Boil for 5 minutes, skimming the surface frequently.

**2** Drain the chicken and rinse under cold water. Rinse out the stockpot to remove the scum, return the chicken to the pot, and cover with cold water.

**3** Add the vegetables, parsley stems, salt and peppercorns, and bring to the boil over a high heat. Reduce the heat and cook, uncovered, at the barest simmer for 2 hours, without stirring or skimming. Remove from the heat and let cool briefly.

**4** Strain the stock through a strainer or colander lined with cheesecloth or muslin, into a large bowl. Let the stock cool completely, then store, covered, in the refrigerator for no more than 24 hours, or freeze in small containers.

**5** Before using, scrape off and discard the fat that forms on the surface.

# meat stock

Strainers and skimmers are vital for successful stockmaking. They remove fat, solid matter and impurities, resulting in a clear, sediment-free stock. For a brown stock, brown the bones first in a hot oven, pouring off any fat before adding them to the stockpot.

MAKES 2 LITRES/2½ QUARTS

| TOOLS | INGREDIENTS |
|---|---|
| cook's knife | 3 kg/6½ lb beef or veal bones |
| stockpot | 2 large onions, chopped |
| skimmer or perforated | 2 large carrots, chopped |
| spoon | 2 celery sticks, chopped |
| colander | 200 g/7 oz mushrooms, sliced |
| large piece cheesecloth | 300 ml/1¼ cups dry white wine |
| | 1 bouquet garni, fresh or dried |
| | ½ tsp black peppercorns |

**1** Put all the ingredients in a stockpot. Add 10 litres/11½ quarts of cold water (a) and bring to the boil. Don't add salt at this stage – it's better to add it to the dish in which the stock will be used.

**2** As the liquid reaches boiling point, a harmless scum forms. Scoop this off with a skimmer or perforated spoon and discard (b). Turn the heat to a simmer and continue to skim off the scum. Cook, uncovered, for up to an hour until the mixture has reduced by at least half.

**3** Remove the pan from the heat and let the stock stand for 30 minutes. This allows debris to settle.

**4** Line a colander with wet cheesecloth. Slowly pour the stock through the cloth, leaving the debris behind (c). For a clearer stock, pour the liquid through the cloth again. Cool the stock, then chill. Scrape off any fat that forms on the surface.

a

b                c

# fruit coulis

**TOOLS** medium/large round bottomed sieve, metal ladle, large mixing bowl

To make a smooth fruit coulis you should use ripe fruits that break down easily, such as raspberries, strawberries or kiwi fruit. Blitz the fruits in a food processor or simmer them first in a little water and sugar, for example blackcurrants or blackberries. Place the sieve over a large bowl then tip the fruits into the sieve, without overcrowding them. Press down on the fruits using the back of a metal ladle or a flat pastry/icing scraper or even a large wooden spoon, rubbing the crushed fruits through so that a smooth, pip-free purée collects in the bowl. Discard the seeds and skins in the sieve. Sweeten the pulp with some icing (confectioner's) sugar to taste and a squeeze of lemon juice, if you think it necessary. Chill until required, but use within 24 hours.

# yoghurt cheese

This is a type of soft cheese popular in the Middle East and India. Yoghurt is tied up in cheesecloth and left to strain for 6–36 hours – the shorter time making for a very soft, mild cheese and the longer a denser cheese with a more pronounced flavour. The end result is similar to cream cheese, but lighter in texture and lower in fat.

Yoghurt cheese is wonderfully versatile, and combines well with either sweet or savoury ingredients. For a tasty snack, spread it on crackers or toast or, if it is quite soft, serve it as a dip with crisp vegetable sticks. For a quick and simple dessert, sweeten yoghurt cheese with a dusting of sugar or a slick of honey, fruit purée or syrup.

Mixing yoghurt cheese with chopped fresh herbs is also delicious. Finely chopped spring onions (scallions) green chilli or a little grated ginger can be mixed in, too. Firm yoghurt cheese can be shaped into balls or logs and then rolled in sesame seeds or coarsely ground black or green peppercorns. Serve with flat bread and olives.

a

# basic yoghurt cheese

The type of yoghurt used will affect the flavour, texture and amount of cheese produced. Natural (plain) yoghurt gives off a fair amount of liquid, so the weight of cheese produced is less than you would get from thicker, set yoghurt. Greek yoghurt is thicker still, giving off correspondingly less liquid. Bio yoghurt is naturally mild in flavour, and produces a mild-tasting cheese, whereas cheese made from yoghurt high in lactic acid has a sharp, acidic flavour. Organic wholemilk yoghurt makes a particularly delicious cheese – mild in flavour, with a slightly grainy texture.

ENOUGH FOR 3–4 SERVINGS

b

**TOOLS**
3 x 50 cm/20 inch squares
   cheesecloth
colander
string
large deep bowl
wooden spoon

**INGREDIENTS**
1 kg/4 cups natural (plain)
   yoghurt

**1** Moisten the three squares of cheesecloth and use to line a colander, draping the corners over the sides (a).

**2** Spoon the yoghurt into the centre of the cheesecloth. Gather up the four corners and twist to squeeze the yoghurt into a ball (b).

**3** Tie tightly with string and fasten onto the handle of a wooden spoon. Rest the spoon over a deep bowl so the yoghurt hangs free, or over a shallower bowl, with supports on either side, as shown here (c). Make sure there is a gap of at least 5 cm/2 inches between the bottom of the cheesecloth and the base of the bowl. Leave in a cool place to drip for 6–36 hours.

c

# yoghurt cheese with pomegranates, spiced sugar and pistachios

In this simple but exquisite dessert, jewel-like pomegranate seeds and a sprinkling of green pistachios adorn a sweetly perfumed mound of yoghurt cheese. The yoghurt should be quite soft and mild, so drain it for about 12 hours.

SERVES 4

**TOOLS**
small bowl
cook's knife
wooden spoon
paring knife

**INGREDIENTS**
6 tbsp pistachio nuts
1 quantity yoghurt cheese
    made with organic
    wholemilk yoghurt and
    drained for about 12 hours
    (see page 131)
1/2 tsp rose water
3 tbsp spiced sugar (see
    below)
1 large pomegranate

**1** Put the pistachio nuts in a small bowl and cover with boiling water. Leave for 5 minutes, then slip off the skins. Roughly chop the nuts and set aside.

**2** Beat the yoghurt cheese with the rose water and spiced sugar. Divide the mixture between four serving bowls.

**3** With a small sharp knife, cut the pomegranate skin lengthways into four segments, taking care not to puncture the juicy seeds inside. Break the pomegranate in half, and then into quarters. Bend the skin back to release the seeds, discarding any bits of membrane. Sprinkle the seeds over the yoghurt and top with the pistachios.

**SPICED SUGAR** Using a pestle and mortar, grind to a powder 6 cloves, 1/2 teaspoon of peppercorns, the seeds from 15 green cardamom pods and 1/2 teaspoon of fennel seeds. Mix with 1/2 teaspoon ground cinnamon. Stir the spices into 350 g/1¾ cups sugar, mixing well. Keep it in a screw-top jar and use as needed.

# pumpkin and girolle soup
## ALAIN DUCASSE

Alain Ducasse, the first male chef to earn six Michelin stars, and mentor to a new generation of chefs who have changed the face of French cooking. A fine-meshed chinois sieve is used to purée the pumpkin for this delicious soup, which is ladled over tiny sautéed girolle mushrooms and topped with crisp lardons and whipped cream.

SERVES 4

**TOOLS**

cook's knife
large saucepan
wooden spoon
chinois sieve and
    wooden pestle
deep bowl
paring knife
mezzaluna
medium frying pan

utility knife
small saucepan
small strainer
small frying pan
paper towel
medium saucepan
balloon whisk
electric mixer

**INGREDIENTS**

3 tbsp olive oil
450 g/1 lb fresh pumpkin, peeled, seeded and cubed
1 small onion, finely chopped
500 ml/2 cups chicken stock
6 tbsp unsalted butter
1/2 tsp fine sea salt, or to taste
1/4 tsp freshly ground black pepper, or to taste
100 ml/scant 1/2 cup double (heavy) cream, lightly whipped
100 ml/scant 1/2 cup double (heavy) cream, whipped until it holds firm peaks (optional)

**FOR THE GARNISH**

1 tbsp olive oil
225 g/8 oz small girolle mushrooms, trimmed and cleaned
1 shallot, finely chopped
2 tbsp unsalted butter
2 tbsp finely chopped chives
75 g/2 1/2 oz bacon or pancetta, cut into 1 cm/1/2 inch cubes (lardons)
4 leafy sprigs fresh chervil

**1** In a large saucepan, heat the oil over a medium-high heat. Add the pumpkin and onion, and stir to coat with oil. Reduce the heat to medium-low and cook until the pumpkin softens and the onions are translucent, about 5 minutes. Pour in enough stock to cover, and cook until the pumpkin is very soft, 10–15 minutes.

**2** Remove from the heat and let cool slightly. Set a chinois sieve over a deep bowl, then pour the soup into the sieve, pressing the vegetables through the mesh with a wooden pestle. Reserve the sieved liquid.

**3** To prepare the garnish, heat the oil in a medium frying pan over a medium heat. Stir in the girolles and shallot and cook, stirring often, until the mushrooms give off their liquid and it evaporates. Add the 2 tablespoons of butter, then the chives. Stir in and remove from the heat.

**4** Put the lardons in a small saucepan and cover with cold water. Bring to the boil over a high heat, reduce the heat to medium-low, and simmer for 1 minute to blanch and remove some of the salt. Drain and rinse briefly in cold water. Drain again and pat the lardons dry. Sauté the lardons in a small frying pan until they are brown and crisp. Transfer to paper towels to drain.

**5** To finish the soup, combine the pumpkin mixture with the remaining chicken stock in a medium saucepan. Bring to a gentle boil, then stir in the 6 tablespoons of butter, and the salt, pepper and lightly whipped cream.

**6** Pour the mixture into the bowl of an electric mixer and beat on medium speed until smooth and creamy. Adjust the seasoning according to taste.

**7** Pour into a warmed soup tureen. Divide the girolle mixture among four warmed soup plates. Spoon in the pumpkin soup. Sprinkle on the lardons, then, if you wish, place a dollop of thickly whipped cream in the centre of each serving. Garnish with sprigs of chervil and serve immediately.

# ramen with pork and vegetables
## EMI KAZUKO

This hearty noodle soup was contributed by leading Japanese food writer Emi Kazuko.
Ramen are Chinese-style noodles served in soup with various toppings. The dish is
one of the most popular in Japan, where there is a ramen museum, a ramen village and
even ramen appreciation clubs. These noodles can be bought from healthfood shops
and good supermarkets. You will need strainers of various sizes for straining the
vegetables, meat and noodles.

SERVES 4

**TOOLS**
medium frying pan
paring knife
medium saucepan
small and medium strainers
cook's knife
small bowl
utility knife
large saucepan
colander

**INGREDIENTS**
*FOR THE BRAISED PORK*
200 g/7 oz pork fillet in one
  piece
1 tbsp vegetable oil
500 ml/2 cups chicken stock
5 tbsp shoyu (Japanese soy
  sauce)
2 tbsp sugar
1/2 tsp salt

2 spring onions, sliced into
  5 cm/2 inch pieces
3–4 cm/1 1/4–1 1/2 inch square
  piece fresh ginger, sliced

*FOR THE RAMEN*
100 g/3 1/2 oz spinach,
  trimmed
60 g/2 1/4 oz bean sprouts
salt and freshly ground black
  pepper

200 g/7 oz dried ramen
  (Japanese noodles)
1 litre/4 cups chicken stock
1/2 pork or beef stock
  (bouillon) cube (optional)
100 g/3 1/2 oz baby sweetcorn,
  cooked
1 spring onion (scallion), finely
  chopped, to garnish
rayu, or chilli oil (optional)

**1** Brown the pork on all sides in the oil over a medium-high heat to seal the meat. Remove from the heat.

**2** Put all the other ingredients for the braised pork in a medium saucepan and bring to the boil. Add the browned meat and
simmer, covered, for about 1 hour. Leave the meat to cool in the liquid.

**3** Lightly boil the spinach, then drain under cold running water for a few seconds. (This makes the green colour bright.) Squeeze
out excess water with your hands, and chop into bite-sized pieces.

**4** Place the bean sprouts in a bowl and pour boiling water over them. Leave for 5 minutes, then drain. Season with a pinch of
salt and pepper.

**5** Remove the pork from the saucepan and thinly slice. Drain the cooking juices and reserve, discarding the other ingredients.

**6** Cook the ramen in a large pan of boiling water according to the packet instructions. Drain under cold running water to rinse
off the starch.

**7** Heat the chicken stock, adding the 1/2 stock cube if a stronger soup is required. Stir until the cube has dissolved.

**8** Warm up the sweetcorn in boiling water and drain.

**9** Put 2 tablespoons of the cooking juices into each of four individual noodle bowls. Add the hot stock to half fill the bowls.
Put a quarter each of the ramen, sliced pork, bean sprouts, spinach and sweetcorn on top. Sprinkle with chopped spring onion
and serve hot with rayu.

# boiling
and
steaming

Along with knives, pots and pans can be your pride and joy, for it is within them that your efforts at chopping, mixing and seasoning culminate, and the alchemy that is cooking takes place. Because of this, they are more complex than knives. Knives are about cutting and the results are instant and obvious; pots and pans require patience and co-operation. For successful results you must get to know how they react with different ingredients and heat levels.

# pots and pans

My earliest pots and pans were mean-spirited affairs made of thin aluminium or coated with quaintly speckled enamel. I did not treat them well, nor they me. However, though they warped and buckled, burnt me and the food, they did not succeed in dampening my embryonic passion for cooking. Since then I have amassed a collection, and the more I cook, the better quality I buy.

There's no denying that good pots and pans are expensive. It's worth starting off with three or four good ones that earn their keep, rather than buying several of inferior quality. Don't be tempted by the growing number of so-called 'chef's sets' on the market. You will inevitably end up with pans you never use because you don't cook the type of food for which they are intended. They also take up valuable storage space. You may, of course, be given a set of pans, perhaps as a wedding present, but this leaves you the problem of having to live up to their demands. If you are new to cooking, you may feel pressured into embarking on recipes that are over ambitious or simply not your style. It is far better to build up your collection of pans gradually and let your culinary repertoire expand at its own pace.

## choosing saucepans

When all new saucepans look shiny and nicely finished, it is hard to know how to choose the best other than be guided by price. The labels may not tell you the full story. Before buying, think carefully about how you will use and store your saucepans. Size, shape, weight and material (see 'materials choice', page 12) are all-important.

A basic set of saucepans might consist of a couple of smallish pans, say 1.7–2 litres/1¾–2 quarts, one or two medium pans (3–4 litres/3–4¼ quarts) and a large pan (5 litres/5¼ quarts). A very small pan (1 litre/4 cups) is useful for melting butter, boiling eggs or reheating small amounts of food, and a small non-stick milk pan is a must for heating milk.

The base should be thick and solid – a thin base will buckle over high heat, making it useless on a sealed cooking plate. The base of a good-quality pan is ground flat as opposed to stamped flat; check for the marks of the grinding machine. Test for flatness by placing the pan on a level surface and pressing to see if it wobbles.

If your hob has radiant rings, measure the rings and buy pans to fit. The perfect pan should fit exactly over the heating element. This keeps the heat where it is meant to be – under the pan.

A pouring lip will cope with a thin liquid like milk, but not a thick sauce or soup. If the pan is to be used by a left hander, you will need a left-handed pan or one with two pouring lips or a continuous pouring rim that lets you pour from any point. A pouring rim also pours large amounts of liquid and thick liquids more efficiently.

Handles should be long enough to distance your hand from the heat. They must be comfortable to hold and firmly attached to the pan. Rivets or a firm weld are better than screws. Pans that hold 3 litres/3¼ quarts or more should have two handles – either a pair of ears, or one ear opposite a long handle. Lid handles and knobs should be heat-resistant. If metal, they should conduct heat less well than the pan. If your pan is intended to go in the oven, the knob and handle need to be heatproof. Lids are essential for steaming, poaching and stewing, and for bringing water to the boil sooner. They should fit snugly, especially if you want to use the pan for steaming.

## 1-3 STAINLESS STEEL SAUCEPANS

These top-quality, American, traditional-style saucepans, with tight-fitting lids and riveted stay cool handles, are manufactured by All-Clad. Made of a 3-ply bonded construction of an inner layer of 18/10 stainless steel and outer layer of magnetic stainless steel, with a core of pure aluminium that runs all the way up the sides of the pan, they are suitable for all types of hobs, including induction ones. Available in a range of sizes from just under 1 litre/1 quart through to 3.5 litres/3¾ quarts, the larger sizes are ideal for boiling pasta, rice and vegetables, as well as making soups and stocks. The larger capacity pans come with a loop handle for safer lifting.

## 4 STAINLESS STEEL SAUTE PAN

This shallower sauté pan, also made by All-Clad, is of the same high quality as the saucepans. The largest sauté pan comes in at a mighty 5 litres/5¼ quarts – perfect for chilli con carne, curries and pasta sauces to feed a crowded house of family and friends.

# materials science

No one metal has all the qualities for a good pan. Aluminium and copper are the best heat conductors, but they are not very hardwearing. Also, aluminium pans can pit and warp, and copper needs to be lined with tin otherwise the metal reacts with acidic foods. However, they can both be combined with other metals. Aluminium can also be strengthened either by anodising with an electro-chemical process or turned into cast aluminium, that is the molten metal is poured into a shaped mould and left to set. Cast aluminium pans have the heating qualities of cast iron but are lighter in weight. Copper pans are very expensive, but because they have good thermal conductivity (and so cook evenly over the whole pan surface) they are hugely popular with chefs for high temperature frying and sautéing. Titanium is forty times harder than stainless steel but almost half the weight, and when combined with aluminium you get a heat efficient, durable pan.

If you have an induction cooker you need special pans with ferromagnetic bases. Copper and aluminium are not suitable but stainless steel can be treated to be magnetic. Some cast iron pans with thick heavy bases are also suitable. Check the label; if a pan is not marked as suitable for induction, then it is not.

## 1 STAINLESS STEEL SAUCEPANS

These sleek, professional pans are made in top-grade 18/10 stainless steel. The base has an aluminium/magnetic steel/aluminium core sealed between two layers of stainless steel, so are suitable for all hobs, including induction ones. The handles are welded to the body of the pan over a large area so cannot come loose. They are comfortable to hold but tend to get hot when cooking at high temperatures. Despite this, these pans are a joy to use. They are available in five sizes, from 1–4.8 litres/1–5 quarts, and it's well worth having all five; otherwise aim for the largest, the smallest and one in the middle.

1

2

3

## 2 NON-STICK ALUMINIUM SAUCEPAN

Sturdily built but not too heavy, this pan is made from non-warping cast aluminium, coated inside and out with a SilverStone® non-stick surface. This makes for fat-free cooking and easy cleaning, so it is a good pan for sauces, porridge, scrambled eggs and other foods that stick. Suitable for all hobs except the induction type, the pan has a thick ground base for fast, even heat distribution. The oven-proof glass lid has a heat-resistant knob. Available in blue, green or black, and in three sizes, from 1.1–2.25 litres/1–2¼ quarts.

## 3 TRI-PLY SAUCEPAN

Tri-ply technology involves moulding a double layer of top quality 18/10 stainless steel with an inner core of conductive aluminium. The extensive Le Crueset range of Tri-Ply pans have moulding that covers the entire pan surface from base to rim so the whole pan gets hot at once and cooks the food from all sides. This also means hot liquids don't splutter or spit when you pour them out over the curved rim. Made in all shapes and sizes, deeper pans carry a useful liquid measures gauge on the inside. Suitable for hob, oven and induction cookers.

#### 4 ANODISED ALUMINIUM MILK PAN

As boiling milk tends to stick to the pan, this is one of the few saucepans that needs a non-stick surface. This one, in heavy-gauge aluminium, has an anodised surface on the exterior and a hard-wearing, easy-to-clean, non-stick interior. The stainless steel handle is firmly riveted. If you are left handed, make sure your pan has a pouring lip on both sides.

#### 5 TITANIUM SAUCEPAN WITH REMOVABLE HANDLE

Titanium-coated pans by German manufacturer SKK are described by many professional cooks as having the best non-stick, scratch-resistant hard-wearing surfaces. A combination of super-hard titanium and aluminium makes for a highly efficient, durable, light pan. The handles in this SKK range are detachable, so the pans are ovenproof. In addition, the milk pan has pouring lips on both sides, perfect for left- and right-handed cooks alike.

#### 6 INFUSED ANODISED SAUCEPAN

American brand Calaphon is described as revolutionary hybrid cookware with the best of all worlds in terms of looks, durability, heating and versatility. The core metal is anodised aluminium and is infused with non-stick PTFE properties, so is tough enough to cope with metal stirring utensils. The triple-riveted handles, including shorter helper handles on larger pans, are made of non-heat conductive stainless steel which means they don't get too hot to handle. And all this topped with beautiful stainless steel lids that fit snugly over the easy-pour flared rims.

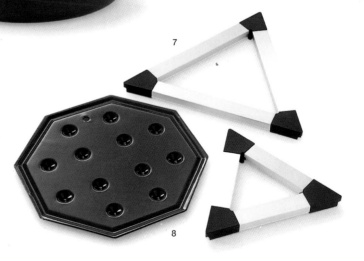

### ACCESSORIES

#### 7 TRIVET/POT STANDS

Trivets protect work surfaces from heat marks caused by hot pans and dishes. Many worktops and tables are increasingly heatproof to a certain degree but it's best, with heavy metal pans in particular, to place a trivet down first. This attractive triangular duo of aluminium with black rubber corners also slot into each other to make a mat and will keep their good looks without staining or buckling.

#### 8 HEAT DIFFUSER

When you need a very low hob temperature for poaching fish, making proper custards, even reheating coffee a heat diffuser can reduce the temperature to below simmering. This model by Austrian company Trukka, is a design classic. It provides an air cushion between two dimpled metal plates to control and hold heat at below 100°C/200°F. Perfect for gas cookers, solid electric plate hobs and even camping stoves, so there should be no more burnt milk saucepans or overcooked scrambled eggs.

# beyond basics

As your cooking skills develop and you gain in confidence, you will undoubtedly start to yearn for more pots and pans. The ones shown here are the next step up from a basic set and will ease tasks such as preserving and making soups and sauces. Buy them according to need. Some of these pans are quite large, which might be off-putting if you have limited storage space. However, because they can perform two or three functions, they may actually help you to economise on space as well as money. For example, a large stockpot is well worth having as it can double up as a pasta pot and, though it does not have the flaring sides that help evaporation, as a preserving pan. A pressure cooker without its lid makes a very useful large saucepan.

## 1 STOCKPOT WITH PASTA INSERT

If you care about good soup, a stockpot is almost a basic requirement. This large stainless-steel pot accommodates a large amount of meat, bones and vegetables. The tall, somewhat narrow shape slows evaporation of liquid and allows solid matter to remain submerged for hours at a time, while coaxing out delicious flavours. A five-layer ground base (see the double boiler, below) permits prolonged simmering without scorching. The generously sized and firmly welded U-shaped handles make for safe lifting.

The perforated pasta insert lifts out easily, leaving the cooking water behind – a process that is easier and safer than carrying a heavy pot from hob to sink. Those who wear glasses will also appreciate steam-free lenses. The insert also doubles up as a strainer when blanching vegetables.

## 2 PRESSURE COOKER

Pressure cookers work by trapping steam by means of a specially designed tight-fitting lid. As pressure builds up, the temperature rises above boiling point and steam is forced into the food, reducing cooking time and cutting down on fuel. This stainless steel model has a domed lid housing a self-regulating valve, which limits the amount of escaping steam. Normal cooking time is reduced by at least one third. The solid ground base is suitable for all hobs, including the induction type.

## 3 DOUBLE BOILER/CASSEROLE

This stainless steel pan has a well-fitting lid and a solid, five-layer base – a core of silver alloy/copper/silver alloy is sandwiched between two layers of stainless steel, giving excellent heat conduction. Simmering water in the lower pan gently heats the base of the upper one without touching it. This is an infallible way of making egg-based sauces such as hollandaise – the gentle heat keeps egg proteins from coagulating, as they do in scrambled eggs, so they are able to emulsify with butter to form a smooth and silky sauce. Used either on its own or with the lid, the bottom part of this pan doubles as a saucepan or casserole.

## 4 COPPER SAUCEPAN

A copper pan is the Rolls-Royce of cookware. This splendid saucepan encapsulates the properties of three different metals: copper for speedy and even conduction of heat, a taint-free stainless steel lining – far more durable than traditional tin – and a stay-cool, cast iron handle. The only drawback is that once you have one copper pan, you'll want more.

## 6 SLANT-SIDED ALUMINIUM SAUCEPAN

Made from heavy-gauge aluminium with a 6 mm/¼ inch ground base, this homely-looking pan is perfect for sauces. The narrow base speeds up boiling, and the splayed-out sides increase the surface area, encouraging evaporation and reduction of liquids. A continuous turned edge means you can pour from any position. The bakelite handle remains cool during cooking. It is best not used for cooking vegetables as uncoated aluminium will cause them to discolour.

## 8 SLANT-SIDED ANODISED ALUMINIUM SAUCEPAN

Altogether smarter with its grey anodised coating and elegant stainless steel handle, this 1 litre/1 quart pan is similar in design and function to the uncoated aluminium pan. Two pouring spouts make it suitable for left- or right-handers. It is also available in a 2.3 litre/2½ quart size, which makes a brilliant sauté pan. The larger size has a continuous turned rim, making it easier to tip out solids and liquids.

## 5 PRESERVING PAN

This capacious, 13 litre/13¾ quart, stainless steel cauldron will satisfy the needs of the most dedicated jam-maker. It has a solid ground, wide base to ensure even heat distribution, and gently flaring sides that increase the surface area and encourage evaporation. The invaluable helper handle assists with lifting and pouring, while the semi-circular handle across the top can be locked in an upright position to keep the pan cooler.

## 7 BAIN MARIE

Any saucepan can be turned into a double boiler with this 'universal' stainless steel bain marie. Place it in the top of the pan above simmering water and it will heat the contents gently and evenly. This is an ideal way of making egg-based sauces and custards, melting chocolate or cheese, or reheating leftovers without scorching them.

## 9 BUTTER WARMER

This neat little stainless-steel pan, measuring just 11 cm/4¼ inches in diameter, is specially designed for warming or clarifying small amounts of butter. It is attractive enough to be brought to the table, for example to pour butter over asparagus. You can also use it for warming brandy or melting chocolate. It has just one pouring lip, so left-handers either have to pour 'backwards' or use their right hand.

## blanching

This is a method of partially cooking vegetables by immersing them briefly in rapidly boiling water. Vegetables that are to be frozen are blanched to halt enzyme activity. It is a method used by chefs to cook vegetables ahead of serving – they can be quickly reheated with no loss of flavour or texture. After blanching, vegetables are best plunged into a bowl of iced water, a process known as 'refreshing'. This also has the effect of heightening the colour, especially of green vegetables.

## simmering

Cooking a casserole or stew at a simmer, with the occasional bubble breaking the surface, helps soften the collagen in meat tissues, making tough meat more tender. The process is further helped by adding acidic ingredients, such as tomatoes and wine. A casserole with a heavy metal base allows for gentle simmering.

## reducing

You can make quick gravy to serve with pan-fried meats, such as chops or steak, cooked in a sauté pan. After cooking, remove the meat to a serving dish and keep warm. Add a small glass of wine to the pan juices and stir well, scraping up any meaty deposits with a wooden spoon or wooden spatula. Boil rapidly to reduce by a third, then pour in 2–3 tablespoons of cream or crème fraîche. Allow the gravy to bubble for a few seconds, add seasoning and pour over the meat.

## gentle boiling

The turbulent action of fast boiling can break up the texture of certain foods, such as floury potatoes, as the starch swells. When boiling point is reached, turn the heat to a gentle boil. Some starchy foods can boil over if the heat is too high, for example pasta and rice. A tablespoon of oil helps to maintain surface tension.

# specialist pans

These pans are marvellous to have for those times when you get the urge to whip up zabaglione or boil caramel, for example. Though they tend to be expensive, it is a pleasure to use pans in which form so closely follows function. The rounded shape of the zabaglione pan perfectly echoes the shape of the whisk used to create the foam. The fondue pot is wide and shallow enough for several people to dip their forks at once without being overcrowded. The flared sides of the polenta pan increase the surface area and encourage evaporation.

## 1 POLENTA PAN

Known as a 'paiolo' in Italy, this beautiful copper pan makes the rather arduous process of stirring polenta a pleasure rather than a chore. The pot heats quickly and evenly, while flared sides make prolonged stirring easier. The shapely wooden handle stays cool and comfortable during stirring. The pan is unlined and should therefore be rubbed with vinegar and salt before and after each use (see 'miraculous meringues', page 101).

## 3 SUGAR BOILER

This attractive copper pan is ingeniously designed to cope with the very high temperatures produced during sugar boiling. The pan is unlined because the traditional tin lining would melt (see 'materials choice', page 12), and sugar does not react adversely with copper. You might expect the handle to be made of wood, which remains cool, but at the temperatures reached wood might catch fire. Even oven gloves are in danger of igniting. The problem is solved by the hollow copper handle, into which chefs traditionally insert a length of broomstick. Because the handle is funnel shaped, the wood is in contact with only a small area of hot metal, so the wood does not catch fire and it prevents heat from being conducted to the end where your hand is.

## 2 ZABAGLIONE PAN

This solid copper pan is designed to froth up the warm, creamy alcoholic custard known as zabaglione in Italy and sabayon in France. Set over a low flame or double boiler, the copper conducts even, gentle heat, which softly coagulates the egg proteins as you whisk. The deep, rounded bowl facilitates the rapid scooping movement needed to create the foam.

## 4 CHEESE-FONDUE POT

A cheese fondue consists of cheese and wine melted together in a pot over a flame. Diners spear chunks of bread on forks and swirl them in the communal pot, which is known as a 'caquelon' in France and Switzerland. As high temperatures make cooked cheese stringy, cheese-fondue pots are traditionally made of glazed earthenware, which withstand only gentle heat. Meat-fondue pots are made of metal.

## 5 FONDUE SET

At one time the ultimate wedding present, fondue sets are becoming popular again for quick and easy entertaining. This modern-style set is made of black enamelled cast iron with a white interior. It comes with a small spirit candle-style burner underneath and shiny stainless steel forks. The spirit burner melts the cheese (a mixture of Gruyère and Emmenthal) white wine and kirsch then keeps it at just the right dunking consistency for cubes of crusty bread.

## 6 CATAPLANA

A traditional Portuguese stewing pot, inspired by Moorish cooks, this is made by hinging together two tin-lined copper wok-shaped pans. You place ingredients for a tasty casserole or stew in one half then lock on the domed lid and simmer gently on a flame or hob. It makes a great holiday memento.

## 7 SAUCIER

To make fresh sauce, chefs like to use a pan that bows slightly outwards with a wider top than bottom. Liquids like wine or stock can then quickly bubble merrily down for maximum flavour. The saucier pan is also perfect for dishes that require stirring, such as risottos and roux-based sauces. This All Clad model has a copper core at the base and so is ideal for cheffy recipes.

## 8 ELECTRIC CHOCOLATE TREAT MAKER

Fresh fruits, marshmallows and biscuits dipped into a smooth, melted chocolate 'fondue' is an increasingly popular dessert at parties. Chocolate, though, can be temperamental if overheated, so remove the anxiety with an electric 'bain marie'. Break good chocolate (70% cocoa solids) into the little saucepan, add warmed double cream for a more milky taste or brandy for a kick and switch on the dial.

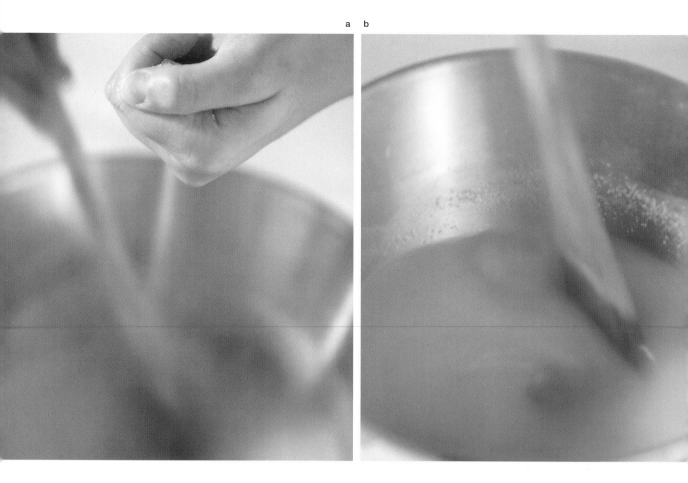

# basic polenta

Polenta is a mild-tasting grain with a deeply satisfying flavour. Cooked to a porridge-like consistency it can be served wet, like mashed potato, or cooled and cut into shapes, then grilled or fried until crisp – delicious for mopping up tasty juices and gravy.

Polenta is traditionally made in a special pan (see page 148), but a large, heavy-based saucepan makes a good substitute. The hot mixture plops enthusiastically as it cooks, so use a long-handled wooden spoon to avoid being scalded.

SERVES 4–6

**TOOLS**
polenta pan or large,
   heavy-based saucepan
long-handled wooden
   spoon
wooden board or wide,
   shallow pan
palette knife (metal spatula)

**INGREDIENTS**
1.5 litres/6 cups water
1 tsp salt
300 g/1²⁄₃ cups polenta

**1** Bring the water and salt to the boil in a polenta pan or large saucepan, then turn down to a medium simmer. Stirring with one hand, use the other to add the polenta in a steady stream, holding your fist in a funnel shape (a).

**2** Continue to add the polenta, making sure each fistful is absorbed before adding another. Traditionally, polenta is stirred in one direction only (b).

**3** Polenta is best stirred for up to 20 minutes. Take care as the hot mixture will spurt upwards as it thickens. It is cooked when it comes away from the side of the pan (c).

**4** To serve polenta wet, simply spoon it into a serving dish. Otherwise, pour it onto a board or a wide, shallow pan, level the top with a wet palette knife (d) and allow to set firm before frying or grilling.

# grilled polenta with musrooms, celeriac and sage

This recipe uses polenta that is slightly stiffer than the basic mix, and is particularly suitable for cutting into shapes before frying and grilling. Use two or three different kinds of cultivated or wild mushrooms such as chanterelles or oyster, shiitake, chestnut or portobello.

SERVES 4–6 AS A STARTER OR LIGHT MEAL

**TOOLS**
polenta pan or large, heavy-based saucepan
long-handled wooden spoon
18 cm/7 inch square roasting tin
palette knife (metal spatula)
cook's knife
grill pan
pastry brush
vegetable peeler
small frying pan
tongs
large frying pan

**INGREDIENTS**
500 ml/2 cups water
1/2 tsp salt
125 g/3/4 cup polenta
2 tbsp olive oil, plus extra for brushing polenta
2 tbsp butter
2 tbsp chopped fresh sage
100 g/31/2 oz peeled celeriac (celery root), cut into 1–5 cm/1/2–2 inch cubes
500 g/1 lb 2 oz assorted mushrooms, cut into bite-sized chunks if large
2 garlic cloves, finely chopped
1 tbsp chopped flat-leaf parsley
squeeze of lemon juice
pinch of cayenne pepper
sea salt and freshly ground black pepper
small sage sprigs, to garnish

**1** Cook the polenta following steps 1–3 of basic polenta (see page 150). Pour the polenta into a small, square roasting tin and level the surface with a wet palette knife. Leave to cool.

**2** Preheat the grill to very hot. Meanwhile, slice the polenta into six rectangles, then halve each rectangle diagonally to make two triangles. Brush both sides with olive oil and spread out in a grill pan.

**3** Heat 1 tablespoon each of the oil and butter in a small frying pan. Add half the sage and gently fry for a few seconds to flavour the oil. Add the celeriac cubes and fry over a medium heat for a few minutes, turning them with tongs until lightly coloured on all sides. Remove the pan from the heat and set aside.

**4** Heat another tablespoon of butter and oil in a large frying pan. Fry the remaining sage for a few seconds, then throw in the mushrooms. Stir-fry over a moderately high heat for 7–9 minutes until most, but not all, of the liquid has evaporated. Add a little more oil if necessary.

**5** While the mushrooms are cooking, grill the polenta pieces until golden and crisp at the edges, then turn them over and grill the other side.

**6** Keeping an eye on the polenta, tip the contents of the celeriac pan into the mushrooms, and add the garlic. Fry for another minute, then add the parsley, lemon juice and seasonings.

**7** Divide the polenta triangles between individual plates and pile the mushroom mixture on top. Garnish with the sage sprigs.

Steaming and poaching are beautifully simple methods of allowing clean, natural flavours to shine through. In fact, steamed food can make a welcome change from a surfeit of chargrilling, searing and stir-frying. If you're on a low-fat diet, steamed food is definitely worth trying, and if you cook in cramped conditions or are without an oven, steaming food in tiered containers can be a lifesaver, as the Chinese have known for centuries.

# steamers and poachers

As the name suggests, steaming is a method of cooking food in the vapours that rise from boiling cooking liquid, which may be water, stock or wine. Virtually any food can be steamed: meat, poultry, seafood or vegetables. It is mainly the Asian cuisines – Thai, Japanese and Chinese – that make the most of the techique. Food is placed on a plate or in a perforated container set above the liquid and covered with a lid to keep the steam in. Because the food is not in direct contact with the liquid, fewer nutrients are lost by leaching. If the liquid is water, it will be nicely flavoured by the food being steamed, and can be used to make a gravy or sauce, or for cooking rice.

If you have never tried steaming, start off with a 'universal' steamer insert, or a fold-out steamer. Then you can progress to a more expensive multi-tiered set. Some items, such as fish kettles or asparagus steamers, are expensive and worth buying only if you are likely to use them regularly. On the other hand, a Christmas pudding ball costs little and is fun to have even if you use it only once a year.

## 1 THREE-PIECE STEAMER
You can cook a complete meal with this 20 cm/8 inch diameter, tiered steamer set. Made of top-quality 18/10 stainless steel, the bottom pan has a thick ground base for maximum heat conduction and for use on any hob, including the induction type. The bottom pan can be used to simmer a stew, while large vegetables such as cauliflower or root vegetables steam in the deep middle container, and smaller vegetables steam in the top. The lid fits all three parts so you can use the base alone or with one steamer basket only.

## 2 BAMBOO STEAMERS
Pleasing and inexpensive, these Chinese steamers can be used for a variety of foods, including whole fish, pieces of poultry, as well as vegetables and dumplings. They come in various sizes and can be stacked as high as you like in a wok or pan of boiling water. New steamers should be soaked for 15 minutes to get rid of the pervasive smell of bamboo.

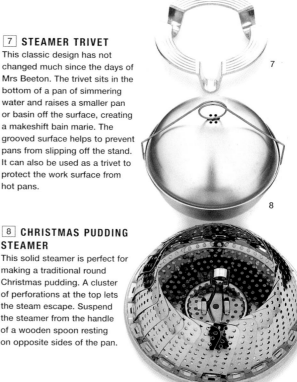

## 6 RICE STEAMER

Save on cleaning the pan and cook rice in a perforated rice steamer. The perforations are small enough to prevent uncooked grains of rice escaping. It is important not to overfill the steamer as rice doubles in volume once cooked. The chain has a hook on the end so you can hang it from the side of the pan.

## 3 COUSCOUSIER

This two-tiered aluminium pot is designed for cooking the North African semolina-based dish couscous. The lower pot stews meat, poultry or vegetables in a fragrant broth, from which steam rises through the upper pot's perforated base to cook the couscous above.

## 4 'UNIVERSAL' STEAMER INSERT

Sit the stepped base of this perforated container in any of your saucepans, and you have an instant steamer for cooking vegetables, fish, meat or poultry. It is an indispensable utensil.

## 7 STEAMER TRIVET

This classic design has not changed much since the days of Mrs Beeton. The trivet sits in the bottom of a pan of simmering water and raises a smaller pan or basin off the surface, creating a makeshift bain marie. The grooved surface helps to prevent pans from slipping off the stand. It can also be used as a trivet to protect the work surface from hot pans.

## 8 CHRISTMAS PUDDING STEAMER

This solid steamer is perfect for making a traditional round Christmas pudding. A cluster of perforations at the top lets the steam escape. Suspend the steamer from the handle of a wooden spoon resting on opposite sides of the pan.

## 5 ELECTRIC STEAMER

A plug-in steamer is invaluable for those who like a lighter style of cooking. This Tefal Vitacuisine model is more than just a steamer, it is a multi purpose table top cooker. At the base is a shallow reservoir in which you heat water until it starts to steam. Then you can either fit on a base cooking plate to steam fish or chicken covered with a clear domed lid, or use a large bowl or smaller baskets for vegetables or rice. Multi purpose and ideal for small families or couples.

## 9 FOLD-OUT STEAMER

Suitable for most saucepans, this compact stainless-steel steamer opens out like the petals of a flower. The perforations and gaps between the overlapping petals allow steam to penetrate well and the feet raise the food above the boiling water. The central stalk limits the ways in which you can arrange the food, but on some models the stalk is removable. The fold-out steamer is available in two sizes, expanding from 14–22.5 cm/5½–9 inches and from 17.5–27.5 cm/7–11 inches.

Poaching is a technique that falls midway between boiling and steaming. Foods such as chicken or fish are laid on a rack in a pan with just enough liquid to cover the bottom, and simmered very gently until they are barely cooked. The food remains wonderfully moist and, because it has not been subjected to vigorous boiling, keeps its shape.

## poaching fish on a rack

**TOOLS** fish kettle/poacher

Ensure the whole fish (salmon, snapper or sea bass) is scaled, gutted and washed, and that it will fit the rack. Then calculate the cooking time by measuring the depth of the fish at the thickest part and allow 5 minutes per cm, e.g. 7 cm depth x 5 = 35 minutes.

Make a court bouillon: simmer 1 shallot, 1 carrot and 1 celery stick, sliced, in 1.5 litres/6 cups water with 150 ml/$2/3$ cup white wine, some thyme sprigs, a bay leaf, $1/2$ teaspoon peppercorns and 1 teaspoon sea salt for 10 minutes in the fish kettle.

Lower in the fish on the rack, return to a gentle simmer, cover and cook gently for the calculated time. Lift out the rack and let the fish stand for 10–15 minutes before serving. The court bouillon can be strained and reused.

**10 ASPARAGUS STEAMER**
Some cooks think that if asparagus stalks are cooked until tender, the tips will be overcooked. This tall, narrow steamer allows the stalks to stand upright in boiling water while the tips cook in the steam. However, if you don't mind stalks a little on the crunchy side, you could just lay the spears flat in an ordinary steamer.

10

11

**11 FISH KETTLE/POACHER**
Small or medium-sized fish can be poached in any pan into which a rack will fit, but large, round fish such as salmon need an elongated pan that allows the fish to lie flat. The fish is placed on a perforated, two-handled rack that lifts easily from the pan, draining the fish without spoiling its shape. Some fish kettles are so large they will straddle two burners. There is also a glamorous diamond-shaped kettle that is designed especially for poaching flat fish such as halibut and turbot.

12

**12 EGG POACHER**
Though it is not a poacher in the strict sense, as the eggs are cooked by steam, this magnificent pan not only cooks faultless eggs but, without the insert, doubles up as a non-stick sauté pan. Made in top-quality 18/10 stainless steel (see 'materials choice', page 12), the poacher has non-stick, removable egg cups, and a 5 mm/$1/4$ inch thick, encapsulated base suitable for all types of hob.

# steamed salmon with ginger, spring onions and bok choy

Steamed on a trivet over a wok, this comforting and easily digested dish is ideal if you are under stress or entertaining in a hurry. It needs nothing more than a simple accompaniment of plainly boiled white rice. Make sure the fish is very fresh.

SERVES 4

| TOOLS | INGREDIENTS | |
|---|---|---|
| paring knife | 4 salmon steaks or cutlets, | 2 large spring onions |
| 23 cm/9 inch plate | each about 2.5 cm/1 inch | (scallions), green parts |
| trivet | thick | included, shredded, but |
| aluminium foil | 2 tsp finely chopped fresh | with green and white parts |
| wok with lid | ginger root | kept separate |
| another wok or large, | 2 tbsp rice wine or dry sherry | 3 heads bok choy, quartered |
| heavy-based frying pan | 1 tbsp soy sauce | lengthways |
| fish turner | 1/2 tsp salt | good squeeze of lime juice |
| small saucepan | 4 tbsp groundnut oil | coarsely ground black pepper |
| | | 2 tsp sesame oil |

**1** Rinse the fish steaks, pat dry with paper towels and place in a single layer on a heatproof plate.

**2** Combine the ginger root, rice wine or dry sherry, soy sauce and salt. Sprinkle this over the fish, rub it into the flesh and leave for 20 minutes, turning once.

**3** Place a trivet in a wok and add enough water to reach halfway up the trivet. Bring to the boil, place the plate of fish on the trivet and cover with a loose tent of foil. Adjust the heat so the water is just boiling and put the lid on the wok. Steam for 10–15 minutes until the fish is opaque and just starting to flake.

**4** While the fish is steaming, heat 2 tablespoons of groundnut oil in a second wok or large, heavy-based frying pan. When the oil is almost smoking, fry the white part of the spring onions for 30 seconds. Throw in the bok choy and stir-fry for 4–5 minutes until the stalks are just tender, but still crunchy. Splash with a good squeeze of lime. Arrange in small mounds on four warmed serving plates.

**5** Using a fish turner, carefully lift the fish pieces from the wok and place on top of the bok choy. Arrange the green spring onions on top and sprinkle with several grindings of black pepper.

**6** Heat the sesame oil and remaining 2 tablespoons of groundnut oil in a small saucepan. When it is very hot, pour over the green spring onions and fish. Serve immediately.

**STEAMING IN A WOK** You will need a metal or wooden trivet (see page 155) and a domed lid, often sold with a wok set. Food is steamed on a heatproof plate set on the trivet in the base of the wok. If you like, you can wrap food such as small chicken breasts or fish steaks in greaseproof paper parcels, as shown. Alternatively, bamboo baskets (see page 154) can be stacked on the trivet; they can also be used on a trivet in an ordinary saucepan.

'A wok is amazingly versatile. It is, of course, the best tool for stir-frying, but is also excellent for deep-frying, braising and steaming.' **SRI OWEN**

# tunisian couscous with greens, red peppers and garlic
## PAULA WOLFERT

The recipe for this traditional Tunisian dish was contributed by Paula Wolfert, the award-winning American food writer whose speciality is Mediterranean and Middle Eastern cuisine. The melange of dill, fennel, celery leaves, red-pepper flakes and spices makes for a light and delicious couscous, which Paula suggests serving with glasses of buttermilk, as is the custom. If you don't have an authentic North African couscousier (see page 155), use a large saucepan with a tightly fitting steamer insert. If fennel leaves are hard to find, increase the amount of dill. Tabil is a Tunisian spice paste, which you can buy from shops specialising in Middle Eastern Food.

SERVES 6

**TOOLS**
cook's knife or mezzaluna
garlic press
paring knife
couscousier or large
    saucepan with steamer
    insert
large frying pan
wooden spoon or turner
long fork
tongs

**INGREDIENTS**
3 tbsp chopped dill leaves
3 tbsp chopped fennel leaves
6 tbsp chopped flat-leaf
    parsley
handful of celery leaves,
    chopped
handful of carrot tops,
    chopped
1 large spring onion (scallion),
    thinly sliced
1/2 small leek, thinly sliced

8 tbsp olive oil
1 small onion, chopped
3 tbsp tomato purée
5 large garlic cloves, crushed
2 tsp sweet paprika
2 tsp salt, or more, to taste
2 tsp ground coriander or tabil
    powder
1 tsp ground caraway seeds
1 1/2–2 tsp dried red-pepper
    flakes, preferably Aleppo or
    Turkish pepper

500 ml/2 cups water
450 g/generous 2 1/2 cups
    medium-grain couscous
1 fresh green chilli, deseeded
    and finely chopped
1 red (bell) pepper, deseeded
    and cut into 6 pieces
6 garlic cloves, peeled and
    left whole

**1** Fill the bottom of the couscousier or saucepan with water and bring to the boil. Put the perforated top or steamer insert in place. Add all the green leaves, spring onions and leeks, and steam, covered, for 30 minutes (a).

**2** Remove from the heat and allow to cool, uncovered. When cool enough to handle, squeeze out the excess moisture and set aside.

**3** Heat the oil in a large frying pan and add the onion. Gently fry for 2–3 minutes to soften, then add the tomato purée. Cook, stirring, until the paste glistens.

**4** Add the crushed garlic, paprika, salt, coriander or tabil, caraway and red-pepper flakes. Cook slowly until the mixture is well blended. Add 250 ml/1 cup water, cover and cook for 15 minutes.

**5** Remove the pan from the heat. Stir the dry couscous into the contents of the pan and stir until well blended (b). Stir in the steamed greens, leeks and spring onions, and mix well. Fold in the green chilli, pieces of red pepper and garlic cloves.

**6** Top up the bottom of the couscousier or saucepan with water and bring to the boil. Put the top or steamer insert in place. Add the contents of the pan and steam, covered, for 30 minutes (c).

**7** Turn out the couscous onto a warm serving dish. Use a long fork to break up any lumps. Use tongs to fish out the whole garlic cloves and pieces of red pepper, reserving them.

**8** Stir 120 ml/1/2 cup water into the couscous, taste for seasoning and cover with foil. Set in a low oven for 10 minutes before serving.

**9** When ready to serve, decorate the couscous with the slices of red pepper and whole garlic cloves. Serve with glasses of buttermilk.

a

b

c

# mussels diablo

## ALDO ZILLI

This spicy dish, contributed by Aldo Zilli, chef patron of Zilli Fish, Zilli Cafe and Signor Zilli Restaurant and Bar in Soho, London, is perfect for reviving jaded palates. Adjust the amount of chilli to suit your own taste and serve with lots of crusty bread to dip into the sauce.

SERVES 4

**TOOLS**
large lidded saucepan
cook's knife
large metal spoon

**INGREDIENTS**
1.5 kg/3 lb 5 oz mussels,
    cleaned
2 tbsp olive oil
3 garlic cloves, finely chopped
6 red chillies, deseeded and
    finely chopped
2 tbsp Italian flat-leaf parsley,
    finely chopped
250 ml/1 cup dry white wine
400 g/14 oz can chopped
    tomatoes
toasted ciabatta, to serve

**1** Discard any mussels that are open. Heat half the oil in a large pan and add the mussels, garlic, chilli and half the parsley. Cover and simmer over a medium heat for 4–5 minutes.

**2** After 4 minutes, begin to remove the mussels that have opened; after 6 minutes, remove and discard any that have not opened.

**3** Clean the pan, heat the remaining oil and add the reserved mussels, wine and chopped tomatoes. Cook for 15 minutes. Stir in the remaining parsley.

**4** Serve the mussels hot in bowls with toasted sliced ciabatta.

Coffee-making at its most basic is simply a matter of pouring boiling or near-boiling water over fresh grounds and allowing them to steep. However, during nine centuries of coffee-drinking, brewing equipment has proliferated. Like coffee, properly made tea needs clean-tasting, freshly drawn and boiled water. A kettle is essential – water is more easily poured from a kettle's spout, and because the water is enclosed, it boils more quickly and uses less fuel.

# coffee and tea

### 2  CAPPUCCINO CREAMER

To create the essential froth for your cappuccino, half-fill the creamer with milk, heat until it is almost boiling, then put on the lid and pump the plunger for about 30 seconds. Alternatively, you can heat milk in a saucepan and froth it with a spiral whisk.

### 3  ESPRESSO COFFEE MAKER

This traditional aluminium machine can be used on the stove top. Fill the bottom container with water, insert a funnel-shaped filter and fill it with medium-ground coffee. Then screw the top section to the lower. Once heated, water and steam are forced through the grounds and on through a narrow shaft in the top container. A high-octane brew then gushes out of the top of the shaft, filling the upper container. It is available in 3-, 6-, 9- and 12-cup sizes.

### 1  DRIP-FILTER COFFEE MAKER

This electric coffee maker has a convenient swing-out filter holder operated by a press button, a front-filling water tank and a magnified water-level indicator. To use, fill the cone-shaped filter with finely ground coffee and then with boiling water, which filters through into the carafe. The cone shape permits fast saturation of the grounds, while the density of the filter slows down the rate at which water passes through. The filter also absorbs some of the coffee's natural oils, resulting in a brew that is light and clear but somewhat lacking in body.

### 4  PLUNGE-FILTER COFFEE MAKER

This provides one of the simplest ways of making a rich brew. Pour boiling water over coarsely ground coffee in the base of the glass beaker. After 5 minutes of steeping, press the plunger – two filter discs attached to a central shaft – down over the grounds. This traps them in the base of the beaker and leaves the coffee ready to pour. Make sure the discs fit tightly into the beaker, or grounds will escape up the side. One drawback is that the coffee does not maintain its temperature while steeping. This can be overcome by using an insulated cover; newer models have an acrylic outer casing, which retains heat better.

Coffee aficionados at home or in offices have fuelled a boom in high tech espresso-style automatic machines, without the need for a trained *barista*. Many of these machines are designed to work with pre-measured fresh coffee 'bags' (known as pods or capsules) which you drop into the filter cup that is then fixed onto the steaming outlet to drip out as coffee into the cups below. Some models do allow you to use loose, finely ground coffee which you tamp down into the filter cup with a press. Machines also have a special frothing device that slots onto the filter cup to help make a good head of coffee froth, known as the *crema*. All machines have a side spout for steaming and frothing milk.

Before you buy, check the bar pressure rating, the higher the bars the more cups of coffee you can make in succession: 12–15 bars is more than adequate for a small household. High users such in would benefit from ratings of around 19 bars.

5

### 5 GAGGIA BABY

One of the best brands on the market, this domestic espresso machine is a perfect size for a home kitchen and produces two espresso sizes cups of coffee at a time. It has a brushed metal body with a removable water tank and side spout for steaming and frothing milk for cappuccinos. The machine can use ground coffee or drop-in pods.

6

7

### 6 NESPRESSO

The Nespresso system (pioneered by coffee giant the Nestle group) uses special sealed capsules of coffee which you buy in bulk in a range of strengths, flavours and aromas. A number of manufacturers make machines that use the capsule system (which means you cannot use loose coffee or the pods). This Magimix Nespresso machine is a cube-size box with cup warmers placed at the top next to the water tank. Neat and chic.

### 7 BEAN-TO-CUP MACHINES

If you prefer to grind your own beans just before making a cup of coffee, as they do in stylish coffee houses, then choose a bean-to-cup machine. Jura Impressa is regarded as the crème de la crème of this style of machine, its single rotary operating switch system leaving you to choose to dispense a shot of espresso or a larger Americano cup. You can also control the height of the water spout for a good head of *crema*.

# tea

There was a time when a kettle was simply a kettle; nowadays there is a wide choice of designs. If you are choosing a kettle to use on the hob, look for one with a broad, flat base to maximise contact with the heat source and speed up boiling. The handle should be positioned well above the lid, and the spout should direct steam away from your hand. If you want an electric kettle, bear in mind that the tall jug type needs less water to cover the heating element, so it boils more quickly and uses less electricity than the traditionally shaped sort. Some are fitted with a fine mesh filter just behind the spout to separate out the sediment that may accumulate in hard-water areas.

There is no doubt that tea is better made from loose leaves that are allowed a 5-minute steep in a teapot, rather than from a teabag pressed hurriedly into a cup. Like kettles, teapots come in a range of styles, materials, colours and shapes. Tea seems to taste better when made in a glazed china or earthenware pot. Glass and stainless-steel pots also work well but are more expensive.

Whatever the material, there are three main features to look for: a non-drip spout, a lid that stays in place as you pour the last cup, and a handle large enough to distance your knuckles from the pot.

1

2

## 1 WHISTLING KETTLE
The Alessi Kettle with Bird, designed in 1985, has become something of a modern design icon. It fulfils all the essential requirements of a stove-top kettle, possessing a wide, thick base, a comfortable, heatproof handle that positions your hand away from the steam, and a cheerful whistle.

## 2 TRADITIONAL KETTLE
This homely looking kettle is made in enamelled steel and comes in a range of bright colours, as well as black or white. The handle and knob are heat resistant. The solid ground base is suitable for all types of hob, including the induction type and the solid heating plates of range cookers.

### 3 CHINA TEAPOT

This classic white porcelain teapot has a pleasingly fat spout, a round knob for lifting the lid and a capacious, curved handle. An integral filter prevents stray tea leaves from escaping into your cup.

### 4 GLASS TEAPOT/TEA PRESS

This elegant teapot works like a plunge-filter coffee maker. Tea leaves are held in a perforated container while steeping. When the tea looks the right colour, press down the plunger and remove the central insert.

### 5 CORDLESS KETTLE

In the old days electric kettles had wires trailing across the worktop from socket to kettle plug. Then a clever designer thought of repositioning the actual plug underneath the kettle on a base unit. So all you need to do is lift the kettle on or off the base unit to connect it. The kettle appears almost cordless with the wire tucked neatly away. No more wet hands fiddling with live kettle plugs.

### 6 JAPANESE TEAPOT

Those who enjoy invigorating whole leaf green teas might like to brew up in a traditional Japanese silky black porcelain tea pot with an attractive dimple-patterned top and lid. The wide oval handle and internal strainer adds a touch of tea ceremony authenticity.

### 7 BALL INFUSER

This stainless steel tea infuser, made of fine mesh in two halves on a spring, is perfect for those who prefer to brew their favourite cuppa with loose leaves but wish to avoid the chore of emptying the soaked leaves left inside a pot. Good, too, for dried tisanes or fresh mint leaves.

# braising
# and
# stewing

These pots form the backbone of any kitchen. They competently brown and simmer fragrant braises and stews, and come in all shapes and sizes, each with special characteristics. Materials are the same as those used for saucepans (see 'materials choice', page 12). However, unlike saucepans, these pots have small, ear-shaped handles, perhaps suggesting less input is required from the cook.

# metal pots

The ideal pot is one you can use on the hob or in the oven, and that is good looking enough to bring to the table. It is also useful to have at least one that can be transferred from freezer to oven. You will need a couple, either in cast iron or stainless steel, for everyday use; a 6 litre/6⅓ quart pot serves 4–5 people, and a 3 litre/3 quart pot serves 2–3 people. A shallow braising pan with a lid is also likely to earn its keep for big weekend breakfasts and for slow-cooked braises, and a Dutch oven is a must for pot roasts and stews.

2

## 2 BRAISING PAN

This braiser can be used either on the hob or in the oven. The domed lid encourages condensation and maintains moist heat within the pot. Without the lid, the braiser can be used for frying. Made of 18/10 stainless steel, with a thick aluminium core extending up the sides of the pan, it conducts heat quickly and evenly.

## 3 BRITTANY POT

Classic French dishes such as moules marinières, as well as stews and braises, are traditionally prepared in these rounded pots with gently flaring sides. Made of enamelled cast iron, this one comes in four colours.

1

3

## 1 POT ROASTER

This magificent 6 litre/6⅓ quart cooking pot is made of 18/10 stainless steel with an aluminium inner core for optimum heat conductivity that extends all the way up the sides of the pan (see 'materials choice', stainless steel, page 12). The pot comes with an internal rack for easy removal of contents. It has ear-shaped, stay-cool handles and a well-fitting lid.

## 4 ENAMELLED DUTCH OVEN

Also known as a 'cocotte', this heavy, enamelled cast iron pot has tall, straight sides for holding substantial quantities of meat, vegetables and liquid. The lid can either be sealed with a strip of dough or set slightly askew to allow steam to escape. A thick base allows for even heat transference on the hob. Use for browning and slowly simmering stews.

## 5 CAST IRON DUTCH OVEN

This handsome pot in pre-seasoned, black cast iron, designed by Björn Dahlström, is destined to become a modern classic. Like the traditional Dutch oven, it has a thick, flat base for browning, and tall sides for holding a large volume of meat and liquid. The sides flare slightly to encourage evaporation. It is available in a 5 litre/5¼ quart size only.

## 6 BRUSHED STAINLESS STEEL CASSEROLE

Another modern classic by Björn Dahlström, this pot has the same minimalist lines as the cast iron Dutch oven. Available in 5 and 8 litre/5¼ and 8½ quart sizes, it is made of superior 18/10 stainless steel with a thick aluminium core that extends all the way up the sides, giving good heat distribution throughout the pan.

## 8 LAFONT ENAMELLED CAST IRON COOKWARE

Originally founded in France by the Lafont family back in 1879, but now relocated to Argentina, these beautifully handcrafted cast iron pots are porcelain enamelled fired at incredibly high temperatures, which gives them an exceptionally high durability and strength. Sold in a selection of casseroles and gratin dishes they also come in an array of positively pretty colours.

## 7 NON-STICK CASSEROLE

Made of titanium, the surface of this casserole is hard enough to withstand the use of metal tools. A rock-solid base browns and crisps at high temperatures but is equally good for gentle simmering. The glass lid, sold separately, is heat resistant up to 260°C/500°F so can be used in the oven. It is suitable for all hobs except the induction type.

### 9 TRI-PLY STAINLESS STEEL CASSEROLE

This multi-function, high-quality stainless steel, double-handled casserole is perfect for cooking on the hob and the oven. Manufactured by Le Creuset, it has tri-ply layers of stainless steel with an aluminium core running up the sides of the pan, which eliminates spitting when it is tilted. This makes for more efficient heating all round the pan. An outer magnetic steel layer means it is perfect for induction hobs.

10

### 10 DOUFEU

The Doufeu is Le Creseut's answer to the traditional Dutch oven or Moroccan tagine and is perfect for long slow pot roasts and casseroles. The secret lies in the lid, which has dimples on the inside and an inverted dip outside, in which you place ice cubes, thus chiling the cast iron lid. During baking, steam rises from the food inside the pan, condenses on the dimples and falls back to moisten the food. Long slow cooking may require the ice cubes to be replaced.

### 11 BABY REMOKSA

Developed in Czechoslovakia in the 1930s, this portable electric cooker on legs was a godsend for those with basic cooking facilities during post-war communist rule. The lid contains the heating element, which heats up the metal casserole. So simple and so clever – we loved it. It's perfect for cooking small portions of stews when you don't want to heat up a whole oven. Great, too, for bedsits and even caravans. Larger models have a glass lid so you can check on your simmering dinner.

11

12

### 12 MUSSEL POT

Mussels make an easy quick meal but need a lot of room with a well fitting lid. This special mussel pot has a domed lid which doubles as a serving dish. The stainless steel pot gets really hot so once the lid is clamped in firmly the mussels cook quickly in the rising steam. After a few minutes, remove the lid and slide out the molluscs and their juices into the lid to serve.

# braising and pot roasting

a    b

**TOOLS** cast iron cooking pot, glass measuring jug

Cuts of meat that benefit from slow cooking, such as stewing beef, shoulder cuts, shin, skirt, etc, can be first browned in a frying pan with oil, onions and root vegetables, then transferred to a heavy cooking pot (cast iron or earthenware) with a close-fitting lid.

Braising is a moist cooking method in which food is cooked with just enough liquid to produce steam. Pot roasting is similar but usually involves whole joints of 1 kg/2¼ lb or more. The method relies on moisture from the food rather than added liquid. Allow at least 45 minutes per kg/2¼ lb of cubed meat and 1 hour per kg/2¼ lb for rolled joints at 150–160°C/300–325°F/gas 2–3. A little stock, water, wine, cider or beer (about 300–500 ml/10–18 fl oz) should be added to a braise (a), along with herb sprigs or whole spices.

The cooking juices can be strained off and boiled down in a clean saucepan on top of the stove, or the meat and vegetables removed with a slotted spoon (b, c) and the whole roasting pan placed on top of the stove for boiling down to reduce the juices to a sauce-gravy (d). If you wish to thicken the juices, make a thin paste of 1 tablespoon of cornflour (cornstarch) mixed with a little cold water then stir briskly into the bubbling juices until they thicken to a glossy gravy.

c    d

# beef pot roast with winter vegetables

Long, slow cooking in the moist environment of a covered pot produces meltingly tender meat from even the cheapest cuts. The meat is first browned and then gently cooked with vegetables and a relatively small amount of liquid. It bubbles away lazily, enriching the liquid in which it sits, and leaving you free to get on with other things. A sprinkling of finely chopped parsley, lemon zest and garlic added just before serving gives a lovely fresh flavour to the dish.

SERVES 4

| TOOLS | INGREDIENTS | | TO SERVE |
|---|---|---|---|
| paring knife | 1.6–1.8 kg/3½–4 lb rolled | 1 bay leaf | 16 baby carrots |
| Dutch oven or casserole into | beef, silverside or brisket | 2–3 strips thinly pared orange | 12 small potatoes, shaped into |
| which the meat fits snugly | 4 fat garlic cloves, thinly sliced, | peel | ovals |
| tongs | plus 1 small garlic clove, | 350 ml/scant 1½ cups red | 1 Savoy cabbage, quartered |
| cook's knife | finely chopped | wine | and cut into ribbons |
| vegetable peeler | about 20 rosemary leaves | 150 ml/⅔ cup meat stock, | knob of butter |
| citrus grater | 2 tbsp vegetable oil | preferably home-made | |
| mezzaluna | 25 g/2 tbsp butter | sea salt and freshly ground | |
| conical sieve | 1 red onion, finely chopped | black pepper | |
| 4 saucepans | 2 celery stalks, finely diced | finely grated zest of 1 lemon | |
| whisk | 2 carrots, finely diced | 3 tbsp chopped flat-leaf | |
| carving knife | small bunch of thyme | parsley | |
| | | ½ tbsp plain (all-purpose) flour | |

**1** Preheat the oven to 140°C/275°F/gas 1. Dry the meat thoroughly and make slits all over it with the tip of a small knife. Poke pieces of sliced garlic and the rosemary leaves into the slits, using the knife tip to embed them (a).

**2** Heat the vegetable oil in a Dutch oven or heavy-based casserole. When it is very hot, add the meat and brown on all sides, turning with tongs (b). Transfer the meat to a plate.

**3** Add half the butter to the pot. When it is sizzling, add the onion, celery and carrots, and gently fry for about 5 minutes until soft. Put the meat back in the pot, together with any juices that have accumulated. Add the thyme, bay leaf and orange peel, then pour in the wine and stock (c). The liquid should come no more than one-third of the way up the meat. Season with salt and freshly ground black pepper.

**4** Bring the liquid to the boil, then cover with a tight-fitting lid and put in the oven. Cook for 3–3½ hours, turning every 30 minutes or so. Towards the end of the cooking time, mix together the lemon zest, parsley and chopped garlic. Mix the flour and remaining butter to a smooth paste. Cook the carrots, potatoes and cabbage until tender but still crisp and brightly coloured. Keep them warm in separate saucepans. Remove the meat from the pot. Put it in a warm dish and leave to rest in a warm place for 10 minutes, loosely covered with foil.

**5** Meanwhile, blot up any fat from the braising liquid with paper towels. Strain the vegetables into a saucepan, pressing them with the back of a spoon to extract all the liquid. Bring the strained liquid to the boil, adding any juices that have flowed from the meat. Whisk in small pieces of the butter and flour paste, continuing to whisk until the sauce is smooth.

**6** Carve the meat and arrange in overlapping slices on a warmed platter. Pour the sauce over the meat and sprinkle with most of the parsley mixture. Warm the vegetables through with butter, season with sea salt and freshly ground black pepper, and sprinkle with the remaining parsley.

a

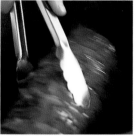
b

c

'Perfect for pot roasting, the cocotte is an indispensable piece of equipment at Le Gavroche.'

**MICHEL ROUX**

# pot roast chicken with beer and mushrooms

## MICHEL ROUX

This simple but delicious recipe was contributed by Michel Roux, who, in 1967, with his brother Albert, opened the acclaimed Le Gavroche in Lower Sloane Street, London. During his long and celebrated career he has received numerous awards, and in 1999 the British Catering Trade voted him 'Man of the Millenium'.

The cast iron enamelled cocotte in which the pot roast is cooked is, according to Michel, 'the cornerstone of all French classics'.

SERVES 4

**TOOLS**
enamelled Dutch oven or
    cocotte

**INGREDIENTS**
1 corn-fed chicken, weighing
    about 1.5 kg/3 lb 5 oz
olive oil
butter
60 g/2½ oz shallots, finely
    chopped
250 g/9 oz button mushrooms,
    washed and sliced
1½ tbsp brandy
2 tbsp beer, preferably bitter or
    ale
2 tsp brown sugar
200 ml/1 scant cup double
    (heavy) cream
salt and freshly ground black
    pepper

**1** Preheat the oven to 220°C/425°F/gas 7. Season the chicken all over and in the cavity. Place in an enamelled cast iron pot with a little olive oil and butter, put into the oven, reduce the temperature to 200°C/400°F/gas 6 and roast for 40 minutes, basting the bird several times during cooking, turning it onto its other side and finally on to its back. When cooked, transfer the chicken onto a plate, breast down, so that the juices permeate the meat while it rests.

**2** Discard the fat from the pot, then add a knob of fresh butter, place over a low heat and sweat the shallots until translucent, stirring with a wooden spoon.

**3** Add the mushrooms and cook for a further 3 minutes. Pour in the brandy and scrape the bottom of the pan with the spoon to lift off the sugars. When almost dry, pour in the beer and sugar, and boil to reduce by half. Add the cream and reduce again to a light sauce consistency. Whisk in 50 g/2 tablespoons cold butter to give the sauce sheen. Pour in any juices that have run from the chicken, season to taste, place the chicken back in the pot and bring to the table.

Together with iron, clay was one of the earliest materials used for making cooking pots, dating back to primitive times when food was cooked over an open fire or a bed of hot ashes. As their origin suggests, these homely pots are designed for simmering over a low gas flame or in the oven. Whatever their shape – tall, shallow, straight or bulbous – their virtue is that they absorb heat slowly and evenly, so food cooks uniformly without burning or drying out.

# clay pots

1

2

3

### 1 BEAN POT/FAIT TOUT
This solid, spacious 4 litre/4$\frac{1}{2}$ quart pot truly lives up to its French name (fait tout, meaning 'does all'). The bulging sides increase both the capacity and the actual heating surface, while the slightly narrower neck helps to slow evaporation. The bean pot is resistant to thermal shock so it can be transferred directly from the freezer to the oven. It is also dishwasher proof.

### 2 MARMITE
The tall, partially glazed marmite is traditionally used for hearty stews such as cassoulet or pot-au-feu. The lid is domed, which allows condensation to drip back into the pot and keep the contents moist. When the lid is removed, the large surface area created by the wide diameter and straight sides encourages evaporation and the formation of the authentic cassoulet crust.

4

### 3 OVAL TERRINE
An oval is a traditional shape for making and serving a rustic terrine or pâté of minced meat or fish. The tightly-fitting lid rests on an inner lip and prevents food from drying out. Some terrines have a lid with a hole for steam to escape. The pot can also be used for stews. It is dishwasher proof, and can withstand temperatures from –20°C/–4°F to 250°C/480°F.

### 4 ROUND TERRACOTTA POT
Fired at 1050°C/1920°F, this classic, straight-sided, glazed pot is resistant to fracturing and fluctuations of temperature. It is ideal for a winter meal for two, or for reheating small portions of leftover stew. It also makes an individual oven-to-table serving dish for hearty soups that need finishing off in the oven – onion soup, for example.

All clay pots are brittle, their strength depending on the temperature at which they were fired. The higher the temperature, the stronger the pot. The most brittle, and cheapest, are earthenware pots.

Glazed clay pots are non-porous, easier to clean and retain heat better than unglazed ones. Conversely, an unglazed surface absorbs heat more readily, so choose one with an unglazed base.

5

## 6 EARTHENWARE POTATO BAKER

Known in France as a 'diable', this porous, unglazed earthenware baker seals in moisture and effectively steam-cooks the contents. By doing so it conserves both flavour and aroma. To work well, the size and shape of the baker should closely follow those of the contents. There are different shaped bakers for cooking chicken and fish.

6

7

## 5 CERAMIC STEW POT

That ceramic is a wonderful conductor of heat is well known, but a revolutionary process used by French maker Emile Henry means their stew pots can be cooked directly on the hob as well as in the oven. This makes them an attractive alternative to heavier cast iron casseroles. Available in mini one-portion sizes up to a 26 cm/10½ inch grande famille stewpot. They make good culinary heirlooms.

8

## 7 TIERRA NEGRA

Described as organic cookware from Colombia, these wonderful touchy-feely pots are produced under Fairtrade policies in the Andes. They are made with coarse grey clay, then fired with a terracotta clay glaze. Finally, grass dust is thrown over the pots in the kilns, which turn the glaze an attractive velvety black. You can cook in them on the hob (electric, gas, Aga), bake in the oven or microwave. They are dishwasher safe.

## 8 TONTOPF POT

This unglazed pot is designed for making deliciously moist, oven-cooked stews with almost no water or fat. Before cooking, the entire pot is soaked in cold water, which is released as steam as the pot heats up. The steam condenses inside the lid and moisture drips onto the food.

## 9 TAGINE

A tagine is a uniquely shaped, thick earthenware pot, used in North Africa for the slow-cooked dish of the same name. The pot is traditionally used on an open fire. Very little liquid is needed as the conical lid provides a large cool surface on which steam condenses and then drips into the food below. The tall shape also keeps the lid cool at the top, so it can be lifted without a protective cloth.

Modified for use on the hob, this tagine has an enamelled cast-iron base that maintains even heat at low temperature; it can be used on any type of hob. The earthenware lid is glazed inside and out, making it durable and easy to clean.

9

## 10 PUCHERO

A Spanish, high-sided, terracotta lidded pot is called a *puchero*, an Andalucian term meaning 'stew pot'. This shape is particularly suited for cooking dried beans slowly in stock or water with onions, oil and herbs. The depth of the pot means the beans remain covered in liquid and don't dry out. Any Spaniard, it is said, who has not a *puchero* is broke.

## 11 CAZUELA

Literally translated, *cazuela* is Spanish for a casserole. Made from terracotta, these attractive rustic pots appear all over Spain in many styles, shapes and sizes. They can be used on the hob, on an Aga, in the oven and even on a barbeque. A *cazuela con punto* is a casserole with a pointed dome in the centre, onto which you can push a small chicken to roast surrounded by vegetables.

10

11

'The high-sided shape of the *puchero* is particularly suited to cooking dried beans; the depth of the pot means they remain covered in liquid and don't dry out.'

# chicken tagine with preserved lemons
## CLAUDIA RODEN

This wonderfully fragrant recipe was contributed by Claudia Roden, the acclaimed food writer who is credited with having 'single-handedly introduced the Western palate to Middle Eastern cuisine'. The word 'tagine' refers to both the stew and the pot in which it is cooked. The tagine pot (see page 180) gives the best results, but you can use a flameproof casserole into which the chicken fits snugly. If you use an earthenware tagine, there is a danger that it will crack if set over a gas flame. A heat diffuser will help prevent this; alternatively, do the preliminary cooking in a saucepan, then transfer the chicken to the earthenware pot and finish cooking in the oven.

SERVES 4–6

**TOOLS**
grater
garlic press
pestle and mortar
mezzaluna or cook's knife
tagine or 4.5 litre/4¾ quart round or oval flameproof casserole
2 large metal spoons
cook's knife

**INGREDIENTS**
1 chicken, weighing about 1.8 kg/4 lb
1 onion, grated or very finely chopped
2 garlic cloves, crushed
¼ tsp saffron pistils, crushed
½ tsp ground ginger
1½ tsp ground cinnamon
salt and freshly ground black pepper
good bunch coriander (cilantro) leaves, trimmed and finely chopped
good bunch of flat-leaf parsley, trimmed and finely chopped
peel of 1½ preserved lemons, cut into quarters
75 g/2½ oz green olives, soaked in two changes of water for 30 minutes, drained and rinsed

**1** Put the chicken in a tagine or casserole with all the ingredients except the preserved lemons and olives. Half cover with water (about 300 ml/1¼ cups) and simmer on a medium to low heat, covered, for 1 hour, turning the chicken over a few times and adding more water if necessary.

**2** Throw the lemon peel and olives into the sauce and continue to simmer for 20 minutes, or until the chicken is so tender the flesh pulls off the bone and the liquid is reduced.

**3** Lift the chicken from the sauce and place in a shallow dish. Cut into serving-sized pieces and place in a serving dish or the base of a tagine. Using paper towels, blot any oil from the surface of the sauce. Pour the sauce over the chicken. Serve with couscous if you like.

**PRESERVED LEMONS** Wash and scrub four thick-skinned lemons. Cut into quarters lengthways but stop short at the stem end so the pieces are still attached. Stuff each lemon with 1 tablespoon of sea salt. Pack into a clean glass jar into which the lemons will just fit, pressing so they are squashed together. Seal and leave for three or four days. They will start to release their juices and the skins will soften. Press them down as much as possible, and add enough fresh lemon juice to completely cover them. Seal the jar and leave in a cool place for at least a month. Rinse before using, to get rid of the salt.

# chicken with vegetables in a pot
## MARK HIX

This deliciously succulent recipe for chicken was contributed by Mark Hix, the award-winning former British chef-director of The Ivy and Le Caprice. He devised it after being given a terracotta *cazuela con punto* by James Sayell of Sayell Foods in Hoxton. 'The great thing with this ingenious pot,' says Mark, 'is that you just stick your chicken, stuffed with herbs, on the protruding cone in the centre of the dish, and place your potatoes and other vegetables round the bottom so that they catch the juices as the chicken cooks. You could also cook ducks, pheasants and guinea fowl in one of these cooking pots with equally effective results.'

SERVES 4

**TOOLS**
cazuela con punto
    or ovenproof dish

**INGREDIENTS**
1 large turnip, peeled and cut into 2–3 cm/3/4–11/4 inch chunks
2 parsnips, peeled and cut into 2–3 cm/3/4–11/4 inch chunks
10–12 Jerusalem artichokes, peeled
3 large carrots, peeled and cut into 1 cm/1/2 inch thick slices on the slant
3 large red onions, cut into 6 wedges with the skin left on
10 garlic cloves, unpeeled
a few sprigs of rosemary and thyme
1 good quality, free-range chicken, weighing about 1.2–1.5 kg/21/4–31/4 lb
3–4 tbsp olive oil
salt and freshly ground black pepper

**1** Preheat the oven to 200°C/400°F/gas 6. Arrange the vegetables and garlic cloves in the cazuela or an ovenproof dish, season and spoon over half of the olive oil.

**2** Put the herbs into the cavity of the chicken, season and brush with the rest of the olive oil.

**3** Place the chicken in the pot, or on the cone if using a cazuela, and cook with the vegetables for 1 hour, basting two or three times during cooking and turning the vegetables so they colour evenly.

**4** To serve, cut the chicken into joints or carve the meat and serve with the vegetables.

**NOTE** You can use any other seasonal root vegetable such as swede or celeriac, as an alternative.

# frying
# and
# grilling

There is an enormous choice of frying pans and a good one is not cheap, so before buying think carefully about the type of food you cook and the type of hob you cook on. Shape is important. Different-shaped pans suit different tasks: high-sided pans help prevent splattering; rounded, outward-sloping sides comfortably accommodate spoons and spatulas, making stirring easier; shallow sides help you to deftly slide the contents out of the pan.

# frying pans

Using a frying pan of the right size makes a marked difference to the cooking process and your finished dish. Small amounts of food cooked in too large a pan will dry and burn; juices will spread too thinly and evaporate. On the other hand, if you crowd food into a pan, it will steam and stew instead of browning and crisping.

## which metal?

To fry food, it must be heated quickly and evenly, so the best pans are made of heavy-gauge metals that are efficient conductors of heat (see 'materials choice', page 12). Copper pans lined with tin or stainless steel are superb, but they are also very expensive. Anodised cast aluminium is one of the best materials as long as it is medium to heavy gauge; lightweight pans tend to buckle and develop hot spots. Stainless steel looks stunning and is easy to clean but, used alone, does not conduct heat well. Combined with a thick layer of copper or aluminium, however, it is hard to beat.

Cast iron is heavy and initially slow to heat, but once hot it maintains its temperature and conducts heat evenly. A small cast-iron frying pan is handy for dry-frying whole spices, but before buying a larger one, check that you can manage the weight – especially if you have weak wrists.

Heavy-gauge, untreated, mild steel is another option. It needs seasoning with oil and in time it builds up a heavy patina that makes the surface non-stick. Until then it needs careful treatment to prevent rusting. Untreated steel pans should never be washed, but simply wiped clean and oiled.

Non-stick pans have improved greatly in recent years, and are worth having not only because they are easy to clean, but also because there is something delectable about the way morsels of food slide around the pan, sizzling in their own tasty juices rather than a bath of oil. A non-stick frying pan not only enables you to cut down on fat, but also allows you to really taste the food.

## choosing frying pans

For a basic set, choose two or three round, heavy-based frying pans for general use: one with a 25–28 cm/10–11 inch diameter base, another with a 20–23 cm/8–9 inch base and possibly a third with an 18 cm/7 inch base – invaluable for a solitary fry-up. You might also consider buying a large, high-sided sauté pan with a lid for poultry quarters or chunky potatoes. A small, sloping-sided pan is essential for omelettes or crêpes. If you like stir-fries, you will also need a wok, though a heavy-based frying pan makes a reasonable alternative.

When buying a new pan, check the handle is firmly welded or riveted. If the pan is very big, an ear-shaped helper handle opposite the long one makes lifting safer. Some handles are cast in one piece with the pan. Though less likely to work loose, integral handles tend to become hotter than handles that are attached separately.

## 1 RIDGED, SQUARE FRYING PAN

Falling midway between a frying pan and a stovetop grill, this pan has a ridged base that lifts food clear of fat and gives appetising stripes to steaks and chops. It is made of cast aluminium with a durable non-stick coating.

## 2 WOK

Designed for continuous movement over high heat, the wok's conical shape tips food continually back to the centre, where the heat is at its most intense. Because the food is constantly on the move during stir-frying, much less oil is needed, making it a healthy option. Round-bottomed woks are suitable for gas hobs; a slightly flattened bottom works better on ceramic or electric hobs. This one has wooden handles, which remain cool despite the intense heat generated from the wok.

## 4 ROUND FRYING PAN

Lightweight does not necessarily mean poor quality, especially when it comes to the metal titanium. When fused with cast aluminium it gives remarkable durability and great heat distribution. German firm SKK produce a range of frying pans described as 'possibly the best non-stick range available'. SKK claim these pans can be heated to a high temperature making it possible to sear and brown meat with little to no fat or oil. Not cheap but good value in the long term.

## 3 STAINLESS STEEL SAUTÉ PAN

Made from superior 18/10 stainless steel (see 'materials choice', page 12), this pan has a thick ground base for maximum heat contact. A wide diameter and high, straight sides allow quick, light frying of chicken quarters or large amounts of potatoes in relatively little fat. The high sides also prevent spattering or spilling as food is turned and shaken. Once the food is evenly browned, the pan can be partly or fully covered, enabling the contents to cook at a more gentle pace.

## 5 DEEP SAUTÉ PAN

A sauté pan is a cross between a deep saucepan and a shallow frying pan, the idea being that with a wide surface area food can first be sautéed and browned, then when stock or wine is added it will bubble and reduce down quickly for a light, delicious sauce. Cristel pans, made of high quality stainless steel and aluminium by French family firm Dodane, have long handles that can be removed to turn the pans into ovenproof casseroles – two pans for the price of one.

## 6 STEEL OMELETTE PAN

Smooth sloping sides and a flat bottom ease the deft manoeuvres necessary for making a perfect omelette. Made from untreated steel (see 'which metal?', page 189), this pan deserves respect – use it only for frying omelettes or crêpes and treat it with care.

## 7 HARD-ANODISED ALUMINIUM CHEF'S PAN

This invaluable pan can be used as a wok or, with its heat-toughened glass lid, as a casserole. It has a heavy ground base for maximum heat conduction, a durable non-stick interior and two stainless-steel handles for easy lifting.

## 8 DIAMOND NON-STICK FRYING PAN

This brand (slogan, 'Diamond's are a cook's best friend') features a revolutionary non-stick coating with tiny diamond crystals. Well, we know from school chemistry classes that diamonds are one of the hardest minerals. In practice, this means that metal stirrers and fish slices can be used in these pans without damaging the surface. Preheat on a medium heat for 2–3 minutes or until a splash of water sizzles when it hits the diamond-hard surface.

## 10 SPLATTER SCREEN

Frying causes splattering and spitting of fat, especially if moist food is being added to hot oil (always pat food dry before frying). When placed over the pan, this fine-meshed screen keeps fat where it belongs.

## 9 NON-STICK FRYING PAN

This premium frying pan, manufactured by Al Clad, is made by a unique bonding of pure metals and alloys. For cooks, this means a very durable, responsive pan with incredible heat conduction, so no more burnt bacon or overcooked eggs. The handle is made of a non-conductive metal and so can be held without thick oven gloves. Not cheap, but then you shouldn't have to replace it for many years. Good for all cookers, including induction hobs.

## 11 HARD-ANODISED ALUMINIUM STIR-FRY PAN

Invaluable for a solo stir-fry, this 20 cm/8 inch pan has a long-lasting, non-stick surface that is covered with minute ridges. The flat bottom is suitable for all hobs.

## stir-frying

**TOOLS** wok, chopsticks/wok stirrer, chopping board, cleaver

The secret of successful stir-frying lies in preparing all the ingredients first as cooking takes very little time.

Thinly slice meats and vegetables, garlic and ginger and lay out on small plates or in bowls. Mix together the flavouring sauces (soy, wine, sesame, Hoisin) in a cup with a teaspoon of cornflour to thicken slightly.

Heat 1–2 tablespoons groundnut oil in the wok. When hot and smoking, toss in the meat with the garlic and ginger, and stir-fry, using long-handled chopsticks, for 1–2 minutes. Remove and set aside. Add denser sliced vegetables, such as carrots, peppers, and spring onions (scallions), and stir-fry for 2 minutes.

Return the meat to the wok, or if using fish or seafood toss these in at this point. Cook for 1 minute, then mix in the flavouring sauce. Stir-fry for a few seconds until thickened, then toss in a handful or so of leafy vegetables, such as spinach or coriander (cilantro). Sprinkle with sesame seeds or chopped cashew nuts or almonds and serve immediately. The whole process should take no longer than 10 minutes.

# making an omelette

a      b      c

**TOOLS** omelette pan, fork, palette knife (metal spatula)

A pan with a heavy base and shallow sloping sides is necessary to make a perfect omelette. A 20 cm/8 inch diameter one is perfect for individual size omelettes. Allow 2 large eggs per person and beat well just before cooking with 2 tablespoons cold water and some seasoning.

Heat the pan slowly over a medium heat and, when you can feel a good heat rising, pour in 1 tablespoon of olive oil and add a small knob of butter. Swirl around the pan and immediately pour in the beaten egg, tipping the pan it so that it coats the base.

Using the back of a fork, lightly scramble the egg and tip the pan each side so the raw egg seeps under the cooked. Also shake the pan over the heat a few times. When the egg mixture is almost cooked and still soft, loosen the sides with a palette knife, tip the pan up and roll the edge nearest the handle to fold over the centre, then over again and out onto a waiting warm plate.

# sweating onions

a      b

**TOOLS** chef's pan with lid, chopping board, cook's knife

Onions are best cooked slowly in a heavy-based pan with a well fitting lid until softened and lightly caramelised. That way tthey develop a natural sweetness and lose their raw harshness.

Finely chop the onions or slice thinly. Heat a good 3 tablespoons light olive oil in a heavy-based pan, stir in the onions and, when they begin to sizzle, sprinkle with a couple of pinches of sugar and season with salt and pepper. Cover and cook on a very low heat for up to 20 minutes, stirring once or twice. The steam during cooking condenses on the lid inside (hence the term 'sweating') and falls back down onto the onions to baste them.

# beyond basics

These pans are tailor-made for a particular use. Some are expensive, and they all take up valuable storage space. Consider them only if you regularly cook, or plan to cook, the food for which they are intended. On the other hand, if you were to buy an oval fish fryer, you might eat fish more often, which is no bad thing; and the chestnut pan would be lovely to have at Christmas . . .

## 1 CRÊPE/PANCAKE PAN

Made of heavy- gauge aluminium with a hard-wearing Silverstone® non-stick surface, this pan will have you tossing pancakes like a pro. The smooth 25 cm/10 inch base allows batter to spread evenly and thinly as you rotate the pan, and the shallow sides facilitate flipping.

## 2 OVAL PAN

This excellent heavy-gauge pan is just right for frying two or three plump fish to crisp perfection. The non-stick surface allows minimal fat to be used and also prevents fish skins from sticking to the pan. It can be cleaned in seconds.

## 3 FAJITA PAN

This oval pan is designed for sizzling the cut of beef (skirt steak, resembling a 'fajo' or belt) after which the dish was named. Made from hard-anodised aluminium, the pan rapidly reaches the high temperature needed. Widely flaring, shallow sides permit quick and easy turning and serving.

## 4 SMALL BLINI PAN

From the same professional range as the crêpe pan, this neat 12 cm/4½ inch pan has smooth, rounded sides that encourage yeast-leavened batter to rise. The handle is long enough to distance your hand from the heat.

## 5 BLINI PAN

Cast aluminium is a firm but lightweight durable metal. Coat it with a non-stick surface and you have a good pancake pan – like this speciality blini pan, perfect for making yeasty buckwheat pancakes. You can also use the pan for Scotch (drop) pancakes or light and moreish American buttermilk pancakes. A light brushing of oil gives extra flavour during cooking.

## 7 KARHAI (INDIAN WOK)

As versatile as a Chinese wok, the karhai is used for frying or, with its lid in place, for slowly simmering meat, poultry, seafood and pulse dishes. Made of heavy-gauge carbon steel with a Xylan® non-stick surface, this karhai has up-tilting handles that enable you to carry it to the table.

## 8 PAELLA PAN

Paella pans feature in many Mediterranean markets now and are not just confined to Spain. The traditional pan is wide and shallow with slightly sloping sides, which allows the plump rice grains to absorb stock quickly with only occasional stirring (unlike risotto, which needs constant attention). Traditionally made of lightweight steel, they are best heated over a gas flame (wash lightly after use, then wipe over with a paper towel and drop of oil to build up a shiny protective patina). Paella pans are also sold in black enamelled steel, and consequently are much easier to care for.

## 9 CHESTNUT PAN

More of a roaster than a fryer, this broad, shallow pan is designed for toasting chestnuts over a gas flame or open fire. The wide perforations allow the skins to remain in contact with the flames and char, while the nut meat inside remains succulent. There is no better way to pass a winter evening.

## 10 DANISH CAKE PAN

With its seven rounded depressions, this hefty lump of cast iron cooks to perfection Danish 'aebleskiver' (apple dumplings). Cast iron conducts and maintains the level of heat necessary for cooking the dumplings right to the centre.

# paella
## SAM HART

Contributed by Sam Hart, co-owner with his brother Eddie of the acclaimed London Restaurant, Fino, this paella is typical of their authentic Spanish-style food. 'Achieving a good crocant,' says Sam, 'takes practice; what you are trying to do is to get the heat right so that the rice is just ready as the last of the stock evaporates. Then the bottom of the rice begins to fry and crisp on the bottom of the pan. Be careful, though, not to burn the rice on the bottom by having the pan on too fierce a heat.'

SERVES 4–6

**TOOLS**
35 cm/14 inch paella pan
paella stirrer/wooden spoon

**INGREDIENTS**
3 tbsp good quality light olive oil
1 large onion, peeled and finely diced
1 red (bell) pepper, finely diced
1 green (bell) pepper, finely diced
2 garlic cloves, peeled and sliced lengthways
2 fresh bay leaves
250 g/9 oz fresh squid, cut into rings
1 tsp sweet paprika
400 g/2 cups paella rice
1 litre/4 cups hot prawn stock
2 small pinches of saffron
300 g/10½ oz fresh mussels
500 g/1 lb 2 oz large tiger prawns/langoustines
300 g/10½ oz fresh clams
1 small bunch fresh flat-leaf parsley, finely chopped
4 tsp good quality extra virgin olive oil
lemons, cut into wedges
sea salt

**1** Place a 35 cm/14 inch paella pan over a medium heat and add the light olive oil. When hot, add the onion and fry for 2 minutes, then add the (bell) peppers, and a pinch of salt, and fry for a further 2 minutes. Add the garlic and fry for a further 2 minutes (a).

**2** Add the bay leaves and squid and cook for 4 minutes, then add the paprika and cook for 2 minutes, stirring well.

**3** Add the rice, mix well, and cook for 2 minutes. Pour in the prawn stock (b) and bring to the boil over a high heat, then simmer vigorously for 10 minutes.

**4** Add the tiger prawns (or langoustines), placing them in a ring towards the middle of the pan, then add the mussels (pushing them down into the rice) around the outer edge of the pan. Add the clams in between the prawns and mussels, also pushing them down into the rice, and cook for 8 minutes (c).

**5** If the paella is in danger of drying out, pour a little more stock over the rice, but remember that you are aiming for a dry, not a soupy, result and that for the last 5 minutes or so of the cooking process there should not be very much stock in the pan.

**6** Remove the pan from the heat, cover with foil and allow to rest for 5 minutes. The steam will cook the rice on the top of the paella, which might be a little underdone at this stage.

**7** Remove the foil, sprinkle with the chopped parsley and add a drizzle of extra virgin olive oil. Serve immediately with lemon wedges on the side.

**NOTE** Your paella will be improved immeasurably if you use home-made stock. Heat some olive oil in a large saucepan and cook the prawn heads, shells and fish head or bones for 1–2 minutes. Break the shells with a wooden spoon. Add a chopped onion, fennel and spring onions, and sweat over a medium heat for 10–15 minutes until starting to caramelise. Add tomatoes, tomato purée (paste) and paprika and cook for 5 minutes. Add a splash of brandy and light immediately, burning off all the alcohol. Deglaze the pan, lifting all the caramelised ingredients from the bottom with a wooden spoon. Add 2 litres/2 quarts water, some thyme and bay leaves and bring to the boil. Reduce to a simmer and reduce the liquid by not quite half (40–60 minutes), to leave about 1 litre/4 cups of stock. Strain through a sieve and discard all the solids. Season the salt and freshly ground black pepper.

a

b

c

# scallop and shiitake stir-fry
## RAYMOND BLANC

Contributed by Raymond Blanc, acknowledged as one of the world's finest chefs, this recipe reflects his insistence on fresh, top-quality produce and light, unmasked flavours. The stir-fry is a wonderful mixture of sweet and bitter, soft and crunchy. It is cooked in a non-stick chef's pan (see page 191), which, as Raymond says, 'epitomises where we are in our cooking today. It has a good design, weight and excellent heat conduction. It's the best non-stick pan I've ever used; I adore the glass lid as I like to see what's going on inside the pan.'

SERVES 4 AS A STARTER OR LIGHT MEAL

**TOOLS**
preparation bowls
cook's knife
paring knife
citrus juicer
large non-stick chef's pan
   or wok
long-handled wooden
   spoon or wok ladle

**INGREDIENTS**
12 large scallops and their
   corals
2 tbsp sesame oil
3 tbsp groundnut oil
200 g/7 oz small shiitake
   mushrooms
2 heads baby bok choy, leaves
   left whole, stalks sliced into
   2 cm/1 inch pieces
150 g/5¼ oz sugar snap
   peas, sliced in half
   lengthways
3 cm/1¼ inch piece fresh
   ginger root, finely chopped
2 garlic cloves, finely chopped
juice of 1 unsprayed lime
salt and freshly ground black
   pepper

**1** Cut each scallop in half and each coral into three pieces.

**2** Heat a high-sided pan or wok with the two oils, add the scallops and corals, and toss for a minute over your highest heat.

**3** Add the mushrooms, then the sliced bok choy stalks and sugar snap peas, and stir-fry for a further minute.

**4** Spoon in the ginger and garlic, along with the bok choy leaves and a little water, and stir-fry all together for another minute or two until the leaves have wilted.

**5** Add the lime juice, season to taste, then serve on four large, warmed plates.

**VARIATIONS** Monkfish makes a wonderful substitute for the scallops, and if you can't find bok choy, use Chinese cabbage, choi-sum or spinach. If shiitake mushrooms are not to your liking, any mushroom can be used instead.

# chicken in red pepper sauce
## MADHUR JAFFREY

The recipe for this colourful chicken dish was contributed by Madhur Jaffrey, best-selling author and authority on Indian food. The dish is cooked from start to finish in a karhai (see page 195), a versatile pan similar to a Chinese wok, and perfect for stir-frying, deep-frying and leisurely braising.

SERVES 4

**TOOLS**
cook's knife
paring knife
blender or food processor
rubber or plastic spatula
karhai or wok with a lid
citrus juicer

**INGREDIENTS**
1/2 large onion, coarsely chopped
2.5 cm/1 inch cube ginger root, coarsely chopped
3 garlic cloves
25 g/1/4 cup blanched, slivered almonds
2 red (bell) peppers, deseeded and coarsely chopped
1 tbsp ground cumin
2 tsp ground coriander
1/2 tsp ground turmeric
1/8–1/2 tsp cayenne pepper
2 tsp salt
7 tbsp vegetable oil, such as sunflower or grapeseed
1 kg/21/4 lb chicken pieces, skinned and cut into small serving pieces
150–250 ml/2/3–1 cup water
2 tbsp lemon juice
1/2 tsp coarsely ground black pepper
fresh coriander (cilantro) leaves, to garnish

**1** Combine the onion, ginger, garlic, almonds, peppers, cumin, coriander (cilantro), turmeric, cayenne pepper and salt in the container of a food processor or blender. Blend, pushing down with a spatula whenever you need to, until you have a paste.

**2** Put the oil in a karhai or wok, preferably non-stick, and set it over a medium-high heat. When hot, pour in all the paste. Stir and fry it for 10–12 minutes or until you can see the oil forming tiny bubbles around it.

**3** Add the chicken with 150 ml/2/3 cup water, the lemon juice and the black pepper. Stir to mix in and bring to the boil. Cover, turn the heat to low and simmer gently for 25 minutes, stirring occasionally, until the chicken is tender. Add a little more water if necessary.

**4** Serve straight from the karhai or transfer to a serving dish. Garnish with coriander (cilantro) leaves before serving.

# deep-frying

The equipment featured here is designed for deep-frying food in boiling fat. An enormous variety of foods, both sweet and savoury, is cooked in this way – batter-coated fish, chips (french fries), fritters, meat balls, Spanish churros, Middle Eastern falafel and kibbeh, Asian rice balls and crispy noodles, Indian pakoras and sweets, to name more than a few.

Because so many different foods can be deep-fried, it is important that the cooking vessel does not absorb odours and is reasonably easy to clean. And as success depends on frying at the correct temperature, the material from which the pan is made must be able to conduct heat evenly and maintain its temperature. Most important of all, because a large quantity of boiling fat is an obvious hazard, the equipment must be safe to use.

## 2 TEMPURA PAN

This beautiful, heavy, iron pan is the secret to making faultlessly crisp tempura and other deep-fried foods. It transfers heat quickly and evenly, and keeps the oil at a stable 170–180°C/340–360°F. It has a spout for pouring off oil, and a rack for draining and keeping morsels of food warm. It comes with a pair of chopsticks for cooking.

## 1 DEEP-FRYING PAN

Made from high-quality enamelled steel, this pan will not absorb smells or grease, and is easy to clean. It conducts heat well, and can be used on any hob, including the induction type. Fat drains easily from the inner wire basket, the handles of which have extensions that rest on the outer handles and lift the food clear of the fat below. The pan can also be used for blanching vegetables.

## 3 POTATO NEST FRYERS

Finely shredded potatoes or other starchy foods are fried in the outer basket, while the smaller basket presses the contents into a nest shape. The inner basket is hinged to the outer one at the bowl end, and the two are held in place by a ring that fits over both handles. The handles are long enough to protect your hand from the heat of the fat.

## 4 ELECTRIC DEEP-FRYER

This sensibly shaped deep-fryer makes efficient use of storage space and allows you to deep-fry a whole fish without bending it. Like all electric fryers, this one is  thermostatically controlled, but unlike most others, it filters cooking scraps into a cold zone between the heating element and the bottom of the pan. This ensures the oil stays clean and fresh for longer. With the exception of the heating element, all components can be put in a dishwasher. The fryer is supplied with a lid.

## successful deep-frying

Successful deep-frying depends on so many variables that it could rightly be called an art rather than a technique. The type, condition and temperature of the oil, type and size of pan, the moisture content of the food, its porosity and surface area, the cooking time – all of these affect the quality of the finished product.

The type of fat or oil is critical. All fats and oils decompose once they reach a certain temperature – some may even spontaneously ignite. Once you can see and smell smoky fumes, or the fat becomes darker or flecked with particles, decomposition is under way. The point at which this happens is called 'the smoke point'. Butter and all animal fats have a low smoke point (about 190°C/375°F), which is why they quickly burn when overheated. Vegetable oils have a higher smoke point (about 230°C/450°F); groundnut oil has one of the highest, which makes it the most suitable oil for deep-frying and stir-frying.

If you don't have a thermometer, you can check the temperature of the oil by dropping a small cube of bread into it. When the bread browns in 1 minute, the oil is ready to use.

The issue of whether oil can be reused is a contentious one. Although some cooks condone it, I would never do so, as successful deep-frying depends on getting the oil good and hot. Once oil has been heated to a high temperature, decomposition takes place rapidly and the flavour becomes tainted. If you do re-use oil, make sure you don't overheat it and that it is thoroughly strained after use.

## chips

After cutting, soak the raw chips in cold water for 30 minutes to remove excess starch. Drain and pat dry. Fill the fryer about a third full of groundnut or sunflower oil. Heat the oil to 160°C/325°F. Place a good handful of raw chips in a wire basket and deep-fry them for 5 minutes, until a pale golden colour.

Drain and increase the oil temperature to 190°C/375°F. Refry the chips for about a minute, until golden and crisp. Drain well and season with salt.

## churros

crisp fried fritters of lemon-flavoured choux batter tossed in caster sugar

**TOOLS** non-stick saucepan, wooden spoon, deep-fat fryer, piping bag with large star nozzle

To make the choux pastry, heat together 1 teaspoon caster (superfine) sugar, 1 teaspoon sea salt, grated zest 1/2 lemon, 250 ml/1 cup water and 100 g/1/2 stick butter, chopped, in a medium-size, non-stick saucepan. Meanwhile, sift 100 g/3/4 cup plain (all-purpose) flour onto a plate and beat 3 large eggs in a bowl.

When the water and butter have melted and start to boil, immediately shoot in all the flour and beat well with a wooden spoon until the mixture comes away from the pan sides in a thick smooth dough. Cool off the heat for 5 minutes, then gradually work in the eggs until you have a smooth dropping consistency.

Heat the oil in a deep-frying pan to about 180°C/350°F. Spoon the batter into a piping bag fitted with a large star nozzle. Pipe squiggles of batter (15–18 cm/6–7 inches long) directly into the hot oil, slicing off the dough with a knife. Cook for about 2 minutes until the squiggles turn golden brown. Drain with a metal slotted spoon and toss immediately into a bowl of caster sugar, ideally flavoured with some aniseed or five spice powder.

c

# tempura

To make Japanese tempura, dip thinly sliced vegetables or large peeled prawns into a lightly mixed batter of 2 egg yolks, 300 ml/1¼ cups water and 200 g/1½ cups plain (all-purpose) flour. Deep-fry two or three pieces at a time in groundnut or sunflower oil at 180°C/350°F, in a tempura pan or wok. Remove the cooked tempura and place on the special rack to drain.

# spring rolls
## SRI OWEN

Contributed by Sri Owen, author of several celebrated books, including *Indonesian Regional Food and Cookery*. A wok is a tool she can't do without. As she says, 'It is amazingly versatile. It is of course the best tool for deep-frying, but it is also excellent for stir-frying and braising, plus a wok with a lid can be used for steaming as well.'

Spring rolls originated in China sometime before the 6th century AD, when they consisted of pancakes rolled up and filled with the new season's spring vegetables, a welcome change from long winter months of preserved foods. Today's spring roll wrappers are thin sheets of pastry, not pancakes, and the range of fillings is enormous. These use cooked vegetables, but by all means add minced pork, chicken or prawns if you wish.

MAKES 20 ROLLS

**TOOLS**
large wok with flat base

**INGREDIENTS**
20 frozen spring roll wrappers, 21–25 cm/8–10 inches square, defrosted
1 egg white, lightly beaten
300 ml/1¼ cups groundnut or vegetable oil for deep-frying

**FOR THE FILLING**
3 tbsp groundnut or sunflower oil
450 g/1 lb carrots, peeled and cut into matchsticks

115 g/4 oz white cabbage, shredded into matchsticks
200 g/7 oz (drained weight) canned bamboo shoots, rinsed and cut into thin sticks
150 g/5½ oz fresh shiitake mushrooms, wiped clean and thinly sliced
225 g/8 oz button mushrooms, thinly sliced
2 tsp finely chopped fresh ginger root

3 tbsp light soy sauce
90 g/3¼ oz cellophane vermicelli, soaked in hot water for 5 minutes, drained, and cut into 5 cm/2 inch lengths with scissors
6 spring onions (scallions), cut into thin rounds
1 egg white
a pinch, or more, of chilli powder

**1** First make the filling. Heat the oil in a wok or frying pan and, then add the carrots, cabbage and bamboo shoots and stir-fry for 2 minutes. Add both kinds of mushroom, the ginger and soy sauce, and stir-fry for a further 3 minutes.

**2** Add the noodles and spring onions, and stir-fry on a high heat for 2 minutes, so that the liquid evaporates but the vegetables are still moist. Season to taste. Remove the mixture from the pan and leave it to cool.

**3** Place one spring roll wrapper on a flat surface, diamond-wise, so that one corner is nearest you. Put 2 tablespoons of the filling on this corner. Press the filling down a little, and roll the corner of the wrapper over it, away from you and towards the centre.

**4** Fold in the two corners that lie to your left and right. Brush the far corner of the wrapper with a little egg white and roll up the wrapper to make a neat, cylindrical, well-sealed parcel. Repeat with the rest of the filling and the wrappers, making your spring rolls as nearly even in weight and shape as possible.

**5** Heat the oil in a deep-fryer, wok or pan to 180°C/350°F. Put four spring rolls into the oil, turn down the heat a little, and deep-fry for 6–8 minutes, turning them several times, until they are golden brown. Remove with a slotted spoon and drain on paper towel.

**6** The spring rolls should be kept warm in the oven until you are ready to serve the whole batch. Alternatively, let them get cold, then re-fry them for a minute or so in hot oil just before serving.

**TIP** Cooked spring rolls can be frozen for up to 4 weeks and reheated straight from the freezer. Heat the oil to 150°C/300°F and deep-fry the frozen rolls for 6–8 minutes so that the filling is heated right through and the wrapper is crisp. If the oil is too hot, the wrapper will blister before the filling has thawed.

Grilling is a method of cooking by direct, dry heat, either under the radiant heat of the grill or directly over the heat of the hob or barbecue. Cooking must be fast enough to simultaneously seal in juices and produce a crisp crust. Successful grilling calls for tender, succulent ingredients, an intense source of heat and, for grilling on the stovetop, pans that heat up fast and can withstand high temperatures without warping.

# grilling

For cooking under the grill, you will need a heavy-gauge metal pan with a rack. The one that came with your oven might be adequate, but if it has warped or twisted, it is worth replacing. Ovenproof baking dishes can also be used under the grill, and are ideal if you want to form a crust or melt a cheese topping on an almost-cooked dish.

For stovetop grilling, you will need a thick, flat, cast iron pan or griddle, with or without ridges. A rectangle or a long oval is the most practical shape as you can load more food onto it. As an alternative to the flat grill pan, there are cast iron pans with shallow, raised sides that look like frying pans, but are in fact much heavier.

## 1 BLOWTORCH
The vogue for blackened and seared food that started in the 1980s has seen the blowtorch migrate from the workshop to the kitchen. It is a useful tool for skinning peppers and tomatoes, caramelising sugar, searing meat, or just adding that extra touch of black to finished dishes. This sleek black model has push-button ignition and an easily adjustable flame.

1

## 2 TOASTERS
Commercial-style stainless steel toasters are increasingly popular because the heating elements are more robust. In addition, many models now incorporate a special sandwich carrier so you can make those favourite cheese toasties at any time of the day or night. A manually operated timer and ejector lever means you have more control over the degree of browning, and a pull-out base tray helps regular crumb clearance.

2

## 3 SALAMANDER
Rather like a branding iron, the small iron disc is heated until it is red hot, then used for browning or caramelising the surface of individual dishes, particularly crème brûlée. Although the same effect can be achieved with a grill, the salamander heats the surface of the food only, so you can enjoy the sensuous contrast of chilled, soft custard and hot, crunchy caramel.

3

## caramelising crème brûlée

**TOOLS** blowtorch

For best results, ensure the baked rich cream is well chilled and firm. Caramelise the top just before serving, otherwise, if you return the dish to the refrigerator, the sugar coating may start to soften.

   Sprinkle the top of each brûlée evenly with either demerara or caster (superfine) sugar. Don't make too thick a layer. Hold a lit blowtorch about 10 cm/4 inches from the sugar layer until it starts to melt and turn golden, then slowly move the flame over the rest of the sugar until it is all caramelised. Do not let it blacken or the sugar will taste unpleasant. Cool until crisp and firm. Crack the top with a spoon just before serving.

## 1 REVERSIBLE GRILL

This cattleman-sized (52.5 x 24 cm/20¾ x 9½ inch) cast iron grill is designed for use across two burners or on the barbecue. The ridged side sizzles steaks, chops, burgers, fish or vegetables with a minimum of fat. Use the smooth side for potato rösti, traditional drop scones, or for a large batch of grilled sandwiches. Both sides of the grill have a gutter for channelling away unwanted fat.

## 2 RIDGED STOVETOP GRILL PAN

Made of vitrified cast iron, this shallow, rectangular grill pan has a ridged surface that produces appetising brown stripes and raises the food slightly to prevent it from sitting in fat. A continuous gutter and a wide pouring lip allow fat to be drained off easily. The steel-wire handle folds over the pan  for convenient storage.

## 3 WAFFLE IRON

This attractive metal mould, known as a 'gauffrier' in France, has two hinged and embossed plates, between which waffle batter is cooked over a source of heat. The handles are held together by a clip to prevent the batter from leaking out, and are long enough to protect your hands from the heat. Hand-operated waffle irons date back to the 15th century; some of them were real masterpieces, embossed with intricate patterns, coats of arms or magical or religious symbols.

### 4 FLAT STOVETOP GRILL

This beautifully designed oval pan is made of stylish matt black cast iron. It has an integral handle and a low-rimmed edge that allows easy access and turning of food. Designed for hob-to-table use, the pan comes with its own heatproof stand, made of hard-wearing rubberwood.

### 5 FLAT GRIDDLE

This 30 cm/12 inch anodised aluminium griddle can be used to grill traditional drop scones and griddle cakes and appetising toasted sandwiches. It will also quickly cook eggs and bacon. The hooped handle packs flat for storage.

### 6 CIRCULAR WIRE RACK

Used on the stovetop, this non-stick rack is handy for grilling chillies, peppers, onion rings and other fresh vegetables, and for heating flat breads and tortillas. The wooden handles remain cool during use. It measures 25.5 cm /10¼ inches in diameter.

### 7 WAFFLE IRON PAN

If your family loves hot fresh waffles and pancakes an electric waffle iron may encourage you to make them more often, not just on Shrove Tuesday. The iron consists of two heavy, cast iron, non-stick grids. You pour batter mix into one, clamp the other on top, set the dial and a beeper lets you know when the light, thick pancake (or waffle) is ready. This pan is great way to introduce children to the joys of cooking.

## grilling vegetables

**TOOLS** chopping board, vegtable knife, mandolin, ridged frying pan, palette knife (metal spatula)

Perfect for strips of (bell) pepper, slices of courgette (zucchini), rounds of onions or asparagus tips.

Quarter peppers, and core and trim the ends so the flesh lies flat. Top and tail courgettes, then cut lengthways into slices 5 mm/ 1/4 inch thick using a mandolin. Snap off woody ends of asparagus tips, and, if liked, peel off tough skin with a vegetable peeler.

Place a ridged grill pan over a medium-high heat. When you can feel a strong heat rising, place the vegetables crossways on the ridges in a single layer and cook for 3–5 minutes until the flesh is chargrilled in stripes.

Loosen with a palette knife and flip over to cook for a further 2–3 minutes (although very thinly sliced courgettes won't need this). Pile the grilled vegetables in a shallow bowl and cover with foil or a lid so the steam softens the flesh further. Drizzle with a little olive oil, fresh lemon juice and seasoning.

# grilling bruschetta

Cut crusty white country-style bread into slices 1 cm/½ inch thick and grill on a hot ridged pan until the bread is toasted on both sides. Rub with a cut large clove of garlic and brush with olive oil.

# grilling steak

Use rump, sirloin, rib eye or fillet steaks at least 1.5–2 cm/¾ inch thick and 150–200 g/5½–7 oz in weight. Heat a ridged grill pan until hot. Brush each side of the steaks lightly with oil then season and immediately place in the pan at right angles to the ridge, so the flesh cooks with attractive markings.

Either cook for 2 minutes or, after 1 minute, loosen with a palette knife and reposition the steaks on the same side to create a crosshatched pattern, and cook for a further minute. Flip over and cook the other side similarly, i.e. a total of 4 minutes, or according to taste.

# grilled squid with chillies
## RUTH ROGERS · ROSE GRAY

With their inspired approach to Italian country cooking, Ruth Rogers and Rose Gray have made London's River Café one of the world's most acclaimed restaurants. Their wonderfully simple recipe uses a cast iron grill or griddle to cook squid in seconds.

SERVES 4

**TOOLS**
cook's knife
serrated knife
paring knife
small whisk
stovetop grill, lightly
    brushed with oil
tongs

**INGREDIENTS**
6 medium squid, no bigger
    than your hand
4–6 mild red chillies, deseeded
    and very finely chopped
extra virgin olive oil
sea salt and freshly ground
    black pepper
2 tbsp lemon juice
225 g/8 oz rocket (arugula)
    leaves

**TO SERVE**
3 lemons, quartered

**1** Clean the squid by cutting the body open to make a flat piece. Scrape out the guts, keeping the tentacles in their bunches, but removing the eyes and mouth.

**2** Using a serrated knife, score the inner side of the flattened squid body with parallel lines 1 cm/ ½ inch apart. Then do the same the other way to make crosshatching.

**3** To make the sauce, put the chillies in a bowl and cover with about 2.5 cm/1 inch of oil. Season to taste.

**4** To make the dressing, combine 6 tablespoons of olive oil with  the lemon juice. Season to taste and whisk until smooth.

**5** Place the squid (including the tentacles) scored-side down on a very hot stovetop grill. Season with salt and pepper. Grill for 1–2 minutes, then turn the squid pieces over; they will immediately curl up, by which time they will be cooked.

**6** Toss the rocket in the dressing. Arrange a squid body and tentacles on each plate with some rocket. Place a little of the chilli on the squid and serve with lemon quarters.

The choice of barbecue equipment grows each year. Before buying, it is vital to do some research and to consider the practicalities. As well as space, location and storage issues, think about how many people you are likely to cook for. If a barbecue is too small the grill will become congested and food won't cook properly; if it's too big, you will waste fuel. For four to six people you need a grilling area at least 30 x 30 cm/12 x 12 inches, or 35 cm/14 inches in diameter.

# barbecues

## choosing a barbecue

Charcoal is by far the best fuel. Though they are convenient to use, gas and electric barbecues do not impart the same flavour. In any case, lighting, fanning, watching and waiting are essential parts of the ritual. Choose lumpwood charcoal or briquettes, which burn for longer. Scattering rosemary twigs on the coals once the food is cooking adds to the fragrance. Avoid instant-lighting charcoal or lighting agents unless you want the food to taste of petrol.

All charcoal barbecues are made up of two components: a firebox that holds fuel and a rack that holds food. Many models include a grate to allow air to circulate under the fuel, and some have vents for regulating heat. Rack height is usually adjustable for controlling the cooking temperature.

Barbecuing at its most basic requires no more than a cake rack set on two bricks. For many years this is what I used, and all I could afford; the results were delectable, or so they seemed at the time. Equally simple, but tidier, is a disposable barbecue, which consists of a heavy foil tray, firelighter, fuel and a rack. All you need is a match.

Cast iron portable barbecues, such as the hibachi, are hard-wearing and easy to use. They have short legs and can be used on the ground or on a heat-resistant surface at table-top height.

The food that can be cooked on small portable barbecues is of necessity rather restricted. If you aspire to cooking a whole fish or a spit-roasted chicken, you will need to invest in a more sophisticated piece of equipment. The free-standing brazier types have an open grill and sometimes come with a wind shield, hood and/or spit-roaster. They are fitted with wheels or detachable legs, and some models are portable, making them convenient to transport to a picnic. Make sure the legs are long enough for you to be able to cook comfortably; it is less back-breaking to squat on the ground than to be half bent over something that is not quite the right height for standing at.

The bulbous kettle barbecues have a domed lid that excludes air, thus reducing the risk of flare-up. The lid also deflects heat onto the food, resulting in quicker and more even cooking, and enabling larger pieces to be cooked with success. Though the rack on kettle barbecues is not adjustable, the firebox has vents that enable you to control the cooking temperature. An enamelled finish is more durable than the heat-resistant paint that some models are treated with.

The pedestal or pillar types of barbecue have a firebed set above an integral flue. The flue is filled with newspaper, which is lit through a ventilation hole, preferably with a long match. The upward draught creates a powerful draw that quickly lights the fuel.

### 1 | DISPOSABLE BARBECUE

Hardly atmospheric but great for a spur-of-the-moment picnic, disposable barbecues are usually ready to use in 15–20 minutes, and will often keep going for up to two hours. They are good for a couple of steaks or chops, or several sausages.

1

### 2 | PEDESTAL BARBECUE

This sleek, stainless steel model is good-looking enough to grace the balcony of the most design-conscious loft dweller. No need for messy chopped kindling, just stuff the flue with yesterday's newspaper and ignite. Billowing smoke may initially annoy the neighbours, but it soon dies down. The barbecue has ventilation holes for regulating temperature, and a windshield with three slots for adjusting rack height. Drawbacks: the outer surface becomes intensely hot and is therefore a hazard to children and pets; the barbecue is tall and the base relatively narrow, so it must be set on very flat, level ground to remain stable.

### 3 | HIBACHI BARBECUE

Originally from Japan, these neat cast iron barbecues are weighty but still portable. They have short legs and can be set on the ground if you don't mind squatting, or placed at table height on a fireproof surface. The fuel sits in a trough close to the rack, the height of which is adjustable. Though convenient and easy to use, hibachis have a small firebed so the fire doesn't last long. They are best used for small pieces of quick-cooking food.

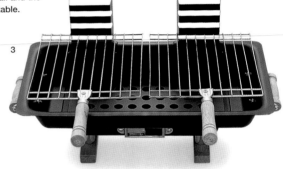

3

### 4 | OVAL PORTABLE BARBECUE

This rugged cast iron barbecue is well suited to outdoor cooking. The rack can be set at two levels and is sturdy enough to support a pan, so can be used for boiling and simmering as well as grilling. A damper regulates heat and the flip-down lid allows you to add more fuel.

2

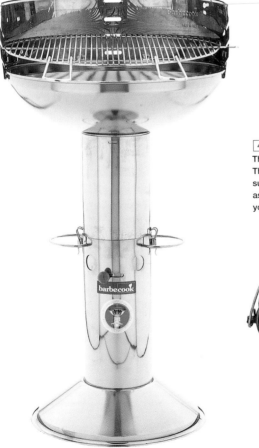

4

## 5  KETTLE BARBECUE

An all-American classic, this outstanding barbecue is made in rust-resisting enamelled steel, and has a thermometer in its lid for accurate monitoring of temperature. The vents open for cooking while the lid is lowered, creating convection heat that produces a tasty crisp exterior and seals in juices. A touch of a button conveniently releases the ashes into a container below the firebox.

## 6  LONG-HANDLED UTENSILS

Tools with extra-long handles allow you to baste, spear and turn while distancing your hands from the heat. The tongs are well sprung and have a ridged surface for efficient gripping. The slotted turner has a cleverly angled edge to prevent food from accidentally slipping off it. The brush allows you to safely anoint food with oil or a marinade without fear of drips and flare-up.

## 7  WIRE HOLDERS

Turning whole items of food is made easier with these specially shaped wire holders. Brush with oil first to prevent sticking.

5

6

7

## successful barbecuing

Line the base of the firebox with foil and cover with sand. This absorbs fat drippings and helps prevent flare-up.

• Light the barbecue with good old-fashioned paper and sticks. Once lit, leave the charcoal alone until it is covered in pale grey ash. Only then is it ready to use.

• To assess temperature, hold your palm 15 cm/6 inches from the grill and count. If you can feel the heat after 2–3 seconds, the fire is hot enough for cooking small thin items such as chipolata sausages, skewered food and fish fillets.

• If you can hold your hand over the grill for 4–5 seconds, the heat is suitable for larger pieces that need longer cooking, such as spare ribs, chops or chicken quarters

• If you can withstand the heat for longer than 5 seconds, the fire is not hot enough.

• Keep tools with extra-long handles within easy reach of the barbecue. You will need tongs, a fork, a spatula and a brush. A pointed knife is useful to test for doneness.

• To reduce the risk of food poisoning, keep one pair of tongs solely for raw meat and poultry.

# barbecued seafood skewers
## WOLFGANG PUCK

Perfect for a summer lunch, this mouthwatering recipe was contributed by Wolfgang Puck, one of an influential breed of chefs who launched new trends in Californian cuisine with an expert blend of fresh local ingredients and classical French technique. Cook the vegetables first, then stoke up the barbecue so it is very hot before you grill the seafood.

SERVES 6–8

**TOOLS**
cook's knife
mezzaluna
large, shallow dish
paring knife
food processor
6 metal skewers, about 30 cm/12 inches long

**INGREDIENTS**
450 g/1 lb swordfish or salmon, cut into 2.5 cm/ 1 inch cubes
450 g/1 lb scallops, halved if large
450 g/1 lb large, raw prawns, shelled and deveined
salt

**FOR THE MARINADE**
7 tbsp olive oil
2 tbsp freshly ground black pepper
4 tbsp finely chopped herbs, including basil, oregano, thyme and parsley

**FOR THE AIOLI**
75 g/2¾ oz sun-dried tomatoes, packed in oil
2 tbsp chopped basil
8 garlic cloves, roasted
2 tbsp balsamic vinegar
7 tbsp extra-virgin olive oil
salt and black pepper

**FOR THE GRILLED SALAD**
225 g/8 oz spring onions (scallions) or leeks, halved lengthways
225 g/8 oz small carrots or sweetcorn, halved lengthways
2 red (bell) peppers, halved and deseeded
225 g/8 oz courgettes (zucchini), halved lengthways

225 g/8 oz Japanese aubergines (eggplant), halved lengthways
1 fennel bulb, cut lengthways into 1 cm/½ inch thick slices
4 large tomatoes, halved and deseeded
salt and freshly ground black pepper
250 ml/1 cup olive oil
1 tbsp finely chopped garlic
1 tsp ground cumin
7 tbsp balsamic vinegar
7 tbsp coarsely chopped fresh herbs, including basil, oregano, parsley and thyme

**1** Mix all the marinade ingredients together. Put all the seafood in a large shallow dish and pour over the marinade. Refrigerate for 2–4 hours.

**2** To make the aïoli, put the sun-dried tomatoes, basil, garlic and balsamic vinegar in a food processor and purée until smooth. With the motor still running, slowly add the olive oil and season with salt and pepper. Refrigerate until ready for use.

**3** For the grilled vegetable salad, mix all the vegetables with salt, pepper and half the olive oil. Place on a hot barbecue and grill until tender and brown (some vegetables may take longer than others). Remove from the grill, cool and cut into 2.5 cm/1 inch pieces. Cut the tomatoes into 1 cm/½ inch cubes and add to the vegetables. Mix the vegetables with the garlic, cumin, vinegar, herbs and remaining olive oil.

**4** When ready to cook the seafood, thread onto skewers, alternating prawns, scallops and swordfish or salmon (about 175 g/6 oz per skewer). Season each skewer with salt.

**5** When the barbecue is very hot, grill the seafood for about 4 minutes on each side.

**6** To serve, divide the vegetable salad between individual plates and place a skewer on top of the salad. Drizzle part of the aïoli over the seafood and serve the rest on the side.

# slightly smoky grilled quails
## PETER GORDON

Brilliant New Zealand chef Peter Gordon combines modern British food with the very best of Pacific Rim flavours. His quail recipe is perfect for the barbecue – as he says, 'Quails are great to barbecue because they're easy to hold in your hands, and they'll dribble just the right amount of juice down your chin.' Though not essential, a barbecue with a lid allows the quails to take on a smoky flavour without burning.

SERVES 4

| TOOLS | INGREDIENTS | |
|---|---|---|
| kitchen scissors | 8 quails | 3 garlic cloves, finely chopped |
| large bowl | a good handful of basil leaves, | 4 tsp Thai fish sauce |
| paring knife | plus a little extra, shredded | 4 tsp mirin |
| long-handled tongs or fork | 3 tbsp plus 1 tsp sesame oil | 4 tsp wine vinegar |
| citrus juicer | 2 tsp sesame seeds | 1 tbsp demerara sugar |
| | thumb-sized piece fresh ginger | lime juice, to taste |
| | root, very finely chopped | |

**1** Hold a quail in your hand, breast-side down, and cut out the backbone with a pair of kitchen scissors (see 'spatchcocked poussins', page 54). Put the bird in a large bowl. Repeat with the other seven.

**2** Add the remaining ingredients to the bowl, reserving some of the basil, and toss together. Cover with cling film (plastic wrap) and leave to marinate in the refrigerator for at least 6 hours. Remove from the refrigerator about 2 hours before you're ready to cook, so the birds have time to come to room temperature.

**3** Once the barbecue coals are glowing, make them into a mound in the centre. Lay the quails, flattened out and breast-side up, on the rack in a ring around this hot mound. Close the lid if you have one, as this will keep some of the heat and the smoke in. Cook for 6 minutes, then open the lid, turn over the quails, close the lid again and cook for another 5–8 minutes.

**4** Test a quail by poking its thigh with a sharp knife at the thickest point. If the juices run clear, it's cooked. If they are still pink, continue to cook for a couple more minutes, then test again. If the bird is black and flaming, you'll be going hungry.

**5** Transfer the cooked quails to a platter and sprinkle with the extra shredded basil and a squeeze of lime.

When manoeuvring food at high temperatures, you need long-handled tools to protect your hands. The tools should grip well or be shaped in such a way that they are compatible with the nature of the food and/or the shape of the pan. Hang them within easy reach of the hob so you don't have to fumble in a drawer. Avoid lifters and turners with wooden or painted handles, and those with rivets and joins. A continuous piece of metal is easier to clean and will last a lifetime.

# tools for lifting and turning

## 1 FISH LIFTER

This efficient tool enables you to lift a whole fish and keep it intact. The bowed blade has a gently chamfered edge that slips easily under the fish without tearing the skin. The perforations allow fat to drain.

## 2 WOK TURNER

The rapid stirring, turning and lifting of food that stir-frying demands are made simple with this shovel-shaped tool. It is available with or without perforations.

## 3 FISH TURNER

A thin, rounded blade allows careful handling of fish and other delicate foods. The slots make the blade flexible and allow fat to drain away as you lift.

## 4 SPRING-ACTION TONGS

Popular with professional cooks, these stainless steel tongs have a positive spring action and ample scalloped heads that allow you to clasp food securely.

## 5 SCISSOR-ACTION TONGS

With their inwardly curved, pincer-like heads, these tongs are ideal for lifting and turning small pieces of food. The plastic-coated handles are comfortable to hold and remain cool in use.

## 6 ANGLED TURNER

Ergonomically designed for comfort, this angled turner is available in right- and left-handed versions.

## 7 NON-STICK TURNER

Even though non-stick pans are more durable than they used to be, it still makes sense to use a non-stick turner. This one is made of die-cast aluminium and has an angled blade with generous slots for efficient fat drainage.

## 8 BAMBOO RICE PADDLE AND FORK

These are used for serving rice or mixing it with other ingredients. The paddle's tapered edge separates rice grains without crushing them.

## 9 TURNING FORK

A five-pronged fork delicately harpoons slippery food.

## 10 GRILLING TOOLS

Having the right shaped tools for cooking burgers, steaks, chops and grilled vegetables makes for effortless cooking without food sticking to pan or grill. Resist the temptation to push food around on the grill too soon but leave to seal and brown for about a couple of minutes then gently nudge, flip or lift. Long handles ensure your arms stay out of range of hot fat spits.

## 11 PAELLA SKIMMER

When making paellas use a long handled skimmer with a thin flat perforated bowl.

# roasting
# and
# baking

Look for good, solid roasting pans and be prepared to pay for them – the one that came with your oven will inevitably warp and you'll end up with the fat gathering in one corner, leaving the rest of the pan high and dry. Roasting pans come in a variety of materials. However, size and weight are more important. Pans need at least 5 cm/2 inches of space around them for air to circulate, so check the size of your oven before buying.

# roasting

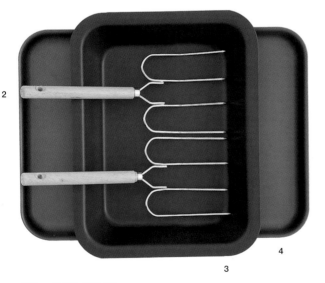

Get several sizes – if you roast a small joint in too large a pan, the juices will spread thinly and burn. Conversely, a large joint in an undersized pan will cook unevenly. Pans should be rigid, with sides high enough to restrict splattering. A non-stick surface is worth having if you are trying to reduce your fat intake. If you like roasted vegetables, get a largish shallow-edged pan too. It will double as a baking sheet.

### 1 ENAMELLED SELF-BASTING ROASTER

This cleverly designed, high-quality roaster has a series of dimples set into the lid. These encourage moisture to gather and drip evenly over the meat, resulting in a particularly succulent roast.

The steel rack lifts the meat out of the fat. Because the meat is completely enclosed, its surface will not become crisp. If you want it to be crisp, remove the lid towards the end of the cooking time.

### 3 ANODISED ALUMINIUM ROASTING PAN

This heavy-duty roasting pan and the shallow roasting tray (4) are guaranteed not to twist or buckle when exposed to high temperatures. The hard surface is resistant to scratches, even from metal utensils. The base is solid enough to stand up to the direct heat of the hob, so you can use the pan for gravy-making on top of the stove. The pan is available in a range of sizes and will last a lifetime.

### 4 ANODISED ALUMINIUM ROASTING TRAY

The ideal pan for roasting vegetables. Sliced aubergines (eggplant), onion rings and (bell) peppers will become deliciously crisp and sticky as the dry heat of the oven circulates over them, unimpeded by a high-sided pan. The generous surface area means you can give them plenty of room. If you cram them together they will simply steam in their own juices and remain disappointingly pallid.

### 2 LIFTING FORKS

A pair of lifting forks ease the transfer of meat from roasting pan to serving platter. Choose forks that have at least three prongs. Any fewer and the meat is in danger of dropping between them.

## 5 STAINLESS STEEL MINI ROASTING PAN

People who live on their own need not deprive themselves of the pleasure of a roast. Just 20 cm/8 inches square, this smart little pan is the perfect size for one. It is also useful for roasting whole onions, beetroot or turnips. Made of top-grade stainless steel, it can also be used under the grill and on the hob.

5

6

## 6 BULB BASTER

Rather surgical in appearance, this glass tube and rubber squeeze ball is used for basting as well as drawing off fat. Fill the tube with meat juices by squeezing the ball, then release and hold the tube upright. The fat will rise to the top and the fat-free juices can be squirted over the meat or used to make a gravy or sauce. Calibrations show exactly how much liquid the tube has sucked up, which can be useful in sauce-making.

## 7 RIDGED OVEN PLATE

A ridged, non-stick pan for open oven roasting, this is perfect for cooks who want to reduce their fat intake. Made of a non-metal liquid crystal polymer the central deep ridges mean meat fats will drip and collect in the side gully to be drained off. You can cook meat or fish along with thinly sliced vegetables and flavourings, although lean meat may need a light marinade. Sold with or without handles it is also dishwasher safe.

7

## 8 PROFESSIONAL QUALITY ROASTING PAN

Made of thick aluminium and anodised for extra strength, these generously sized, deep, non-stick roasting pans with easy-to-grip handles are large enough to take a medium-size turkey and can be used also for baking big family-size lasagnes and shepherd's pies . They will give a great many years of good service to the keen cook.

8

## 9 V-SHAPED ROASTING RACK

Fully adjustable, this rack lifts any size of bird or joint well away from the base of the pan. Ordinary flat racks do little more than raise the meat a centimetre or two above the pan, which is of little use if you are cooking a goose or a duck, for example, as they produce copious amounts of fat. The V-shape not only facilitates clearance of fat but allows air to circulate under the meat, resulting in faster, more even cooking and crisper skins.

9

## 10 DOUBLE OVEN GLOVES

All-in-one oven gloves are easier to use, store and find than a pair. The deep pockets are triple-lined on the palm side and double-lined on the back, protecting your hands and wrists even if you happen to brush against the insides of the oven.

10

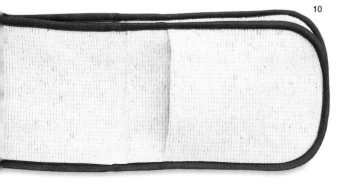

11

## 11 SILICONE OVEN MITT

The magic material, silicone, used in so many kitchen utensils, is also heatproof when pressed into a mould to make a thick oven mitt. Looking a little like a beaky hand puppet, it is flexible enough for a cook's hand to grasp the edge of a hot roasting pan and lift it out. Better still, it won't wear thin or get smelly and grubby because any spills can be easily wiped off.

## ⑫ TRUSSING NEEDLE

Resembling a giant darning needle with an eye large enough to take a piece of string, a trussing needle makes a more secure job of sealing flaps and openings in poultry or tying a joint into a neat, compact shape. Unlike a skewer, it can pass all the way through the meat, drawing the string with it.

12

13

## ⑬ VERTICAL ROASTER

Chicken may be a favourite roast dinner, but roasting the legs until tender whilst the breast remains moist can pose a problem. The solution? Stick a bird onto a vertical metal roaster so it cooks from the inside at the same time as the outside. This version contains a central infuser that can be filled with aromatic herbs or lemon wedges. The juices trickle down over the flesh during cooking to moisten and flavour and collect in a big puddle that can then be used as a 'jus' gravy.

## ⑭ GRAVY SEPARATOR

This ingenious jug works on the very simple principle that oil and water do not mix. All gravy separators are basically heatproof jugs with spouts that come out from the base. You pour in the cooking juices from your hot roasting pan, wait a couple of minutes for the oily fat to settle on top, then pour out the natural meat juices, either to trickle over carved roasted meat as a 'jus' or to use a gravy base.

14

15

## ⑮ FAT SEPARATOR

As fat always rises to the top as it cools, a utensil with a spout that joins the jug at the base allows you to draw off liquid, leaving the fat behind. This elegant porcelain fat separator is designed to pour fat-free gravy from a deep spout at one end and the risen fat from a shallow spout at the other.

# trussing a bird

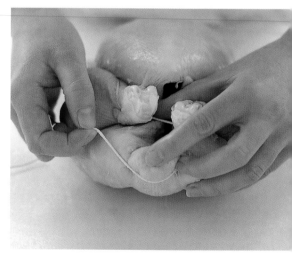

**TOOLS** trussing needle, kitchen twine

Trussing a chicken or stitching a boned and stuffed joint shapes it into a neat package for even cooking. Most chickens are now sold ready trussed, but if you do need to truss one, cut a length of kitchen twine 1 metre/1 yard long and thread a trussing needle.

Cut off the scaly leg joints, leaving behind the drumsticks and thighs. Place the bird breastbone up and hold up the legs together (a). Push through the needle and thread at the joint between drumstick and thigh. Pull through the thread, knotting it at the end.

Tuck the wing joints along the backbone, fold the neck flap over, then push the needle through the wing joints and neck flap. Pull the twine out the other side (b), pulling tightly to hold the

b

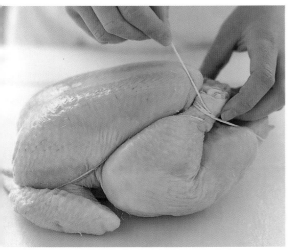

d

## making gravy

a

b

**TOOLS** roasting pan, wooden spoon

After a joint or bird has roasted, remove it to a platter, cover with foil and allow it to rest whilst you make gravy.

Place the roasting pan on the hob over a medium heat. Add a small glass of wine or dry cider and scrape it into the meaty deposits. Cook for 1 minute, then sprinkle over 1–2 tablespoons flour, depending on how thick you like your gravy. Stir this into a paste with a wooden spoon and heat for a minute or so.

Have ready about 500 ml/2 cups hot vegetable water or stock and slowly stir this in until it thickens. Season to taste, then strain through a sieve into a warm gravy jug.

ng joints down, then bring the twine over to the leg joints on
e other side.

Tuck the parson's nose up into the body under the legs (c) and
 the legs firmly together with the twine (d). Tie in a double knot
d trim the twine.

or boned rolled joints, such as  stuffed lamb leg or shoulder
nts, ensure the joint is boned as a neat pocket and fill with your
epared stuffing so it is slightly bulging. Thread a trussing needle
ith kitchen twine and stitch securely and secure with double
anny knot.

## slow roasting tomatoes

**TOOLS** roasting pan

Preheat the oven to 100°C/200°F/gas ¼. Halve about eight large plum tomatoes and snip out the upper cores. Place cut side down in a roasting pan and drizzle over 4–5 tablespoons olive oil. Then sprinkle with thyme or snipped rosemary leaves, sea salt flakes and ground black pepper, plus 2–3 sliced fat garlic cloves. Roast slowly for about 2 hours then remove from the oven and allow to cool in the pan. Serve at room temperature in salads or as a side dish.

## roasting potatoes

**TOOLS** saucepan, roasting pan, long-handled spoon

For perfect roast potatoes, first peel and cut the potatoes into 3–4 cm/1¼–1½ inch chunks. Preheat the oven to 190℃/375℉/gas 5. Parboil the potatoes in a pan of salted water for 5 minutes, then drain well. Meanwhile, heat 3–4 tablespoons olive oil or goosefat in a heavy roasting pan for 5 minutes until it begins to 'smoke'. Immediately tip in the drained potatoes and turn quickly in the hot fat using a long-handled spoon. Season, sprinkle over some thyme leaves or snipped rosemary leaves and roast for 45 minutes, turning once or twice in the hot fat until crisp and golden. Drain on paper towel and serve immediately.

a

## roasting chicken

**TOOLS** vertical chicken roaster, roasting pan

Using a vertical chicken roaster is ideal if you wish to replicate a spit-roasted chicken but have no rotisserie.

Press the chicken, which should weigh about 1.5 kg/3 lb 5 oz, leg-side down, onto the vertical trivet, and place in a roasting pan. Brush the bird all over with olive oil, seasoning and spices, such as paprika or curry powder. Roast in an oven preheated to 190°C/375°F/gas 5, allowing 25–30 minutes per kg/2¹⁄₄ lb. The cooking juices will drip down into the pan and can be used for making gravy (see page 231).

b

a

# pan-roasting duck fillet

**TOOLS** frying pan, tongs

Pan-roasting involves two cooking
methods – first sealing the meat in a frying
pan and then transferring it to a preheated
oven to ensure it is nicely caramelised
on the outside and pink and juicy inside.
Finally, the meat should be allowed to
stand so the fibres relax. Timings depend
on the thickness of the steaks or fillets.

Preheat the oven to 200°C/400°F/gas 6.
Heat a heavy-based frying pan with an
ovenproof handle until you can feel a
strong heat rising. Meanwhile, brush a lean
steak, lamb fillet or duck breast lightly with
oil (a) and season. Place in the hot pan
and cook on a medium-high heat for 1–2
minutes until well browned (b), then flip
over and cook the other side for a further
1–2 minutes.

Transfer the pan to the oven for 3–4
minutes. Press the meat with the back of
a fork to check for doneness (c) – medium
rare is when the meat feels slightly springy.
Allow the meat to stand for 3–4 minutes
before serving.

b

c

# pork and crackling
## JAMIE OLIVER

Jamie Oliver is one of Britain's most talented chefs, and this recipe perfectly captures his feisty, no-fuss style. Boneless pork is roasted flat, directly on the bars of the oven shelf, with a roasting pan beneath to catch the juices.

This produces succulent meat, the crispest, crunchiest crackling ever, and gravy that will have you licking your plate. Ask your butcher to take the meat off the bone and then to score the skin across in deep lines about 5 mm/¼ inch apart. Ask for the bones to be chopped up so you can use them to make the gravy.

SERVES 8

| TOOLS | INGREDIENTS | |
|---|---|---|
| pestle and mortar | ½ pork loin, roughly | 2 tbsp olive oil |
| large roasting pan | 3 kg/6½ lb on the bone | pork bones, chopped |
| medium roasting tray for | sea salt flakes | 5 outer celery sticks, roughly |
| browning bones | 1 tbsp chopped fresh | chopped |
| aluminium foil | rosemary | 1 large carrot, roughly |
| large frying pan or saucepan | ½ tbsp fennel seeds | chopped |
| for making gravy | 5 garlic cloves | 1 large onion, roughly |
| wooden spoon | 8 tbsp balsamic vinegar | chopped |
| sieve | 4 bay leaves | |

**1** Rub some salt and rosemary into the pork skin, pushing it into the scored lines.

**2** Using a pestle and mortar, smash up the fennel seeds, then the garlic and remaining rosemary. Rub this mixture into the meat – not the skin, or it will burn. Place the meat in a large roasting pan with the balsamic vinegar, bay leaves and olive oil. Leave for about 30 minutes to marinate.

**3** Preheat the oven to its highest temperature and brown the bones. Rub the pork skin with more salt.

**4** Place the pork directly onto the bars at the top of the oven. Put the browned bones and vegetables in the roasting pan with the left-over balsamic marinade and add 600 ml/2½ cups water. Set the pan in the oven directly under the pork, so that as the pork cooks, all the goodness drips from it into the pan. This liquid will then become your gravy. You also get quite nice charred bar marks on the base of the pork.

**5** The pork will take about 1 hour to cook. After 20 minutes, turn the temperature down to 220°C/425°F/gas 7. Once the pork is cooked, remove it from the oven on the rack and place on a piece of foil to save any juices. Allow to rest for at least 10 minutes.

**6** To make the gravy, put the bones, liquid and vegetables from the roasting pan into a large frying pan or saucepan. Add some water to the roasting pan, as there will be some Marmite-like, sticky stuff on the bottom of the pan, which is very tasty. Bring to the boil on the hob, scraping all the goodness from the bottom of the roasting pan, then add this to the bones and vegetables.

**7** Bring the gravy to the boil, shaking occasionally. Remove any oil or scum from the surface, then strain the contents, discarding all the vegetables and bones. You can reduce and then adjust the seasoning to taste.

# honey-glazed roast barbary duck

Barbary ducks are not so fatty as ordinary ducks and have more flesh on the breast. Repeated brushing with a fragrant coating produces a wonderfully crisp skin with a deep, rich glaze. Allow several hours for the duck to dry; you can speed things up with a cool hair-dryer if necessary. This is delicious served with julienned leeks and carrots, and 'sweet potato mash' (see page 79).

SERVES 3–4

**TOOLS**
colander
paring knife
pestle and mortar
ginger grater
wire rack set over a shallow
    dish
wide, flat brush
30 x 24 cm/10 x 12 inch
    roasting pan with rack
lifting forks
carving knife
poultry shears
small saucepan

**INGREDIENTS**
1 barbary duck, weighing
    1.6–1.8 kg/3 1/2–4 lb
20–25 thin shreds orange
    peel, 1 cm/1/2 inch long
150 ml/2/3 cup clear honey
4 tbsp rice wine or dry sherry
4 tbsp white wine vinegar
4 tbsp soy sauce
2 tsp sesame oil
2 tsp fennel seeds, ground to
    a powder
4 cm/1 1/2 inch piece fresh
    ginger root, grated
200 ml/1 scant cup duck or
    chicken stock, preferably
    home-made
sea salt and freshly ground
    black pepper

**1** Discard any lumps of fat from the duck's cavity. Put the duck in a colander and scald all over with boiling water. Pat dry thoroughly with a paper towel. Pierce the flesh evenly all over with the tip of a knife and insert the orange-peel shreds. Place the duck on a rack set over a dish.

**2** Pour the honey into a small measuring jug. Stir in the rice wine or dry sherry, vinegar, soy sauce, sesame oil, fennel seeds and ginger root. Paint the mixture over the entire surface of the duck, including the crevices under the wings; reserve the remainder. Leave the duck on the rack in a cool, airy place to dry completely.

**3** Preheat the oven to 220°C/425°F/gas 7. Brush the duck once more, using the liquid that has dripped into the dish.

**4** Place the duck, breast-side up, on a rack in a roasting pan. Roast for 10 minutes, then turn the duck over, brush again with the coating mixture and roast for another 10 minutes.

**5** Reduce the heat to 190°C/375°F/gas 5. Turn the duck breast-side up, brush, and roast for 30 minutes. Turn and roast for another 30 minutes, brushing every 10 minutes. Protect any blackened tips with foil.

**6** Raise the heat to 200°C/400°F/gas 5 and turn the duck breast-side up. Brush again and roast for a further 10 minutes. Carefully lift the duck onto a heated dish and leave to rest in a warm place for 10 minutes.

**7** To carve the duck, remove the legs and the wings, leaving some of the breast meat attached to each wing. Remove the breast meat in two long pieces, then cut into bite-sized chunks, making sure a crispy piece of skin is attached to each chunk. Place all the duck pieces in a shallow serving dish and keep warm.

**8** Pour any juices that have accumulated during carving into a small saucepan. Add the stock and the remaining coating. Bring to the boil and simmer briskly until slightly reduced. Pour over the duck pieces and serve.

# roast leg of spring lamb, studded with garlic and rosemary
## GARLTON BLACKISTON

Galton Blackiston has run the Michelin-starred hotel and restaurant Morston Hall, set on the stunningly beautiful North Norfolk coastline, since 1992. His critically acclaimed cooking has evolved by following a simple cooking philosophy that he believes in passionately – a philosophy that is all about using fresh, seasonal, locally sourced produce to create simple yet stunning meals, as is demonstrated in this delicous roast.

SERVES 6

**TOOLS**
deep-sided roasting pan
trivet

**INGREDIENTS**
1 leg of lamb, weighing about
    3 kg/6½ lb, with the chump
    left on (ask your butcher to
    remove the aitchbone)
4 garlic cloves
sprigs of rosemary and thyme
50 g/2 tbsp butter
50 g/2 tbsp  redcurrant jelly
sea salt flakes
coarsely ground black pepper

**1** Preheat the oven to 200°C/400°F/gas 6.

**2** Using a sharp knife, make incisions about 2.5 cm/1 inch deep all over the lamb and insert the garlic, rosemary and thyme. Remember to do the underside as well. Smear the lamb with the butter, then season.

**3** Sit the lamb on a trivet in a roasting pan, and place in the preheated oven. After 1 hour, remove from the oven, coat well with redcurrant jelly, then return to the oven for a further 20 minutes.

**4** Allow the lamb to rest in a warm place for at least 10 minutes before carving.

These dishes are designed for baking food in the oven or browning toppings of bubbling cheese, crisp potato or crunchy breadcrumbs. Made of good-quality materials, such as porcelain or cast iron, gratin dishes conduct heat well and are not stressed by high temperatures. They are usually brought to the table so are made in attractive shapes and colours.

# baking and gratin dishes

## 1 RECTANGULAR CERAMIC GRATIN DISHES

These glazed dishes are strong enough to be transferred directly from freezer to oven. The rectangular shape makes efficient use of oven and fridge space, while gently sloping sides maximise the area for crusty topping and also allow stacking. A thick rim assists with lifting.

The large gratin dish is deep enough to take four or five layers of lasagne. The slightly rounded interior makes serving and cleaning easier.

## 2 OVAL CERAMIC GRATIN DISHES

These are the classic shape for a gratin and are versatile enough to be used as serving dishes or even for carving a small roast. The dishes can be transferred directly from freezer to oven. They conduct heat evenly and retain it well, ensuring food remains warm at the table.

## 3 PORCELAIN SOUFFLÉ DISHES

Round, deep and straight-sided, these dishes expose soufflé mixtures to maximum heat. This coagulates the egg proteins before the air incorporated during whisking has time to escape. The smooth porcelain interior allows the expanding mixture to rise up the dish. They are available in several sizes, but the preferred one is 0.9 litre/1 quart. Anything larger and you risk the inside not being properly cooked.

## 4 ENAMELLED CAST IRON EGG DISH

This shallow dish is specially designed for cooking eggs, either in the oven or on the hob. Widely flaring sides make serving and cleaning easier but, more importantly, they increase the surface area and expose the eggs to maximum heat so they cook evenly.

## 5 ENAMELLED CAST IRON BAKING DISH

The deep sides of this dish make it particularly useful for baking eggs that have a layer of vegetables, such as spinach, underneath, or for individual portions of lasagne.

## 6 PORCELAIN RAMEKINS

These smooth, straight-sided ramekins are used for individual soufflés, as well as baked custards or crème brûlées. Egg-based dishes such as these are cooked in a roasting pan filled with enough hot water to come halfway up the sides of the ramekins. The ramekins have a slightly roughened base to prevent a vacuum forming , which would make it difficult to lift them from the water.

## 7 PORCELAIN OVAL GRATIN DISHES

Available in several sizes, these classic white gratin dishes have a beautiful shape. The fluted handles merge with the sides of the dish, which slope gracefully outwards to increase the surface area for browning. The sloping sides increase the surface area.

## 8 PORCELAIN CHOCOLATE POTS

These elegant pots are traditionally used for rich chocolate desserts, as well as for baked creams and custards.

## 9 CAST IRON RECTANGULAR TERRINE

This dish is designed for baking and shaping the dense mixture of finely chopped vegetables, meat or fish that constitutes a terrine. Cast iron permits the necessary slow, even cooking, while the elongated shape facilitates slicing the terrine into neat, cracker-sized portions.

## 10 ALUMINIUM PUDDING BASINS

These basins can be used for old-fashioned steamed puddings and as cold moulds for chilled custards and mousses. Aluminium is not a suitable material for cooking fruit puddings unless lined with greaseproof (waxed) paper (see 'materials choice', page 12).

## 11 GLAZED EARTHENWARE BASINS

These are the classic basins for traditional steamed puddings. The mixture is covered with pleated greaseproof (waxed) paper, held in place with string tied under the thick rim, which is designed for the purpose. These basins are also ideal for chilled summer pudding, and can double as mixing bowls.

## 12 NON-STICK STEEL MEAT LOAF PAN

This two-part pan has a ridged, perforated base for draining away the fatty liquid that is the bane of cooking a meat loaf. The outer pan doubles as a bread pan.

# spinach soufflé

**TOOLS** saucepan, souffle dish, bowl, whisk

For four people, cook 250 g/9 oz washed spinach, without extra water, until wilted. Drain, squeeze dry and chop finely. Heat the oven to 180°C/350°F/gas 4. Butter a 1 litre/1 quart souffle dish and dust with 2–3 tablespoons dried breadcrumbs.

Sauté a small chopped onion in a little oil in a large, non-stick pan for 3 minutes, then mix in 25 g/1 tablespoon butter, melt, and stir in 2 tablespoons flour, 1 teaspoon dry mustard and 1/2 teaspoon mild curry powder. Cook for 1 minute, then gradually beat in 200 ml/1 scant cup hot milk (a) until smooth and thickened. Cook for a minute or so, then remove from the heat.

Stir in 100 g/1 cup grated mature Cheddar and 2 tablespoons grated Parmesan (b), then 4 egg yolks and the spinach. Check seasoning.

Whisk 5 egg whites until stiff but not dry. Fold into the mixture (c), spoon into the dish, level the top and scatter with 2 tablespoons grated Cheddar (d). Bake for 20–25 minutes until risen and slightly wobbly in the middle. Serve immediately.

a    b

## steamed lemon puddings

**TOOLS** metal pudding basins, steamer, wooden spoon, mixing bowl

Grease 4 x 150 ml/2/3 cup metal pudding basins with softened butter (a). Place a teaspoon of golden syrup or honey in each base.

Beat together 125 g/4½ oz each softened butter and golden caster (superfine) sugar, 100 g/¾ cup self-raising flour, 2 medium organic eggs and the grated zest of 1 lemon until light and creamy. Mix in 50 g/½ cup fresh white breadcrumbs, the juice of 1 lemon, adding a little milk, if necessary, for a soft dropping consistency. Spoon into the basins (b), level, cover each with a disc of non-stick baking parchment, then over wrap in foil, pleating the centres to allow for expansion (c).

Place the basins in a steamer basket set over a pan of gently boiling water (d). Cover and steam for 30–35 minutes, checking the water level once or twice and topping it up with boiling water, if necessary. Uncover, allow to stand for 5 minutes, then un-mould onto dessert bowls. Serve with warm real custard or cream.

c    d

# fresh shell bean gratin
## ALICE WATERS

Alice Waters is one of America's favourite chefs. Described as 'poetic', 'visionary' and 'passionate', her cooking is based on the belief that optimal flavour and environmental harmony go hand in hand. This comforting supper dish is typical of her cooking. You will need a gratin dish about 5 cm/2 inches deep and 23 cm/ 9 inches square. Fresh shell beans are available in late summer and early autumn. Use a mixture of beans of varying colours. You will need 900 g–1.3 kg/2–3 lb in their pods. You can also make the gratin with dried beans. Soak 225 g/8 oz beans (separately, if using a mixture) overnight. Drain and boil rapidly in fresh water for 20 minutes. Drain again and begin cooking with step 1.

SERVES 4–6

**TOOLS**
medium-sized saucepans
strainer
jug or bowl
cook's knife
paring knife
medium frying pan
wooden spoon
1.5 litre/1½ quart gratin
   dish

**INGREDIENTS**
450–500 g/1–1½ lb podded
   fresh shell beans, such
   as cannellini, flageolet and
   borlotti
salt
6 tbsp olive oil
½ onion, finely chopped
4 garlic cloves, cut into slivers

1–2 sage leaves, chopped
115–140 g/4–5 oz greens,
   such as chard, broccoli
   raab, mustard greens,
   turnip tops, sliced into
   ribbons (optional)
2 tomatoes, roughly chopped
8 tbsp toasted breadcrumbs
   (see below)

**1** Put the beans in separate saucepans with just enough water to cover by 2.5 cm/1 inch (fresh shell beans absorb very little water). When they have come to the boil, add salt and 2 tablespoons of the olive oil, and lower the heat to a simmer. Cook until the beans are tender, about 30 minutes. Drain the beans in a strainer set over a measuring jug, and save their liquid.

**2** Preheat the oven to 180°C/350°F/gas 4. While the beans are cooking, gently fry the onion in 2 tablespoons of olive oil, with the garlic, sage leaves and some salt, until the onion is soft and translucent. If you wish, cook a small bunch of greens with the onion; add a little of the bean water along with them if you do.

**3** When the onion is cooked, add the tomatoes, raise the heat, and cook for 1–2 minutes.

**4** Combine the beans in a gratin dish with the onions, tomatoes and greens, if using. Add enough bean water to almost cover. Taste, correct the seasoning, and pour the rest of the olive oil over the gratin.

**5** Cover the top with toasted breadcrumbs and bake for 45 minutes. Check occasionally and moisten with more bean water if the gratin seems to be drying out too much.

**TOASTED BREADCRUMBS** Preheat the oven to 150°C/300°F/gas 2. Remove the crust from stale levain bread or other country-style bread. Shred into small pieces and either chop it by hand or in a food processor, or leave in rough chunks depending on use. Toss with a pinch of salt and a little olive oil to coat the bread. Spread the crumbs on a baking sheet in a thin layer. Bake until golden brown, tossing every 10 minutes.

# vanilla soufflé with chocolate sauce
## CHRIS TANNER · JAMES TANNER

A breathtaking dessert with a guaranteed wow factor contributed by top UK chefs the Tanner Brothers. The secrets to a good soufflé are a well buttered and sugared dish, the crème pâtissière should always be at room temperature and the mixing bowl meticulously clean. Most importantly, you need good company to share it with.

SERVES 6

**TOOLS**
2 small saucepans
4 mixing bowls
balloon whisk
wooden spoon
cling film (plastic wrap)
6 large ramekin dishes
pasty brush
large metal spoon
baking sheet

**INGREDIENTS**
*FOR THE CRÈME PÂTISSIERE*
480 ml/2 cups milk
125 g/heaped 1/2 cup caster (superfine) sugar, plus extra for dusting
1 vanilla pod (bean), split and seeds scraped out
6 organic eggs, separated

60 g/1/2 cup plain (all-purpose) flour
softened butter, for greasing

*FOR THE CHOCOLATE SAUCE*
350 ml/scant 1 1/2 cups whipping cream
150 g/5 1/2 oz dark chocolate
cocoa powder, for dusting

**1** Put the milk, half the sugar and the vanilla pod and seeds in a saucepan and gently warm. Remove from the heat and leave to infuse for 15 minutes.

**2** In a mixing bowl, whisk together the egg yolks, flour and remaining sugar until it forms a smooth paste.

**3** Pour over the milk and mix well. Transfer to a clean pan and heat gently for 10–15 minutes, stirring continuously, until the mixture begins to thicken. Transfer to a clean bowl, cover with cling film and leave to cool.

**4** Preheat the oven to 200°C/400°F/gas 6. Brush the insides of six large ramekin dishes with softened butter – always brush up the sides. Add a tablespoon of sugar to each ramekin and tilt and rotate until the insides are coated in the sugar. Pour out any excess sugar, then chill.

**5** Whisk the egg whites until they form stiff peaks. Put the crème pâtissière into a large bowl and whisk well. Add half the egg whites and whisk well until the mixture forms a smooth paste. Add the remaining egg whites and fold in with a large metal spoon.

**6** Spoon the soufflé mixture into the prepared ramekins, filling them up to the top. Carefully tap down the dishes (this releases any trapped air). Place on a baking sheet and bake for 10–15 minutes – do not open the oven door during cooking since this allows the hot air to escape.

**7** Meanwhile, make the chocolate sauce. Gently bring the cream up to the boil. Pour onto the chocolate and stir until melted. Set aside.

**8** When the soufflés are ready, carefully but quickly remove from the oven. Dust with cocoa powder and serve immediately with the chocolate sauce.

# dough making

Cake baking is a precise skill requiring accuracy of weighing, temperature and tin size. Tins of the same volume can have different dimensions – one may be wide and shallow, another narrow and deep. A mixture intended to cook quickly in a shallow tin will not cook properly in a tin that is too deep, and vice versa. A good recipe will specify the dimensions of the tin, not just the volume.

# cake tins and trays

The most useful tins to have are a pair of round, shallow, 20 cm/8 inch tins for sponge cakes, a deep, 23 or 25 cm/9 or 10 inch tin for fruit cake, a Swiss (jelly) roll tin and perhaps a 23 cm/9 inch springform tin for easy release of moulded cakes and desserts. One or two 12-cup trays are useful for muffins, small cakes and tarts, or dough left over from a large cake. Tins with a non-stick surface may not be foolproof, but are worth having nevertheless. For choice of materials, see 'bread-tin materials', page 279.

1

### 1 SILICONE MUFFIN TRAY
Non-stick flexible silicone has revolutionised the cookware business. Made by fusing silicon (from common sand) with oxygen, the resultant chemically inert material is a modern miracle. With an amazing temperature tolerance of -40°–250°C/-40°–500°F, it cooks and browns evenly, and is wonderfully flexible for easy turning out. Microwaveable and dishwasher safe, this deep-sided muffin tray comes in a funky red colour to liven up your bakeware drawer.

### 2 JOINED SMALL TINS
These differently shaped individual tins are joined together in a row for convenience. Choose from boats, rectangles, waisted ovals and many more. Once you have one sort, you'll want to collect more.

### 3 FOIL AND PAPER CUPS
Useful for light mixes that cook very quickly, these can be placed on a baking sheet or in the indented cups of a muffin tray. If they are left in place until ready to eat, paper cups prevent the cakes from drying out. Children love peeling them off.

2

3

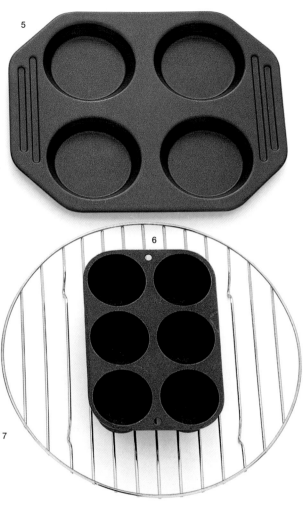

#### 4 ENGLISH BUN TRAY

This 12-cup, non-stick tray is ideal for small cakes (cupcakes), tarts and mini quiches. The ridged handles make the tray easier to grip when sliding it in and out of the oven.

#### 5 YORKSHIRE PUDDING TRAY

Similar to the English bun tray, this one has four shallow, flat-bottomed cups for making single portions of Yorkshire pudding. The tray can also be used for baking small sponge cakes, tarts and quiches.

#### 7 COOLING RACKS

An elevated wire rack speeds cooling of cakes by allowing steam to evaporate from all surfaces. A very fragile cake may be damaged by the wires, so cover the rack with a layer of greaseproof (waxed) paper first. The paper will absorb evaporating steam.

#### 6 CAST IRON POPOVER/ MUFFIN TRAY

Air circulates quickly between these individual cups pressed into a heavy, cast iron sheet, promoting rapid rising and setting of dough. The flared, 4 cm/1½ inch deep sides increase surface area, which encourages dough to rise and moisture to evaporate.

dough making **253**

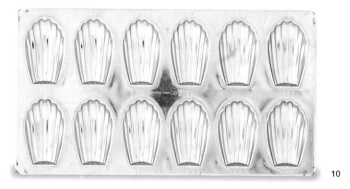

### 8 SQUARE CAKE TIN

It is rarely recognised that square cake tins are actually one size bigger than round; thus a 23 cm/9 inch round and a 20 cm/8 inch square tin of the same depth are the same capacity. This shallow, 4 cm/1½ inch deep tin is made from heavy-duty, chef's quality, hard-anodised aluminium, and is perfect for brownies or light sponges.

### 9 DEEP SQUARE CAKE TIN

This 8 cm/3 inch deep version of (8) is also made from hard-anodised aluminium, which does not warp during baking. It is perfect for large fruit cakes, which need long cooking.

### 10 MADELEINE TRAY

The scallop-shaped, fluted indentations increase the area that is exposed to heat. This allows the batter to rise quickly in the middle and produce the characteristic madeleine shapes.

### 11 ANGEL FOOD CAKE TIN

The tube allows heat to penetrate to the centre of the cake and provides another surface for the mixture to cling to as it rises. The tube projects beyond the rim so when the tin is inverted to cool the cake, air can pass beneath it. Some tins have small feet on the rim for better balance when inverted.

### 12 SPRINGFORM TIN

This is invaluable for fragile cakes that are hard to unmould. When the clip is unbuckled, the sides of the tin move out from the base, leaving behind a perfectly formed cake. Made of heavy-gauge steel with a durable non-stick coating inside and out, this heavy-duty tin comes with an additional tube base embossed with swirling flutes. It is ideal for cheesecakes or mousse-like cakes or for making *kugelhopf* – said to be Marie Antoinette's favourite cake, maybe because it reminded her of her Austrian homeland.

### 13 DEEP, ROUND CAKE TINS

Dense fruit-cake mixtures need long cooking, so should be baked in a deep, heavy-gauge tin to prevent scorching. These tins have a removable base and a reinforced, rolled rim that helps to maintain their shape.

11

13

12

14

15

## 14 SWISS ROLL TIN

Extremely shallow, this rectangular tin is specially designed for cooking the thin layer of sponge needed for a swiss (jelly) roll. It is made from heavy-gauge tinned steel, which conducts heat quickly and evenly, and will not warp or twist.

## 15 SHALLOW CAKE TIN

This is used for quickly cooked mixtures such as sponge cakes and sponge sandwiches (round cake layers). It is best always to buy a pair. Although it has a non-stick surface, it still needs greasing.

a b
c

## making yorkshire puddings

**TOOLS** Yorkshire pudding tray, bowl, whisk, jug

For light puffy puds, first make a batter by whizzing together in a food processor (or by hand in a large bowl with a big balloon whisk) 100 g/¾ cupplain (all-purpose) flour, ½ teaspoon fine sea salt, 250 ml/1 cup milk and 1 large organic egg, then transfer the mixture to a jug.

Preheat the oven to 200°C/400°F/gas 6. Grease a 4-hole Yorkshire pudding tray with a little oil or melted lard and place in the oven for 3–5 minutes until smoking. Pour the batter into the holes until three-quarters full (a and b). Bake until risen and crisp, about 12 minutes (c). Serve quickly. The remaining batter can be used for a second batch!

# preparing a sandwich tin

**TOOLS** cake tin, baking parchment

It is always necessary to prepare a cake tin, whatever its size, to ensure the cooked cake can be turned out without sticking to the base or sides. To this end, cooks often will grease and line a tin with oil and non-stick baking parchment. Non-stick tins will not need such involved preparation, but will still benefit from a light brushing of oil before baking.

To line a shallow cake tin, first place the base of the tin on a sheet of baking parchment and draw around the base (a). Cut out just within the drawn line, so the shape fits neatly. Brush inside the tin with a little oil, then line with the baking parchment. Fill with the cake mixture (b) and bake as required. When ready to turn out, loosen the sides with a small palette knife (metal spatula) and invert onto a wire rack to cool.

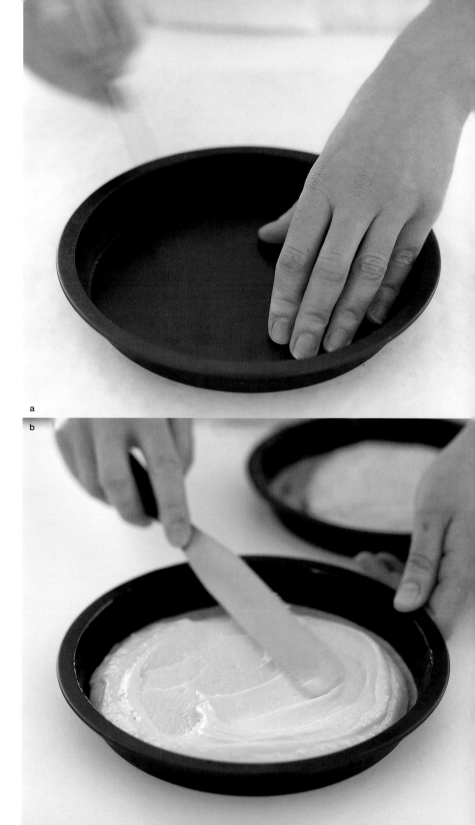

a

b

# lemon and lime roulade
## MICH TURNER

**Roulades are deceptively easy to make and look very impressive. Contributed by Mich Turner of the acclaimed Little Venice Cake Company, London, this roulade combines the fresh zest of lemons and limes for a very light, refreshing dessert.**

SERVES 4

**TOOLS**
swiss (jelly) roll tin
large mixing bowl
whisk
sieve
metal spoon
palette knife (metal spatula)

**INGREDIENTS**
*FOR THE ROULADE*
25 g/1 tbsp butter, plus extra
    for greasing
4 eggs
115 g/heaped 1/2 cup golden
    caster (superfine) sugar
zest of 2 lemons
zest of 2 limes
115 g/scant 1 cup plain (all-
    purpose) flour

*FOR THE FILLING*
200 ml/scant 1 cup whipping
    cream
zest of 1 lemon
zest of 1 lime
6 tbsp lemon curd

*TO DECORATE*
icing (confectioner's) sugar,
    for dusting
fresh, edible flowers, to serve

**1** Heat the oven to 180°C/350°F/gas 4. Butter a 40 x 30 cm/16 x 12 inch swiss roll tin and line the base and sides with non-stick baking parchment. Dust lightly with flour and chill.

**2** Melt the butter, then set aside to cool. Place the eggs and sugar in a large mixing bowl and whisk until the mixture forms a thick trail (5 minutes), then briefly whisk in the lemon and lime zest. Sieve the flour into the mixture and gently fold in with a metal spoon. Pour in the cooled, melted butter and gently fold in until well mixed.

**3** Scrape the mixture into the prepared tin and spread with a palette knife until it forms an even layer approximately 1 cm/1/2 inch thick. Bake in the oven for 6–8 minutes until just cooked.

**4** Invert the roulade onto a fresh piece of non-stick baking parchment placed on a clean, damp tea towel and lightly dusted with golden caster sugar. Carefully roll up the roulade and set aside whilst you prepare the filling.

**5** Whip the cream and fold in the lemon and lime zest. Unroll the roulade and discard the baking parchment. Spread the lemon curd and then the cream over the roulade, and re-roll tightly.

**6** To serve, heavily dust the top with sieved icing sugar and decorate with fresh edible flowers.

**NOTE** Alternatively, fill the roulade with fresh summer berries and lightly whipped fresh cream. It can be made up to a day in advance and filled just prior to serving.

# mocha brownies
## NICOLA GRAIMES

**Made without flour, these chocolate-coffee brownies have a temptingly, moist, fudgey texture.**

MAKES 12 SQUARES

**TOOLS**
20 cm/8 inch square
cake tin

**INGREDIENTS**
150 g/5½ oz plain chocolate
(70 per cent cocoa solids),
broken into pieces
100 g/3½ oz butter
1 tsp strong instant coffee

1 tsp vanilla extract
100 g/3½ oz ground almonds
175g/scant 1 cup caster
(superfine) sugar
4 eggs, separated

**1** Preheat the oven to 180°C/350°F/gas 4. Grease, then line a 20 cm/8 inch square cake tin with baking parchment.

**2** Place the chocolate and butter in a heatproof bowl set over a pan of gently simmering water – make sure the bottom of the bowl does not touch the water. Stir gently, very occasionally, until melted.

**3** Carefully remove the bowl from the heat and stir in the coffee and vanilla extract. Add the almonds and sugar and mix well until combined. Beat the egg yolks lightly then stir them into the chocolate mixture.

**4** Whisk the egg whites until they form stiff peaks. Carefully fold a large spoonful into the chocolate mixture, then fold in the rest until completely mixed in.

**5** Spoon the mixture into the prepared tin and bake for 35–40 minutes until risen and firm on top but still gooey in the centre. Leave to cool in the tin, then turn out, remove the baking parchment and cut into 12 pieces.

# double lemon muffins
## NICOLA GRAIMES

**The secret to good, light muffins is to not over stir the mixture – a few lumps don't matter.**

MAKES 8

**TOOLS**
large paper cases
deep muffin tray
mixing bowls
whisk

**INGREDIENTS**
225 g/scant 1¾ cups plain
(all-purpose) flour
1 tsp baking powder
pinch of salt
150 g/¾ cup golden caster
(superfine) sugar
zest of 1 lemon

5 tbsp milk
2 eggs
140 g/5 oz unsalted butter,
melted
2 tbsp lemon juice
3 tbsp good-quality lemon
curd

**1** Preheat the oven to 200°C/400°F/gas 6. Place nine large paper cases in a deep muffin tray.

**2** Sift the flour, baking powder and salt into a mixing bowl. Add the sugar and lemon zest and combine.

**3** Place the milk, eggs and melted butter in a separate bowl and whisk until combined. Gradually add the milk mixture to the flour, stirring gently. Add the lemon juice and mix gently until combined.

**4** Spoon a heaped dessertspoonful of the muffin mixture into the paper cases, then top each one with a teaspoonful of lemon curd. Cover the lemon curd with the remaining muffin mixture, leaving room for the muffin to rise.

**5** Bake for 20 minutes until risen and golden, then cool on a wire rack.

For a meltingly crisp, golden-brown pastry case, use a fluted metal tin with a removable base. Some cooks use a bottomless metal ring set directly on a baking sheet. Though they are attractive, tart dishes made of fluted porcelain absorb heat more slowly than metal and do not produce such a crisp crust. The most useful diameters for tart tins are 23 and 25 cm/9 and 10 inches. If you ever need to cater for a crowd, you might also want to consider a 30 cm/12 inch tin.

# tart tins and pie plates

A high-sided tart tin comes in handy for making quiches. If you are partial to pies, deep and shallow ceramic pie dishes are worth buying, as is a metal pie plate for that spur-of-the-moment pie.

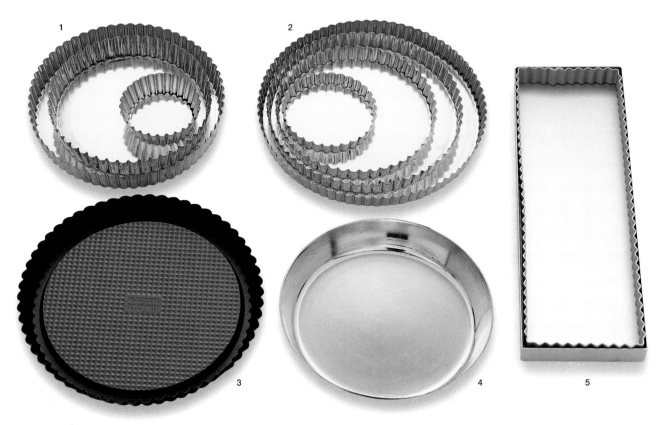

Rigid metal baking trays or sheets are essential for baking small pastry shapes, biscuits and hand-formed breads. They also provide porcelain dishes with a boost of heat from below, which helps to cook the base. It's worth buying two baking trays so you can load one while the other is in the oven. Never put two in the oven simultaneously – the top one will prevent heat circulating over the lower, and you'll end up with unevenly cooked food. Buy the largest baking tray your oven will accommodate, but allow at least 5 cm/2 inches all round for air circulation.

### 1 DEEP FLUTED TART TINS

The fluted sides of these metal tins almost double the surface area exposed to heat. This encourages the crust to set more quickly. Being deep, the sides make a particularly strong crust, which is useful for cream- or egg-based fillings containing solid pieces of food. The bases of these tins are removable (see 2).

### 2 SHALLOW FLUTED TART TINS

Perfect for glazed fruit tarts or shallow custard-filled tarts, these tins are available in sizes ranging from 11–31 cm/4 1/2–13 inches. As with the deep-fluted tins, the bases are removable. Stand the tin on a jam jar and ease the outer ring down. You can leave the tart on the base when you transfer it to a serving plate.

### 3 NON-STICK SPONGE TART TIN

This warp-free tin with a raised centre is used for baking those slightly old-fashioned whisked sponge cases that you load up with whipped cream and fruit. Once turned out, the base is left upside down, leaving a raised rim surrounding a circle for the filling. The base has a dimpled surface, which makes unmoulding easier.

### 4 TARTE TATIN TIN

Made of copper lined with stainless steel, this elegant pan is ideal for baking the upside-down apple cake known as 'tarte tatin', because copper quickly conducts the high heat necessary for caramelising syrupy juices. A wide base and shallow sides provide a large surface area, which allows the tart to cook evenly through to the centre.

### 5 RECTANGULAR TRANCHE TRAY

Recreate classic French patisserie tarts and savoury quiches with a long silver anodised aluminium tart tin. Measuring 36 x 12 cm/14 1/2 x 4 1/2 inches, with a loose base, the tin comes either with plain, straight-sided edges (traditional for sweet tarts) or fluted for savoury ones. Cut the tarts either in slices (tranches) or triangular wedges.

### 6 CERAMIC CRINKLE-CRUST PIE DISH

Perfect for the enthusiastic pie-maker, this family-size ceramic dish has an attractive, crimped edge, so there is no need to struggle and pinch your own pastry. You can use it to make either a double crust pie, such as traditional ham and egg, or a top-crust fruit or steak pie. Very versatile, it can also double up as a gratin dish for creamy pastas and fish pies.

### 7 CERAMIC TART/PIZZA DISH

This classic French ceramic plate has a variety of uses. Round and flat, measuring between 30–37 cm/12–14 1/2 inches diameter, and ovenproof, it can be used as an oven-to-table pizza baking plate. It will also show off a large fruit flan to elegant perfection – the mill-pond flat surface means flans and tarts will not dip in the centre – and serve as a cheese platter.

6

7

8

### 8 SILICONE BAKING MOULDS

Made from superbly non-stick and flexible silicone (see page 252), this cheerful red tart dish conducts heat evenly and quickly, ensuring your pastry cases are crisp. Dishwasher and freezerproof.

## 9 DEEP PIE DISH

This is one of those impeccably designed dishes that get handed down from generation to generation. It is made of thick, glazed ceramic, which allows steady heat to penetrate the centre of the pie without burning the crust. The wide, flat rim supports the top layer of pastry and gives a generous seal, while the gently rounded interior makes serving and cleaning easier.

## 10 PIE BIRD

The purpose of this porcelain bird is to support the top crust and vent the steam that would otherwise make the crust soggy. The slightly arced base allows steam to travel upwards and out through the beak. Make sure the beak is wide open. You can also buy special funnels that serve the same purpose.

## 11 SHALLOW PIE DISH

Like the deep dish (9), this classic piece of bakeware is made of thick, glazed ceramic with a flat rim for sealing double-crust pies. The round, shallow shape makes it a versatile dish – it can double up as a gratin dish and is elegant enough to be used as a serving bowl for vegetables, salad or fruit.

9

10

11

## 12 PIE PLATES

These lovely traditional tinned-steel plates are for baking shallow, double-crust pies or open tarts – the kind your grandmother used to make. They are available in a range of sizes, from a single serving to a family-sized 30 cm/12 inches.

## 13 NON-STICK PIE PLATE WITH INSERT

This pie plate is supplied with a useful perforated insert that can be used instead of baking 'beans' (see page 271) when baking an unfilled pastry case.

12

13

## 14 BAKING SHEETS

These heavy-duty baking sheets absorb and transmit the heat necessary for setting, crisping and browning doughs of various kinds. The upper sheet is made of tinned steel and the lower of blackened steel (see 'bread tins', page 279). They are rigid enough not to warp or twist, and have a slightly inclined edge that makes them easier to grip. Biscuit or baking trays perform a similar function, but they have a shallow, fully turned-up edge to prevent runny doughs from overflowing and cooked biscuits from sliding off the tray.

14

# double-crust pie

**TOOLS** rolling pin, pie dish, pie bird, small sharp knife, pastry brush

A double-crust pie has a base and a top crust. To ensure the top crust is crisp and golden, the filling should be nicely rounded on top. Alternatively, a pie bird or funnel can be placed in the centre to hold up the pastry. Allow a good 350 g/12 oz of pastry dough for a 20–22 cm/8–8½ inch round dish.

Divide the pastry into two-thirds and one-third. Roll out thinly so both pieces will overhang the dish by an ample 2–3 cm/¾–1¼ inches. Press the larger circle into the dish base, fit in a pie funnel if liked, and fill with thinly sliced apples or other fruits, or a savoury filling (a).

Beat an egg yolk with 2 teaspoons of cold water to glaze and brush around the edge. Then lift over the smaller circle and lower over the top (b). Trim the edge with a small sharp knife(c). To seal, either press around the edge with the back of a fork or pinch into the edge, pressing down with two fingers of one hand while pushing in with the thumb of the other hand (d).

Cut a cross in the centre of the pie, then glaze evenly with the remaining yolk using a pastry brush. Place the pie on a baking sheet. Bake in a preheated oven at 200°C/400°F/gas 6 for 15 minutes, then reduce the heat to 180°C/350°F/gas 4 and bake for another 30–45 minutes.

a

b

c

d

# leek and peppercorn tart

A mouthwatering supper-time treat, this tart is made with rich shortcrust pastry. For maximum crispness, the pastry is rolled as thinly as possible and baked directly on a baking sheet at a high temperature. The leeks must be small and thinly sliced so they cook through. They will be tender but still crisp. The smoky flavour of green peppercorns is delicious with leeks and cheese.

SERVES 4–6 AS A LIGHT MEAL

| TOOLS | INGREDIENTS |
|---|---|
| flour sifter or sieve | 225 g/scant 1¾ cups plain |
| mixing bowl | (all-purpose) bleached flour |
| pastry blender | ¼ tsp each salt and sugar |
| coarse grater | 150 g/5½ butter |
| pestle and mortar | 3 tbsp iced water |
| cook's knife | 100 g/3½ oz Cheddar |
| utility knife | 100 g/3½ oz mozzarella |
| flour dredger | 1½ tsp dried green |
| rolling pin | peppercorns |
| baking sheet | 3 small leeks, weighing about |
| small flat whisk | 250 g/9 oz in total |
| pastry brush | 50 g/1¾ oz pancetta |
| | 2 tsp fresh thyme leaves |
| | beaten egg yolk, to glaze |

**1** Sift the flour, salt and sugar into a bowl. Using a pastry blender if you wish, work in half the butter until the mixture resembles coarse crumbs (a). Briefly work in the remaining butter, leaving it slightly unevenly mixed. Lightly stir in the water to form a soft dough. Wrap in cling film (plastic wrap) and chill for 1 hour.

**2** Grate the cheeses, using the coarse blade of a grater. Crush the peppercorns with a pestle and mortar. Trim the leeks and slice in half lengthways, then crossways into 2 cm/¾ inch slices. You will need 175 g/6 oz of prepared leek. Cut the pancetta into bite-sized pieces.

**3** Preheat the oven to 240°C/475°F/gas 9. Roll out the dough on a floured surface as thinly as possible to form a 31 cm/12½ inch square (b). Carefully drape the dough over a rolling pin and place on a baking sheet (c). Trim the edges neatly.

**4** Leaving a 1.5 cm/⅔ inch border all round, scatter the cheeses evenly over the dough. Sprinkle with the peppercorns and a little salt to taste, then add the leeks, spreading them out evenly. Sprinkle with the pancetta and thyme.

**5** Fold up the edges of the pastry to slightly enclose the filling, folding the corners to a pleat. Brush the edges with the egg yolk.

**6** Bake for 20 minutes until the pastry is golden and the leeks look slightly charred. Serve hot or warm.

a

b

c

# tarte tatin

**TOOLS** tart tatin tin, swivel peeler, rolling pin, chopping board, knife

First, thinly peel three large Cox's apples with a swivel peeler, then cut into quarters and remove the cores. This can be done ahead of time, because even though the apples will oxidise and turn a little brown, they will dry out slightly and be coated in sugar as they bake.

Preheat the oven to 200°C/400°F/gas 6. Roll out about 300 g/ 10½ oz ready-made puff pastry (or unravel a sheet of ready-rolled pastry) and cut out a circle 23–24 cm/9–9½ inches in diameter, using a dinner plate or cake tin as a template. Place on a flat sheet, prick the base several times with a fork and chill for 1 hour.

Place the tarte tatin tin over a low heat and add 40 g/1½ oz unsalted butter, 75 g/⅓ cup caster (superfine) sugar and ½ teaspoon ground cinnamon or nutmeg (a). Shake the pan occasionally to mix the butter and sugar, then lay in the apple quarters, cored side up (b). Cook for about 10 minutes, by which time a caramel should have begun forming in the pan.

Remove the pan from the heat and drape over the pastry round (c), tucking it in around the edge (d), then place in the oven and cook for 15 minutes or so until golden brown and crisp. Remove from the oven, allow to cool for 5–7 minutes, then carefully invert onto a large heatproof plate.

a

b

c

d

Making pastry is a multi-stage process. You will need tools for blending, rolling, cutting, crimping, brushing and scraping. Though much of this work can be done with your hands, using these tools makes life easier and gives a neater result. Pastry-making is a specialist craft and the tools reflect this. Their functional design has changed little over the years but modern technology has introduced new materials that make the tools more durable and easier to keep clean.

# pastry tools

## choosing tools

A rolling pin is a must. Pastry can be rolled with a broom handle or milk bottle, but neither are the ideal texture, length or diameter. Rolling pins should be smooth to the touch, and longer than the area covered by the dough once it is rolled out. Metal pins are cooler than wooden ones, but as wood is a poor conductor of heat, a wooden pin is pretty cool too. The pin should be heavy enough to do its job without needing undue pressure from you. Though they can make pins more comfortable to use, handles reduce the width of the rolling surface or result in an unnecessarily long pin, which may be difficult to store.

Pastry is best rolled on a cool smooth non-stick surface such as marble or granite rather than wood. It's possible to have a rolling area cut into a work surface; otherwise buy a separate board. A silicone pastry mat is another option. It is easy to wash and can be rolled up for convenient storage.

You'll need a pastry brush for greasing tins and anointing pastry. Silicon bristles are durable, heatproof and easy to clean, but make sure they are fine enough and close enough to deliver an even slick of grease or liquid. Traditional hog's hair bristles do the job perfectly, provided the bristles stay where they belong – attached to the brush rather than the pastry.

A tool for rubbing chilled fat into flour helps to keep it cool rather than using warm hands. Then after rolling out the dough various cutting tools will help with finishing touches – from round cutters, to a serrated pastry wheel for crimping pie edges and even a roller cutter that gives an instant lattice look. Although you can use an upturned saucer or glass, proper metal cutters, with their thin, sharp cutting edges, deliver the best definition; plastic cutters produce thicker, duller edges. To help scrape off the pastry cut outs, use a dough scraper for easy lifting and to keep the dough from stretching. If you choose well, these tools can last a lifetime.

**1 DOUGH SCRAPER**
Originally used for measuring and dividing dough into equal pieces, this traditional tool is now more often used as a scraper, though it still comes in handy for checking your dough is the right size.

**2 PASTRY WHEEL**
A fluted wheel gives a zigzag edge to lattice strips, pasta ribbons and ravioli squares. The safety guard prevents your finger slipping onto the wheel.

**3 LATTICE CUTTER**
This ingenious tool saves the work of hand-weaving a lattice topping for a tart. Toothed wheels produce a series of broken lines as you roll the cutter over the dough. Gently lift and stretch the dough to open out the lattice.

**4 FLEXIBLE PALETTE KNIFE**
Use this tool, also known as a metal spatula, for evenly spreading and smoothing the surface of soft mixtures and toppings. Wetting the blade helps prevent sticking.

### 5 | PASTRY BLENDER
A blender is useful for working fat into flour if your fingertips aren't up to it.

### 6 | NATURAL BRISTLE PASTRY BRUSHES
Bristles reach into crevices and coat surfaces evenly. These brushes are indispensable for anointing pastry, dusting flour or greasing tins. Wash and dry them carefully after use.

### 7 | MARBLE PASTRY BOARD
Cool, smooth marble is the ideal surface on which to roll pastry. It needs very little flouring to prevent sticking.

### PASTRY CUTTERS

8 | This set of three crinkle cutters is a favourite of home cooks. Make sure you wash and dry them carefully after use to avoid rusting.

9 | This covetable professional set includes cutters of every conceivable size. Use them to cut circles not only from dough, but also from firm-fleshed vegetables, pineapple, aspic and hard-boiled eggs. A rolled top edge maintains their shape.

10 | This double-ringed doughnut cutter prevents the off-centre holes that may occur when using two separate cutters.

### 11 | BAKING BEANS
Open tarts often require the pastry base to be baked 'blind' (see page 273) using high heat conductive beans, either ceramic (as shown here) or aluminium. They will last for decades.

11

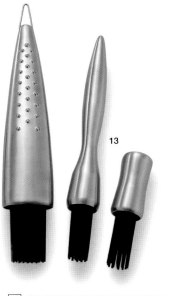

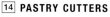

**PASTRY CUTTERS**

Make baking fun with shaped metal cutters – great for children and adults alike. Use them for stamping out biscuit dough or bread croûtes. Pastry stars can also be pressed into shallow bun tins and baked as crown-shaped jam tarts.

12

13

14

12 **WOODEN PASTRY BRUSH**

Natural bristle is best for painting an even glaze on pastry or fruit tart tops. This classic cook's pastry brush has a varnished handle and is perfect for glazing pie tops with egg glaze, fruit flans with jam glaze and cake tins with oil to grease. Do not use on heated pancake pans as the bristle will shrivel.

13 **SILICONE PASTRY BRUSHES**

Versatile silicone can be extruded into long, flexible strains for brushing off loose flour or glazing pastry tops prior to baking. They come fitted into state-of the-art aluminium handles of various sizes and, being heatproof, are perfect for use with hot syrups or barbecue marinades. Dishwasher safe, they neither wear out nor clog up with grease.

15 **ROLLING PINS**

The best pins have smooth surfaces that do not dent and are scratch-resistant. They can come either as long, handle-free pins or as revolving rollers with handles. Heavy stainless steel pins keep cool and can be chilled ahead to keep pastry dough at an even temperature. Silicone rolling pins are non-stick, thus eliminating the need for dusting with flour, which can lead to tough, heavy pastry. Dolly-size pins are best for rolling out dough balls into small circles to fill and shape.

15

# baking blind

a

b

c

d

**TOOLS** rolling pin, tart tin, baking parchment, baking beans, small sharp knife

Shortcrust and sweet pastry used to line open pie or tart tins is often baked 'blind' so it is crisp.

First, roll out the pastry on a lightly floured surface to a round that is the diameter of your tin, plus the height of the two sides, plus 2 cm/1 inch, i.e. a 20 cm/8 inch tin with 1.5 cm/¾ inch sides will require a circle of pastry approximately 25 cm/10 inches in diameter (a).

If the tart tin is not non-stick, either rub it with some softened butter or line the base with non-stick baking parchment. Lift the pastry into the tart tin over a rolling pin and gently press into the tin, allowing a good 1–2 cm/½–¾ inch to overhang. Press

the pastry well into the sides (b) and prick the base. Do not trim, but do save a small ball of raw dough for patching.

Tear off a large sheet of non-stick baking parchment that will amply fill the tin with a good overlap and press on top of the pastry. Fill with baking beans (c) or old raw rice or beans. Chill whilst you heat the oven to 200°C/400°F/gas 6.

When ready to bake, place the tart tin (still filled with the beans) on a flat, heavy metal baking sheet and bake 15 minutes. Remove the paper and beans and return to the oven for a further 5 minutes until pale golden.

Now, you may trim the edges with a sharp knife to the top of the tin (d). If there are any holes or cracks then fill with small pieces of raw pastry dough, moistened with water.

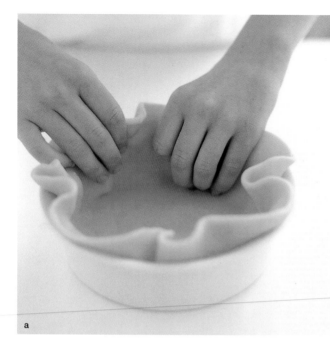

a

b

## double-crust lattice pie

Line a pie dish following the steps given for making a double-crust pie on page 265 (a). Roll out a circle of pastry for the top crust that is about 2 cm/³⁄₄ inch wider than the dish. Roll a lattice cutter over the round (b), then gently lift it up over a rolling pin, stretching it slightly, and let it fall on top of the filled pie dish (c). It will ease open as it falls to create a neat lattice effect. Seal, trim and glaze as on page 265.

c

# bakewell tart
## ROGER PIZEY

This delicious recipe for an English classic is contributed by Roger Pizey, a hugely influential baker who trained as a chef pâtissier with Albert Roux before going on to work for many years with Marco Pierre White, creating award-winning desserts and pastries. He now bakes for Peyton & Byrne, providing pâtisserie for the Heals Building, London, and the National Gallery Dining Room and Café.

SERVES 4

**TOOLS**
mixing bowls
pastry scraper
rolling pin
hand-held mixer
sieve
piping bag

**INGREDIENTS**
**FOR THE SWEET PASTRY**
125 g/4¹⁄₂ oz butter, softened
50 g/¹⁄₄ cup icing
    (confectioner's) sugar
2 egg yolks
1 tbsp water
170 g/1¹⁄₃ cups plain (all-
    purpose) flour

**FOR THE FILLING**
145 g/5 oz butter
145 g/²⁄₃ cup caster
    (superfine) sugar
40 g/scant ¹⁄₃ cup self-raising
    flour
40 g/scant ¹⁄₃ cup rice flour
75 g/scant ²⁄₃ cup ground
    almonds
2 organic eggs
450 g/1 lb seedless raspberry
    jam
200 g/7 oz flaked almonds

**1** First make the sweet pastry. Put the butter in a mixing bowl and beat in the icing sugar. Gradually stir in the egg yolks and half the water. Slowly add the flour and the remaining water. Mix well, scraping down after each stage. Remove from the bowl and knead a little on a cool, lightly floured surface to strengthen the pastry. Leave to rest overnight.

**2** Grease a 26 cm/10¹⁄₂ inch tart ring. Dust the pastry with flour and roll out to a thickness of 3–4 mm/¹⁄₈–¹⁄₄ inch. Line the tart ring, ensuring the pastry is pushed well down at the base of the ring, then leave to rest in the refrigerator for 3 hours.

**3** Meanwhile, make the filling. Cream together the butter and sugar, remembering to scrape down regularly with your pastry scraper. Sieve together the flour, rice flour and ground almonds. Add to the butter and sugar and mix thoroughly. Gradually add the eggs, beating well to produce a light mix. Leave to rest.

**4** Preheat the oven to 160°C/325°F/gas 3, then blind bake the pastry case (see page 273) using baking beans or lentils for 20 minutes until it is just coloured on the inside. Leave to cool.

**5** Meanwhile, heat the raspberry jam and reduce slightly, to intensify the flavour and to thicken it, then spread over the base of the pastry case. Pipe the filling into the tart ring until it is full. Bake in the oven at 160°C/325°F/gas 3 for about 40 minutes. After 20 minutes, remove the tart from the oven and sprinkle on the flaked almonds then return to the oven and continue cooking until the almonds are golden brown and the filling just set. (You'll find the almonds will burn if they are cooked for the full 40 minutes.) Serve warm with fresh vanilla anglaise or cream.

Although bread dough is dense enough to retain its shape when baked on a flat sheet, you can control its shape more precisely, and even the density of crumb, by using a tin. An open rectangular tin confines the base and sides of a loaf, while allowing the top to expand upwards and develop a crust. An enclosed tin limits the amount of expansion and produces a loaf with a denser crumb.

# bread tins

If you are new to bread making, start off with two or three rectangular, medium-sized tins – after all, if you are making one loaf, you might as well make two or three. As you progress, you may want to add a larger tin, and possibly tins for baguettes or brioches.

Rectangular tins should have firmly welded seams and a reinforced, rolled rim. A dimpled surface helps prevent sticking. A non-stick lining also helps in this respect, but is unlikely to be foolproof, and will eventually wear out. Brushing or spraying non-stick tins with oil is always a good idea.

If you bake bread regularly it is worth buying professional, heavy-grade tins. They will not warp or twist, and in time will develop a smooth patina of their own, so you won't need to grease them.

Bread tins come in a range of sizes; make sure you choose the right size for the loaf you intend to cook. The tin should be just over half full when the knocked-back dough is placed in it.

**BREAD-TIN MATERIALS** Blued or blackened steel has been heated to a very high temperature, which creates an ultra-smooth oxidised surface that has some resistance to rust. It is an excellent conductor of heat. Tinned steel bread tins have a coating of tin, as the name suggests. Before use,they need to be washed and dried carefully. Aluminium is a lightweight material and an excellent conductor of heat, but it lacks strength on its own. To compensate, manufacturers sometimes use aluminium to coat bread tins made of steel plate.

### 3 BRIOCHE TIN

This tin has flared, fluted sides and is used for baking brioche, a soft dough enriched with butter and eggs. The sides are taller than the width of the base, which permits maximum rising and exposes a large area of dough to the heat, so the edges set quickly. Tins come in seven sizes, from 7.5–20 cm/ 3–8 inches in diameter.

### 4 SILICONE LOAF TIN

Because of its flexibility, silicone bakeware filled with raw bread dough or batter can be tricky to handle. To overcome this problem, some manufacturers insert a microwave-safe, encapsulated metal rim for easy lifting that doesn't compromise the ease with which breads are unmoulded. The moulds are also easy to store because they simply spring back into life if squashed in a drawer.

### 1 NON-STICK BREAD TINS

Solidly made, these rectangular tins have corners reinforced by their own pleats, sturdy rolled rims and two layers of non-stick coating. They are available in several sizes, and are useful pans for beginners.

### 2 NON-STICK FRENCH BREAD TIN

This 40 cm/15¼ inch, finely perforated tin is designed to hold two medium-length baguettes. If you choose a longer tin, make sure it will fit into your oven.

### 5 EXTENDABLE LOAF TIN

Keen bakers may find they lack suffcient storage space for all their bakeware. An extendable tin such as this anodised metal model with a non-stick surface, which can range from 20 cm/8 inches (around 1 litre/1 quart capacity) to a generous 35 cm/14 inches, is perfect for making family-size cut-and-come again cakes.

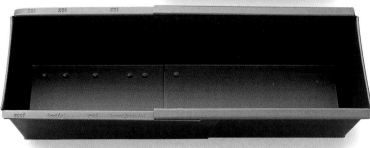

# Swedish dill bread
## ERIC TREUILLE · URSULA FERRIGNO

Successful food writers in their own right, Eric Treuille and Ursula Ferrigno have collaborated on a bestselling breadmaking book and they have both taught baking – Ursula in her native Italy and Eric at the popular Books for Cooks Cookery School in London. Their recipe for Swedish dill bread is, quite simply, superb. Enriched with cream cheese, butter and eggs, and subtly scented with dill, this bread has a moist crumb, light texture and a golden crust studded with toasted onion. It makes a wonderful accompaniment to smoked salmon. A lightly greased non-stick loaf tin guarantees a cleanly turned out loaf.

a

MAKES 1 LOAF

| TOOLS | INGREDIENTS | |
|---|---|---|
| small and large bowls | 2 tsp dried yeast | 150 g/2⁄3 cup cream cheese, at room temperature |
| sieve | 100 ml/scant 1⁄2 cup tepid water | 2 onions, roughly chopped |
| wooden spoon | 500 g/1 lb 2 oz strong white flour | 25 g/2 tbsp unsalted butter, at room temperature, plus extra for greasing tin |
| flour dredger | 1 tsp salt | 1 egg, beaten |
| brush for greasing | 2 tbsp chopped fresh dill | |
| 19 x 12 x 9 cm/81⁄2 x 41⁄2 x 3 inch non-stick loaf tin | | |
| wire rack | | |

b

**1** Sprinkle the yeast into the water in a small bowl. Leave for 5 minutes, then stir until dissolved. Sift the flour and salt together into a large bowl. Make a well in the centre and add the dill, cream cheese, onions, butter, egg and yeasted water. Use a wooden spoon to mix all the ingredients together with the flour to form a stiff, sticky dough.

**2** Turn out the dough onto a lightly floured work surface. Gather into a ball and then flatten. Shape the dough by folding one half over the other, bringing the top towards you.

**3** Use the heel of your working hand to push the dough away from you (a). At the same time, use the other hand to rotate the dough slightly towards you, guiding it slowly round in a circle. Repeat the folding, pushing and rotating for at least 10 minutes until the dough is silky smooth. Put the dough in a clean bowl and cover with a tea towel (dishcloth). Leave the dough to rise until it has doubled in size, about 11⁄2 hours.

c

**4** Grease a loaf tin with butter. Knock back the dough, then leave to rest for 10 minutes.

**5** With the lightly floured palm of your hand, flatten the dough to expel any gas bubbles (b). Keep it in a round shape by exerting even pressure. Fold one edge of the dough to the centre. Press gently to seal the fold.

**6** Fold the other half of the dough inwards so the two folds overlap along the middle of the loaf (c). Gently press along the length of the outer seam to seal the two folds together.

**7** Place the dough seam-side down on the work surface. Shape to an even thickness. Lift the dough, tuck under the ends and place it in the prepared tin, seam-side down (d). Cover with a tea towel. Leave to prove until the dough has risen 1 cm/1⁄2 inch above the top of the tin, about 11⁄2 hours.

**8** Preheat the oven to 180°C/350°F/gas 4. Bake the loaf for 45 minutes to 1 hour until deeply golden and hollow-sounding when tapped underneath. Turn out on a wire rack.

d

# brioche
## STEPHEN JACKSON

This recipe, contributed by Stephen Jackson, owner of West Yorkshire restaurant Weaver's Shed, is an adaptation of one he was taught at his alma mater, Leith's School of Food & Wine. 'It's a nice fast brioche,' says Stephen, 'and by no means the classic method, but it works brilliantly.'

MAKES 2 SMALL LOAVES

**TOOLS**
mixing bowls
food mixer
brioche mould/tin

**INGREDIENTS**
20 g/3/4 oz fresh yeast
60 g/1/4 cup unrefined golden
    caster (superfine) sugar
150 ml/2/3 cup full cream milk,
    at blood temperature
1 kg/21/4 lb plain (all-purpose)
    flour, sieved

2 tsp sea salt flakes
12 small–medium eggs
seeds of 1 vanilla pod (bean)
500 g/1 lb 2 oz butter, at room
    temperature (perfectly soft),
    finely diced
a little top-of-the-milk, for
    glazing

**1** Preheat the oven to 190°C/375°F/gas 5.

**2** Cream the yeast with the sugar. Add a little milk until it becomes smooth, then add the rest of the milk gradually. Tip the flour and salt into the bowl of your food mixer, and set the mixer to stir gently, using the dough hook. Pour in the yeasty, sugary milk and allow the mixture to come together.

**3** Add the eggs individually, allowing each one to be incorporated before adding the next. Then add the butter in tablespoon-sized amounts, kneading all the time until the dough comes together. Add the vanilla seeds. It will be a sticky but workable dough. Add a little more flour in it's too sticky to even contemplate touching.

**4** Turn out the dough into a warm, lightly-floured bowl, cover with oiled cling film (plastic wrap), and leave to rise for about an hour or until airy and light. With as little fuss as possible, divide the dough into your floured loaf tins and allow to rise again, for about 30–40 minutes.

**5** Lghtly brush with the creamy milk, then bake for 35–45 minutes or until the loaves are well-risen and golden. If you tap the brioche lightly on the bottom it should sound nicely hollow. if needs be, flip the loaves over and bake them upside down, just resting in the moulds, for a few minutes until finished. Unmould them and cool on wire racks. Try to avoid slicing off a thick slab and wolfing it down immediately, though, quite honestly, I wouldn't blame you.

There is no mystique to making the doughs for these all-time comforters – just chemistry, patience and a sense of touch. The most important piece of equipment is your hands, which carry out the rhythmic kneading essential for silky, compliant dough that can be rolled wafer-thin. Other tools just help things along.

# pizza and pasta tools

For success with home-made pizza dough, bake your pizza on a baking stone preheated in an oven set at the highest temperature possible. With luck, the result will match the deliciously crisp crust produced by the intense heat of a wood-fired brick oven.

Making your own pasta dough takes time but is a particularly relaxing and satisfying experience. The result will be far superior to the so-called 'fresh' pasta sold by supermarkets.

1

2

3

## ☐1 PERFORATED PIZZA PAN
The holes in this pan allow heat and air to reach the centre of the dough, resulting in a crisper crust than is possible with a solid baking sheet. The pan is particularly good for large pizzas.

## ☐2 PIZZA STONE
Preheated in a very hot oven, this thick, unglazed ceramic slab draws moisture from the dough, producing a crisp yet chewy crust. It is available in diameters of 30–40 cm/12–16 inches.

## ☐3 PIZZA PEEL/PADDLE
This flat tool has a chamfered edge that slides smoothly under a pizza as you lift it from the stone. Peels are also made of wood, which remains cooler in use.

## 4 WOODEN ROLLERS

These pleasing wooden rollers are deeply etched for hand-cutting dough into ribbons of various widths. The cutting edges are quite fragile and may chip if not handled with care.

## 6 PASTA MACHINE

This hand-cranked pasta machine speeds the process of rolling and cutting dough. The machine has graduated openings that are used successively to reduce the dough to the desired thickness. Attachable cutters slice it into ribbons of different widths.

6

## 5 PASTA CUTTING WHEELS

This superb hand-crafted tool has two detachable brass wheels – one plain and one zigzagged for cutting saw-edged ribbons or ravioli. Unlike mass-produced cutters, the wheels have well-defined edges that produce a very clean cut. Being thick and heavy, brass remains cooler in use than lighter metals. This also contributes to a clean cut.

## 7 RAVIOLI TRAY

Made of cast aluminium, this 36-square tray produces ravioli of a uniform size and shape. The wide, flat edges between the indentations increase the area of contact between the layers of dough and reduce the risk of leaks.

7

8

## 8 RAVIOLI CUTTER

If you like extra-large pillows of ravioli, this 6.5 cm/2½ inch square cutter, made of cast aluminium, is the tool to use.

# fresh pasta

Making fresh pasta is really no more of a challenge than making pastry, especially if you use a machine to help you thin and cut the dough. The secret is in the kneading and gradual thinning. You must close the rollers a notch at a time, resisting any temptation to skip a notch.

Pasta responds to warmth, so never work it on a marble or metal surface. Use a large wooden board or other smooth, relatively warm material. You need plenty of space for laying out the strips of pasta, and plenty of clean, dry tea towels on which to lay them. For the best results use Italian '00' flour, allowing 100 g/⅔ cup for each large egg. That said, it is almost impossible to predict exactly how much flour will be needed. You need enough to produce a dough that is neither too dry nor too sticky. Start off with a little less flour – you can always add more. If you add it all at once and the dough is too dry, you will have to start again.

SERVES 4–6

| TOOLS | INGREDIENTS |
|---|---|
| large wooden board | 300 g/2½ cups Italian '00' flour |
| dough scraper | 3 large eggs, at room |
| hand-cranked pasta machine | temperature |

**1** Pour the flour onto a wooden surface, shaping it into a mound with a central well. Break the eggs into the well and beat lightly with a fork. When evenly mixed, start drawing some of the flour over the eggs (a). Continue doing so until the eggs are no longer runny.

**2** Quickly draw the sides of the mound over the eggs, leaving a little flour on the side to use if the dough is too sticky. Work the eggs and flour together until smoothly integrated, adding the reserved flour if necessary (b). Wrap the dough in cling film (plastic wrap) and scrape the surface clean.

**3** Knead the dough by pushing forward against it with the heel of your hand, then fold it in half, give it a half turn and push forward again (c). Repeat, turning in the same direction, for 15 minutes or until the dough is silky smooth and elastic.

**4** Cut the dough into at least six pieces. Flatten one and wrap the rest separately in cling film. Fold the flat piece in three (d) and pass it lengthways through the pasta machine, set at the widest opening (e). Repeat three or four times, folding the dough in thirds each time. Put the strips on a tea towel (dishcloth) and repeat with the remaining pieces of dough.

**5** Close the rollers by one notch and run all the strips through again, this time without folding them. Close the opening by another notch and repeat the procedure. Continue until the rollers are at the narrowest setting.

**6** To make ribbons, cut the pasta into 30 cm/12 inch strips and feed through the cutter of your choice (f). As the ribbons emerge, separate them carefully and spread out on tea towels.

**7** To dry the pasta, coil a few ribbons into a nest and leave to dry for 24 hours, making sure the nests do not touch. Store in an airtight container.

d

e

f

a       b       c       d

# ricotta and mint tortelloni
## MARCELLA HAZAN

Marcella Hazan is the doyenne of Italian cookery and one of the world's most respected food writers. In her delectable home-made tortelloni, silky, golden egg pasta is stuffed with ricotta cheese, mint, onion and garlic. A bay leaf-scented tomato sauce provides the perfect complement.

MAKES ABOUT 36 TORTELLONI TO SERVE 6 AS AN APPETIZER OR 4 AS A MAIN COURSE

**TOOLS**
cheesecloth
wooden spoon
tall jug or bowl
mixing bowl
nutmeg grater
small frying pan
several large tea towels

hand-cranked pasta machine
  with 15 cm/6 inch rollers
fluted pastry wheel
utility knife
medium frying pan
pasta pot
perforated spoon or wire strainer
colander
Parmesan grater

**INGREDIENTS**
*FOR THE STUFFING*
225 g/8 oz wholemilk ricotta
1/8 tsp freshly grated nutmeg
4 tsp chopped fresh mint
1 egg yolk
salt and freshly ground black
  pepper
15 g/1 tbsp butter
2 tbsp finely chopped onion
1/2 tsp chopped garlic

*FOR THE WRAPPERS*
150–200 g/1 1/4–1 1/2 cups
  Italian '00' flour
2 large eggs at room
  temperature
1 tbsp milk

*FOR COOKING AND SAUCING THE PASTA*
25 g/2 tbsp butter for the
  sauce, 15 g/1 tbsp for
  tossing
1 1/2 tbsp extra-virgin olive oil
  for the sauce, 1 tbsp for the
  pasta
1/2 small onion, finely chopped
4 bay leaves
340 g/12 oz large, firm, ripe
  tomatoes, skinned,
  deseeded and chopped
salt and freshly ground black
  pepper
50 g/1/2 cup grated Parmesan

**NOTE** Pasta that is going to be stuffed should be soft and sticky, so the procedure given on page 286 must be adjusted as follows: take one piece of dough at a time through the entire thinning process and, before going on to the next piece, cut it and stuff it as described below.

**1** Wrap the ricotta tightly in a layer of cheesecloth and drain for 30 minutes, as in the recipe for 'yoghurt cheese' on page 131. Place the ricotta in a bowl, add the nutmeg, mint, egg yolk, salt and pepper, and mix well.

**2** Put the butter and onion in a small frying pan, turn the heat to medium, and cook the onion, stirring occasionally, until it turns a pale gold. Add the garlic and cook it, stirring frequently, until it is a shade of gold paler than the onion. Empty the contents of the pan into the ricotta mixture, stirring with a wooden spoon until uniformly mixed.

**3** Make the pasta dough following the instructions on page 286. Cut it into four pieces and take one piece through the entire rolling, folding and thinning process, taking it down to the thinnest notch setting. Keep the rest of the dough covered in cling film.

**4** Lay a 15 cm/6 inch wide, long strip of dough on a clean tea towel. Dot with a row of cherry-sized pellets of stuffing, setting them down 6 cm/2 1/2 inches apart and 3 cm//1 1/4 inches from one long edge of the rectangle (a).

**5** Distribute as many dots of stuffing as will fit along the strip, then bring the edge furthest from the stuffing over them and join it to the other edge (b). Force the air from between the bulges with the edge of your hand and press the edges together gently but firmly. Run a pastry wheel down the edge to trim and seal it, then run it crossways, midway between each bulge (c). Press the edges with your fingertip, then spread out on tea towels, making sure they do not touch. Repeat with the remaining pieces of dough. The tortelloni can be cooked immediately or after several hours. If you are going to cook them later, turn them over every 15 minutes.

**6** To make the sauce, put the 25 g of butter and 1 1/2 tablespoons of oil in a medium frying pan over a medium-high heat. Cook the onion, stirring, until it turns a medium gold. Add the bay leaves and cook for a few seconds, turning, then add the tomatoes, salt and pepper. Cook at a steady but gentle simmer, stirring periodically, for about 15–20 minutes, until the fat floats free of the tomatoes.

**7** Cook the tortelloni in a large saucepan of boiling, salted water, adding 1 tablespoon of olive oil. If you are cooking them some hours after making them, they will take a little longer than when very fresh. Taste one after about 3 minutes and, if necessary, continue cooking until they are tender, but retain some firmness to the bite. Retrieve them from the saucepan with a perforated spoon or wire strainer, gently transferring them to a colander (d). As soon as the tortelloni are done, place in a warm serving platter, and gently toss with 15 g of butter, the tomato sauce and grated Parmesan. Serve at once.

# pizza with wild mushrooms and fontina
## PAUL GAYLER

This potato flatbread, contributed by Paul Gayler, is actually a pizza-style dough made from baked or mashed potatoes with butter. The resulting dough is light and makes a great base for a variety of toppings. Here sautéed wild mushrooms and Fontina cheese are the preferred choice.

MAKES 2 X 25CM (10 IN) PIZZA

**TOOLS**
sieve
2 large mixing bowls
large metal spoon
rolling pin
cling film (plastic wrap)
25 cm/10 inch pizza dish
    or baking sheet
cook's knife
frying pan
vegetable peeler, for the
    Fontina shavings

**INGREDIENTS**
*FOR THE PIZZA*
2 medium baking potatoes
25 g/2 tbsp butter, softened
225 g/scant 1¾ cups plain
    (all-purpose) flour
7 g/¼ oz easy blend (active
    dry) yeast
1 tsp sugar
150 ml/⅔ cup warm milk

*FOR THE TOPPING*
50 g/½ stick unsalted butter
1 shallot, finely chopped
1 garlic clove, crushed
350 g/12 oz mixed wild
    mushrooms
salt and freshly ground black
    pepper

400 g/14 oz new potatoes,
    preferably a purple variety,
    cooked, peeled and thinly
    sliced
100 g/1 cup Fontina cheese,
    thinly shaved
2 tbsp olive oil

**1** Preheat the oven to 200°C/400°F/gas 6. Wrap the potatoes in foil and bake for 1 hour or until soft. Remove them from the foil, leave until cool enough to handle, then remove their skins. Push the skinned potato through a sieve, then weigh it – you will need 200 g/7 oz in total.

**2** Place the potato in a large bowl, add the butter, flour, yeast and sugar, and mix thoroughly. Mix in the warm milk and combine to form a dough. Turn out onto a lightly floured work surface and knead for 5–8 minutes until smooth and elastic.

**3** Place in a lightly oiled bowl, cover with cling film (plastic wrap) and leave in a warm place for 1 hour or until doubled in size.

**4** Turn out the dough and knock back, to expel the air. Roll out the dough to fit a 25 cm/10 inch round pizza dish or baking sheet.

**5** For the topping, heat the butter in a frying pan, add the shallot and garlic, and cook for 2 minutes. Add the mushrooms and sauté for 2–3 minutes until cooked and golden. Season to taste. Reheat the oven to 200°C/400°F/gas 6.

**6** Distribute the potatoes and mushrooms evenly over the pizza base and sprinkle over the shaved Fontina. Cook for 20–25 minutes until golden and puffed up. Serve straight from the oven, drizzled with olive oil and cut into wedges.

**OTHER TOPPING IDEAS**
spiced tomatoes with red
    onion and rocket
grilled vegetables with grated
    mozzarella
preserved artichokes,
    mushrooms and crumbled
    goat's cheese

# moulding
# and
# shaping

Moulded foods such as mousses, custards and jellies seem to hark back to a more leisurely era when there was time for the setting and chilling these dishes need. Whether sweet or savoury, such foods are by their very nature soft and delicate, and perhaps have been somewhat ousted from modern cooking with its insistence on speed and bold assertive flavours.

# moulds

Despite changing trends, moulds do have a place in today's kitchens, even if for only a simple concoction such as a child's birthday jelly. And let's not forget the most basic of modern moulds – the ice-cube tray. Moulds may either be decorative or utilitarian, tall or shallow, patterned or plain. They are often made of metals such as aluminium or copper, because these react very quickly to heat or cold; porcelain or glass is used where heat or cold needs to be retained. Confectionery moulds are made of tinned steel, plastic or rubber. Moulds are often made in the shape of a fish or fruit to indicate the nature of the dish.

## 1 RING MOULDS
These seamless aluminium moulds are designed for baking savarins and babas – rich, yeasted cakes that are drenched in syrup or rum after cooking. The cake remains upside down after turning out and the depression in the centre is piled high with whipped cream and/or fruit. A wide, shallow trough and a thick central tube allow maximum exposure to heat, so the mixture cooks quickly as it rises. Ring moulds can also be used for mousses, custards or rice.

## 2 GIANT ICE-CUBE TRAY
This brilliant ice-cube tray is flexible so you can remove cubes individually, and is supplied with a metal tray so it stays flat in the freezer.

## 3 FISH MOULD
Ornate and versatile, this mould is equally suitable for a grown-up fish mousse or a bright orange children's jelly.

Mixtures for tall or ornate moulds need to be more firmly set than for shallow ones, as they are more likely to collapse or leave part of their contents trapped in an intricate crevice. The smoother and shallower the mould, the easier it is to turn out.

### 4  BOMBE MOULD

This smooth, spherical mould with a rounded top has a tightly-fitting lid to prevent ice crystals forming during storage.

### 5  DARIOLE MOULDS

These small, simple aluminium moulds are good conductors of heat or cold. Use them for making tiny rum babas (but fill only halfway and allow the dough to rise before baking), small sponge puddings, timbales, jellies and crème caramels.

### 6  CHARLOTTE MOULD

To make a charlotte, this bucket-shaped aluminium mould is lined with buttered bread or sponge fingers and then filled with a fruit purée or mousse. The outwardly sloping sides make it easier to line and also allow it to be lifted free of its contents once inverted. Charlottes may be served uncooked and chilled, or baked in the oven and served hot – hence the mould's two heart-shaped handles. Either way, aluminium is an excellent conductor, speeding the penetration of heat or cold as appropriate.

### 7  HEART MOULD

A tool for romantic cooks, this mould is ideal for sweet or savoury dishes to celebrate Valentine's Day or anniversaries.

### 8  JELLY/BLANCMANGE MOULDS

These aluminium moulds are embossed with simple but decorative patterns well suited to a jelly or blancmange. Make sure the top of the unfilled mould is level so that when inverted it does not wobble while the contents are setting.

# jelly

More properly described as a gelatine dessert, jelly gets its characteristic wobble from the flavourless, collagen-based setting agent gelatine. Available in powdered or leaf form, gelatine should be soaked in cold liquid before dissolving in hot liquid. The preliminary soaking allows the gelatine particles to swell evenly which, in turn, allows them to gel in the maximum amount of liquid. If added to hot liquid first, the outer edges of the particles expand too quickly, forming a sticky coating which prevents the inside from softening. The result is a grainy jelly that doesn't set properly.

For successful jellies, you'll need exactly the right amount of gelatine. The setting strength depends on the brand, so it's best to use the amount recommended on the packet, although you might need a bit more for towering jellies or complex moulds.

If you are making a jelly on a hot day, it's a good idea to chill the mould or serving glasses before filling them. Another tip is to fill a large, deep roasting pan with ice cubes to surround the moulds. This method is particularly helpful when making layered jellies that need to set in stages.

Uncooked pineapple, papaya, kiwi fruit and figs all contain enzymes that prevent gelatine setting properly. If you want to use these fruits to flavour your jellies, you'll need to lightly cook them first to stop the enzymes wreaking havoc.

# jelly moulding

**TOOLS** jelly mould, pastry brush, platter

If filling a mould with a fruit and water jelly (i.e. no added cream or milk), rinse it out with cold water and pour in the prepared mix (a). Place on a plate in the refrigerator so it remains flat and cannot be tipped over. Allow to set at least overnight until firm.

To set a creamy or milky blancmange, brush the mould lightly with a little sunflower oil using a pastry brush and fill with the prepared mix. Place on a flat plate in the refrigerator and set overnight.

To unmould jellies, have ready a bowl of very hot water. Wet a platter with cold water. Using your fingertips, pull on the edge of the jelly to ease it away from the mould at the top (b), then dip the mould into the hot water to the count of three. Lift it up, place the platter on top, invert still holding the platter to the mould, and shake firmly two or three times. Lift up the filled mould (c), shaking it lightly; you should feel the set jelly or mould releasing from the sides. If not, repeat the steps again.

a

b

# passionfruit curd
## CHRISTINE MANFIELD

Christine Manfield is one of Australia's most celebrated chefs, a perfectionist inspired by complex flavours and a writer whose successful books, *Paramount Cooking*, *Christine Manfield Desserts*, *Christine Manfield Originals*, *Spice and Stir*, have spiced up the lives of keen cooks from Melbourne to Manchester and Manhattan.

SERVES 6

**TOOLS**
200 ml/7 fl oz dome (dessert) moulds, or 150 ml/2/3 cup dariole moulds
saucepan
fine sieve

**INGREDIENTS**
450 ml/16 fl oz pouring cream
180 g/scant 1 cup caster (superfine) sugar
60 ml/1/4 cup passionfruit juice
2 tsp Mandarine Napoleon liqueur
5 g/1/4 oz gelatine leaves, softened in cold water
350 ml/scant 1 1/2 cups thick natural (plain) yoghurt
pulp from 4 passionfruit, to serve

**1** Gently bring the cream and sugar to simmering point in a saucepan. Remove from the heat and stir in the passionfruit juice and liqueur.

**2** Add the softened gelatine and stir until dissolved, about 2 minutes.

**3** Stir through the yoghurt until the mixture is smooth. Strain through a fine sieve, then pour the mixture into the dariole moulds.

**4** Refrigerate until set, about 5 hours.

**5** Dip each mould in hot water for 20 seconds to loosen the contents, then turn out onto a plate. Spoon the passionfruit pulp over the top the curds and serve with tropical fruit, such as mango, papaya, pineapple or lychees.

These tools compress mixtures into a flattish shape, sometimes embossing or sealing it in the process; otherwise they force the mixture through a nozzle or a specially shaped cutter. None of the tools are essential, unless you regularly ice cakes, but they are fun to use and do not cost the earth.

# presses and extruders

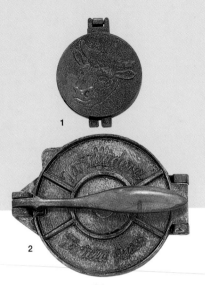

**1 METAL BURGER PRESS**
This hinged, cast-aluminium, cow-embossed press produces a compact, perfectly round burger. The press eliminates the air pockets that causes burgers to crack when turned.

**2 TORTILLA PRESS**
As you pull down the handle of this ingenious press, two cast-aluminium hinged discs uniformly flatten a small ball of masa harina dough into a paper-thin tortilla.

**3 TURNOVER PRESS**
Making meat, fruit or vegetable turnovers is easy with this hinged, semi-circular, plastic press, which simultaneously moulds, crimps and seals the pastry.

**4 SHORTBREAD MOULD**
Beautifully and precisely carved, this hand-made sycamore mould embosses a traditional thistle design on top of shortbread. Sycamore is a dense wood that is particularly suitable for carving intricate designs and producing a crisp imprint.

**5 FALAFEL MAKER**
Home-made falafel made with fresh (not canned) ground chick peas, tahini, garlic, herbs and spices are a revelation and simplicity itself. Presses for making neat falafels are the sort of tools one can pick up on holiday in the Middle East. Press spoonfuls of ground falafel mix into the cup of the mould, level with the back of a knife and press out straight into a frying pan of oil.

**6 BURGER PRESS**
Getting an even, rounded shape for your burgers is made much easier if you simply push the meat into a round mould, press lightly to compact, then demould and stack interleaved with wax paper. Freshly ground steak mince makes the best burgers but also consider using minced fish or seafood flavoured with garlic, grated onion, herbs, spices and a slug or two of Worcestershire sauce.

## 7 RÖSTI/FOOD PRESENTATION RINGS

If you wish to 'plate' your food like the professionals, then metal food rings help to give depth and form to grated potato rösti to salads, risottos or flaked fish. Use deep rings for leafy salads and shallow ones for creamed potatoes, grated potato rösti, flaked crab or fish. You can even use them (placed on non-stick flat trays) for set mousses and pâtés. Very versatile and useful for giving food eye appeal.

## 8 FOOD RING MATE

If you use metal rings for that neat compacted look, use an open metal press that fits just inside the metal rings. Press down to compress the ingredients in the ring, ensuring a neat finish. Perfect for the keen entertainer or caterer.

## 10 BISCUIT/COOKIE PRESS

There is no easier way to make biscuits than with this sturdy aluminium press. A plunger forces dough through a decorative cutter, producing flawless biscuits of various shapes. The gun is supplied with nozzles (tips) for piping fillings and decorations.

## 11 ICING SYRINGE

Icing (frosting) is forced through the cylinder and nozzle (tip) by a plunger attached to a central shaft that passes through the lid. To operate the plunger, put your thumb through the central loop, hook your forefinger and middle finger through the loops on the lid, and press down.

## 9 FORCING/PASTRY BAGS

Forcing bags are used in conjunction with a nozzle (tip) for piping semi-fluid mixtures that hold their shape. The bags are soft and pliable, and respond to the slightest pressure, so may require patience at first. These professional-quality bags are made of waterproof nylon and have a loop for hanging them up to dry. Nylon bags are easy to keep clean and are available in several lengths.

## MAKING A PAPER FORCING BAG

A quickly made paper forcing bag comes in handy for small jobs such as piping decorative curlicues or writing 'Happy Birthday' across a cake.
*To make:*
1. Fold a 25–30 cm/10–12 inch square of greaseproof paper or baking parchment in half diagonally to form a triangle.
2. With the long edge facing you, fold up the right-hand point to meet the top point at the top, without making a crease. Hold the two points together with your finger and thumb.
3. Fold the left-hand point across and over the right-hand section, pivoting it to meet behind the right-hand and top points.
4. Hold the three points together and open out to make a cone.
5. Fold over the points to secure the cone, or use a piece of adhesive tape.
6. Snip off the tip to make a small opening for piping.

## 12 FORCING/ICING NOZZLES

These conical nozzles (tips) shape the mixtures that are forced through them. Made of metal, nylon or plastic, they come in a range of sizes and shapes. Those with well-defined, sharp edges produce the most clean-cut designs. Use them for writing or for piping decorative shapes such as stars, rosettes, ribbons or shells.

# falafel
## SAM CLARK · SAM CLARK

Although considered Egyptian in origin, falafel are common throughout the Middle East. In this recipe from the acclaimed husband and wife duo from Moro, dried fava beans have been used in place of chickpeas as they have a nuttier flavour, though chickpeas are just as good.

SERVES 4

**TOOLS**
falafel press

**INGREDIENTS**
250 g/9 oz dried fava beans, soaked overnight
3 garlic cloves, crushed to a paste with salt
1 large bunch fresh coriander (cilantro), roughly chopped
1 medium bunch fresh flat-leaf parsley, roughly chopped
1½ tsp cumin seeds, roughly ground
1 tsp coriander (cilantro) seeds, roughly ground
½ onion, grated
50 g/⅓ cup chickpea flour or plain (all-purpose) flour
1 egg
¼ tsp bicarbonate of soda (baking soda)
sea salt and freshly ground black pepper
4 tbsp sesame seeds (optional)
750 ml/3 cups sunflower oil for deep-frying

**1** Drain the beans well and place half of them in a large saucepan. Fill with fresh cold water and bring to the boil. Reduce to a gentle simmer and cook for 5–10 minutes or until tender, skimming off any scum as rises to the surface.

**2** Meanwhile, place the raw beans in a food processor and pulse until more or less smooth. Transfer to a mixing bowl and repeat the process for the cooked drained beans. Add the garlic, fresh coriander, parsley, cumin and coriander seeds, onion, flour, egg and bicarbonate of soda. Mix well and season with salt and pepper to taste.

**3** Shape into balls no larger than a walnut, then gently flatten each one into a disc about 2 cm/¾ inch thick and 5 cm/2 inches in diameter, making sure the edges do not crack. Place the sesame seeds on a plate and dip the falafel until coated all over.

**4** Heat the oil in a large saucepan and, when the oil is hot but not smoking, add the falafel in batches. Fry until golden brown on both sides, remove and drain on paper towel. Serve with flatbread, tahini sauce, a wedge of lemon and some pickled chillies.

measuring
and
weighing

It was not until relatively recently that recipes began to specify exact amounts of ingredients. In the past, it was a matter of taking 'some' of one ingredient, throwing in a handful of this and a pinch of that, and heating 'until cooked'. Nowadays, though, we go to the other extreme and probably over-specify. To complicate matters, some cookbooks specify two, sometimes three, measuring systems: metric, imperial and American.

# weight and volume

American recipes specify the majority of ingredients by mass or volume, even though measuring by weight is more accurate and in some cases easier. For example, how do you measure a cup of tomatoes? Or a cup of something that does not easily fit into the shape of a measuring cup? Recipes from other countries specify solid or dry ingredients by weight, and liquid ingredients by volume. Small amount of dry ingredients are also measured by volume, in teaspoons or tablespoons.

Measuring equipment is not expensive so it is worth investing in a set of scales and measuring jugs marked in imperial and metric measurements, particularly if you use recipes from different countries. You can then use either of the two systems; they are not necessarily interchangeable.

It is also worth buying several sets of measuring spoons, if only to save having to wash a single spoon each time you measure sticky or greasy ingredients.

When buying scales, the choice is between balance, electronic and spring scales – each has its advantages and disadvantages. Balance scales look great, but are fiddly to use. The weights are sold separately, and you will need to buy two sets if you use both metric and imperial measurements. Electronic scales are the most accurate type, but you will need to keep replacing the batteries. Spring scales are easy to use, but need to be well built – once the spring breaks they are useless.

### 1 BALANCE SCALES

Made to a traditional design, these attractive scales work by force of gravity: when the ingredients in the pan weigh the same as the metal weights on the platform, the beam is horizontal. Balance scales are accurate and built to last, but they are not quite as easy to use as either spring or electronic scales. They are also somewhat unwieldy, so are best kept on the work surface for convenience.

1

When choosing measuring jugs, remember that a more accurate measurement can be obtained from a tall, narrow jug than from a wide one. A narrow shape causes the contents to rise higher up the jug, so there is a greater distance between the calibrations printed on the side. The wider the space between each increment, the easier it is to see when the contents reach a particular level. Clear jugs are more useful than opaque ones, as they allow you to see the contents at eye level.

## 2 SPRING SCALES

Good looking and practical, these stainless steel scales weigh up to 4 kg/9 lb of ingredients – about 500 g/1 lb 2 oz more than most kitchen scales. The dial is clearly printed with metric and imperial measurements, and large enough to read 20 g or 1 oz calibrations with ease.

## 3 NUTRITIONAL VALUE ELECTRONIC SCALES

These scales have a database of values for over 1400 foods and can evaluate and record your daily food and nutritional intake for up to seven days. You place a portion of food on the scale unit, press the appropriate food or ingredient button and up come the calories, protein, carbohydrate, fat, fibre, cholesterol values. It's then up to you to decide whether to eat it.

## 4 JUG SCALES

Manually operated, these scales are reset by revolving the base once the jug is in place on top. With a capacity of 1 litre any ingredient can be spooned or poured into the jug and the measure noted. Then the base can be revolved again to zero for the next ingredient. It is also a good way of measuring the weight of liquids as chefs like to do. The jug can be inverted onto the base for storage.

## 5 BLOCK DIGITAL SCALES

Battery operated digital scales are perhaps the most accurate way of weighing food, from amounts as small as 1 g/less than 1/16 oz up to a hefty 5 kg/11 lb. You place an empty bowl on the scale, reset the scale to zero, then add the food to be weighed. They are marvellous for weighing ingredients all in the same bowl. If you then want to weigh another ingredient on top, you press zero again and add the next ingredient. The slim design means it can be tucked away in a drawer.

## 6 INFRARED SCALES

This state-of-the-art set of scales uses infrared technology and has won several awards. Consisting of two discs, the inner one contains digital marking with a zero button that resets as required. The outer rim is the detachable base unit that can be placed anywhere within a 1.25 m/4 ft range. You place a bowl on a flat worktop, set the zero button then weigh as normal.

### 10 DRY MEASURING BEAKER

The inside of this classic aluminium beaker is printed with different scales showing the equivalent volume of a particular weight of various dry ingredients. It also shows American cups and pints, English cups, pints and gills, as well as millilitres. The outside of the beaker is printed with metric/imperial conversions. Cheap, cheerful and extremely useful.

### 7 POLYPROPYLENE MEASURING JUGS

Invaluable in the kitchen, these tall polypropylene jugs can be used for measuring and pouring anything from a beaten egg to a large volume of stock. Very durable, they will withstand boiling liquids, and will not break if dropped. They are available in 500 ml/2 cups, 1 litre/1 quart and 2.2 litre/2 1/3 quart sizes.

### 8 WIDE POLYPROPYLENE MEASURING JUG

This wide, polypropylene jug can double up as a mixing bowl. It is especially useful for ingredients that need to be whisked, then poured in measured amounts – pancake batter, for example.

### 9 PYREX MEASURING JUG

A small Pyrex jug is useful for transferring hot soup or stock from one container to another. It is heat-proof, easy to keep clean and will not absorb grease or smells.

### 11 COCKTAIL SHAKER

Shaken, not stirred, anyone? The art of cocktail making is fast becoming fashionable again, especially for those who like to create their own mixes. You measure the spirits, juices and cordial into the sturdy glass measure, pour into the stainless steel beaker, add ice, clamp the two together in a tight seal, and shake.

### 12 ANGLED MEASURING JUG

It can be difficult to gauge accurately the levels of liquid in a measuring jug, especially smaller amounts. This angled jug brings the level up so it is easier to read. Heatproof, it is available in two sizes: 500 ml/2 cups and a smaller size with increments of 5 ml/1 teaspoon.

### 13 EUROPEAN MEASURING CUPS

These charming liquid measuring cups are made of aluminium and have finger-friendly handles. They hold 50 ml, 100 ml and 250 ml.

### 14 BRITISH MEASURING SPOONS

Sensibly designed, these plastic spoons are narrow enough to reach inside spice jars. This comprehensive set includes the elusive 1/8 teaspoon and 1/2 tablespoon. It is worth buying at least three sets.

### 16 FLAT-BOTTOMED MEASURING SPOONS

Balancing round-based spoons on a work surface whilst trying to shake in flour, sugar or spices can be messy. Flat bottoms keep the spoons level. This set consists of five spoons from tablespoon through to teaspoons and fractions of spoons.

### 15 AMERICAN MEASURING CUPS

These stylish stainless steel cups are used for measuring liquids. The top measurement is printed just below the rim of the cup so the liquid does not overflow. (Dry measuring cups are filled to overflowing and then levelled off with a knife.) They hold 1/4, 1/3, 1/2 and 1 cup.

### 17 MEASURING LADLE

Measuring small amounts of liquids can be awkward when using a large measuring jug. This flat-bottomed ladle makes this job much easier, but it only comes in US standard measures.

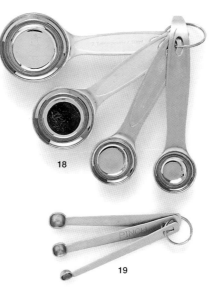

### 18 ODD-SIZE MEASURING SPOONS

As the name suggests, these spoons cope with sizes in between the usual ones: 1 1/2 teaspoons, 2 teaspoons, 1 1/2 tablespoons, 2 tablespoons.

### 19 TINY AMOUNT SPOONS

Adding a dash, a pinch (large or small), even a smidgen can be done with confidence with these measuring spoons. Not standard terms – one cook's dash is another's dollop – but a good approximation.

# saibhaji, dilled vegetables
## MONISHA BHARADWAJ

The success of Indian cooking, according to award-winning cookery writer
Monisher Bharadwaj, depends on the ability to layer flavours. As she
demonstrates in this subtly flavoured dish, it is very important to measure
spices correctly – too much can kill the taste of the main ingredient,
whereas too little results in a flat, lifeless dish.

SERVES 4

**TOOLS**
frying pan
measuring spoons
whisk

**INGREDIENTS**
2 tbsp sunflower oil
1/2 tsp cumin seeds
2 tsp ginger and garlic paste
(see below)
4 tsp split gram lentils (channa
dal), washed and drained
600 g/11/4 lb spinach, washed
and chopped
handful of dill leaves, chopped

2 tomatoes, chopped
1 small potato, peeled and
chopped
2 small aubergines (eggplants),
or 1/2 a large one, chopped
2 carrots, peeled and chopped
1/2 tsp chilli powder
1/2 tsp turmeric powder
salt

**1** Heat the oil in a frying pan. Add the cumin seeds. After a minute or so, as they begin to
darken, add the ginger and garlic paste.

**2** Stir in the lentils, spinach, dill and vegetables. Mix in the chilli and turmeric powders and salt.
Pour in 150 ml/2/3 cup water and cook for about 35 minutes, until the lentils are cooked.
The vegetables will be mushy by now.

**3** Remove from the heat and whisk gently to blend into a smooth but thick consistency.
Serve very hot.

**GINGER AND GARLIC PASTE** Scrape the skin off a 1 cm/1/2 inch piece of fresh ginger root and peel
four garlic cloves. Grate them finely and mix together. The paste should have a balanced aroma and
should not be dominated either by the ginger or the garlic.

Degrees and minutes matter. A few seconds can turn toasted almonds into blackened fragments; a few degrees can dry out a moist braise. Whatever the dish, it is always worth checking the oven temperature with a thermometer before starting to cook. Thermostats are notoriously inaccurate so you may find the actual temperature differs from the one you have set it to. Liquid-in-glass thermometers (with a graduated glass tube) are more accurate than spring-loaded ones (with a pointer).

# temperature and time

Thermometers are also essential for food safety. Some foods, such as pork, chicken and microwaved meals, must reach a specific internal temperature to destroy harmful bacteria. A meat thermometer and a microwave thermometer are invaluable for checking this. Fridges and freezers need to be kept below specific temperatures to slow the growth of harmful organisms. As neither appliance will necessarily maintain the correct temperature, a fridge/freezer thermometer is a worthwhile purchase.

A timer with a loud ring is invaluable for reminding forgetful cooks that food needs checking or removing from the oven or hob. A timer is also invaluable if you are cooking several dishes at once, or if you have the type of oven that does not transmit smells to warn you that food is burning.

## 1  SPIRIT OVEN THERMOMETER
This is the most accurate and reliable type of oven thermometer. It shows heating zones as well as temperature (wording not shown), has a clear spirit tube and hangs or stands in the oven.

## 2  CANDY/FAT THERMOMETER
This well-made thermometer is designed for confectionery and for deep-fat frying. The probe is immersed in boiling liquid and held in place by a spring clip attached to the side of the pan. The thermometer has a movable red clip attached to the rim to make it easier to see if the pointer has reached the correct position.

## 3  MEAT THERMOMETER
Though your senses will usually tell you when meat is cooked, a thermometer is useful for moments of doubt. Insert the probe so the tip is close to the centre of the meat. The meat is ready when the pointer moves to the appropriate wording (not shown). Like the candy/fat thermometer, it has a movable clip.

## 4  SPRING-LOADED OVEN THERMOMETER
As the oven heats up, a metal spring expands and moves the pointer. This one is sturdily made and is designed to hang or stand in the oven. It has a wide base to prevent it slipping between the racks.

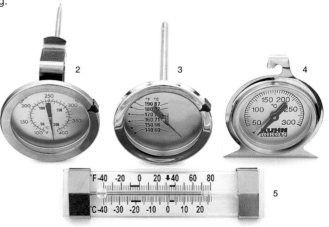

## 5  FRIDGE/FREEZER THERMOMETER
This well-designed thermometer usefully indicates the optimum range of temperatures at which fridges and freezers safely operate.

### 6 DIGITAL PROBE THERMOMETER

A digital readout and a fold-away probe are two useful features of this thermometer. It also operates through an impressive range of temperatures – from minus 49.9°C to 199.9°C/minus 57.8°F to 392°F.

### 7 WATER/CHOCOLATE THERMOMETER

The scale on this goes up to 60°C/140°F, which is the optimum temperature for tempering chocolate – the process of heating and cooling that stabilises emulsified fats. The thermometer is also useful for checking the temperature of water intended to simmer rather than boil – in a bain marie, for instance. It is protected by a removable nylon cage.

### 8 SUGAR/JAM THERMOMETER

Made to a traditional design, this thermometer is indispensable when making jams and confectionery. It indicates the point at which sterilisation takes place, and the stages in jam boiling and syrup making (wording not shown).

### 9 MICROWAVE THERMOMETER

When defrosting food or cooking in a microwave oven, it is vital that the food reaches a safe temperature through to the centre. This plastic thermometer is specially designed so that it can be inserted deep into the food. The metal pin supplied with it is used to penetrate frozen food before the thermometer is inserted.

### 10 CLOCKWORK TIMER

With its resounding ring, this compact 60-minute timer is easily heard. It is also easy to use. It hangs by magnetism or by a convenient hook, and if you are venturing far from the kitchen, you can keep it on a string round your neck.

### 11 HOURGLASS TIMER

Designed by Robert Welch, this is a classic, gravity-based timer for those who like their eggs cooked for exactly three minutes. An enamelled cast iron frame protects the glass.

6

7

8

9

10

11

### 13 STAINLESS STEEL TIMER

This 60-minute mechanical timer makes a sleek accessory for a gleaming modern kitchen. It has an extended alarm to summon you back to the stove should you stray too far, and a black rubber turning knob? easy to grip if your hands are greasy.

12

13

### 12 ELECTRONIC TIMER

This battery-operated 'egg timer' is designed for those who like to have electronic gizmos in the kitchen. A bit fiddly to work, compared with the traditional sand funnel timer which simply needs to be turned, but it does come in a nice bright green.

# jam-making

Successful jam-making needs careful measurement of weight and volume, as well as time and temperature.

- Sllightly under-ripe fruit contains more pectin and so will set better.
- Jam made from fruit which has been picked while wet is likely to go mouldy in a short time.
- Make jam in small quantities – no more than 1.3 kg/3 lb raspberries at a time or 1.8 kg/4 lb strawberries. Small quantities boil in a few minutes, so both the colour and jam itself are perfect.
- Ideally you should use a preserving pan, as the depth of the contents and the rate at which they boil determine the length of time the jam cooks. Use a pan with sides at least 23 cm/9 inches deep.

- Use the correct proportion of sugar – too little and the jam may ferment, too much may cause crystallisation.
- Fruit should be simmered until the sugar is added, and then boiled as fast as possible until setting point is reached.
- Citrus fruit peel, blackcurrants and gooseberries must be thoroughly softened before sugar is added, otherwise they will toughen and no amount of boiling will soften them.
- Sugar must be completely dissolved before the jam comes to the boil, otherwise the jam will crystallise on top. For this reason, it is better to add heated sugar (warm in a baking tray in the oven), which dissolves more quickly, and to stir with a wooden spoon until the 'gritty feeling' disappears.

- If necessary, skim near to the end of cooking or, if there is only a little scum, dissolve it with a lump of butter stirred in after the jam has reached setting point.
- Test for setting frequently so that the jam is not allowed to overcook (see page 316).
- Make sure your jam jars are spotlessly clean inside and out. Sterilise in the oven before filling.
- Fill jam jars to the top to allow for shrinkage on cooling (use a jam funnel, to avoid drips).
- Press a round of waxed paper onto the surface of the jam immediately after filling, placing the waxed side next to the jam.
- Wet the cellophane paper on one side, then stretch over the pot and secure with an elastic band. Label and store in a dry, airy cupboard.

## 1 JAM JARS
Glass jam jars are heatproof, but it is still best to warm them in a low oven first. Screw-on lids give a good seal but must be screwed onto the jars whilst the jam is still very hot for an airtight seal.

## 2 WIDE NECK FUNNEL
Ladling boiling hot jam from the pan is made safer with the use of a metal funnel that fits on top of the glass jars. Don't consider using a plastic funnel, it will melt.

## 3 STRAINER
To make clear jelly, cooked fruit pulp needs to be strained. This cloth, stitched to a round hoop with strong cloth handles, can be hung over a heatproof bowl and left while the clear liquid slowly drips through. Don't be tempted to press on the pulp or the liquid will become cloudy. Let it take its time or leave it overnight.

## 4 COVERS
The old-fashioned method of sealing jam jars is to cover them with a clear cellophane round, seal with an elastic band, then over-wrap with a pretty cloth top tied with string. These packs of pot covers also contain a selection of thin waxed paper discs to be placed waxed side down on the hot jam before the jar is covered with cellophane. If you are using screw-onlids instead, there is no need to use wax discs.

**NOTE ON PECTIN** Pectin is the substance in fruit which sets jam. It is contained in the cell walls of fruit in varying degrees. It is higher when the fruit is under-ripe. Acid, often in the form of lemon juice, helps in the extraction of pectin. Some fruits are higher in pectin than others, for example plums, damsons, gooseberries, blackcurrants and apples, while others contain little or none, for example marrow. In these cases, it is necessary to add acid in the form of lemon juice or commercial pectin.

'Raspberry jam is the easiest and quickest of all jams to make, and one of the most delicious.'

**DARINA ALLEN**

# raspberry and cassis preserve
## DARINA ALLEN

Contributed by Darina Allen, Ireland's most famous cook, and the founder of the celebrated Ballymaloe Cookery School at Shanagarry, County Cork, this quick and easy recipe for raspberry jam can be used for loganberries, boysenberries or tayberries with equal success.

MAKES 1.3 KG/3 LB

| TOOLS | INGREDIENTS |
|---|---|
| jam jars | 900 g/2 lb sugar |
| wide stainless steel pan or | 900 g/2 lb fresh raspberries |
|    copper preserving pan | 4 tbsp cassis |
| jam thermometer | |
| wide neck funnel | |
| long handled wooden | |
|    spoon | |
| ladle | |
| waxed discs | |

a

**1** Wash, dry and sterilise the jars in a moderate oven preheated to 180°C/350°F/gas 4 for 15 minutes. Heat the sugar on a baking tray for 5–10 minutes.

**2** Put the raspberries into a wide stainless steel saucepan and cook for 3–4 minutes until the juice begins to run, then add the hot sugar and stir over a gentle heat until fully dissolved. Increase the heat and boil steadily for about 5 minutes, stirring frequently. If using a jam thermometer the temperature should be around 105°C/220°F

**3** Test for a set by putting a teaspoonful of jam on a cold plate, then leave it for a few minutes in a cool place. It should wrinkle when pressed with a finger.

**4** If ready, remove the pan from the heat immediately. Skim then stir in the cassis. Ladle the hot jam carefully into clean, warmed jam jars through a wide necked funnel, then seal, and leave to cool. Store the jam in a cool place, or put on a shelf in your kitchen.

b

c

# sugar syrups and caramel

**TOOLS** heavy-based saucepan, sugar thermometer, large heatproof bowl

Syrups are dissolved sugar and water, to which flavourings such as spices, lemon zest, etc can be added. They have many uses in dessert making, from sorbets to fruit salads. The strength depends on the proportion of sugar to water. A high-strength syrup consists of equal parts sugar and water; for a medium syrup, use two partss water to one part sugar; a lighter strength syrup would be three parts water to one part sugar.

To make a syrup, sugar and water are heated slowly, with occasional stirring (a), until the sugar dissolves, then the heat is raised and the syrup is boiled for a few minutes to concentrate the density of the syrup.

A caramel is made by dissolving the sugar only in a heavy-based pan and letting it boil until the sugar caramelises, altering the flavour, colour and, ultimately, the texture. It is important that all the sugar crystals dissolve before the temperature is raised to boiling point, otherwise the syrup will crystallise.

To make a caramel, heat a shallow empty pan and, when you feel a strong heat rising, shake in caster (superfine) sugar evenly to cover the base (b). The sugar will start to dissolve around the edges (c). Swirl the pan gently but do not stir it and watch the heat, turning it down if the sides become too dark and burn. Inexperienced cooks may find it helpful to add 2–3 tablespoons hot water to the sugar first before it dissolves to start the melting, but do not stir it or it will crystallise.

Once the sugar has dissolved it can be heated to various temperatures for sugar craft and sweet making: 118°C/244°F is soft ball (when a spoon of hot syrup dropped into ice-cold water forms a soft lump); 121°C/250°F is hard ball; 138°C/280°F is small crack and 175°C/347°F caramel.

Have ready a large bowl of iced water to plunge the pan base into as soon as the molten sugar reaches the required stage. This stops further heating. At all times be very careful when boiling sugar.

a

b

c

storing
food

All food should be covered, regardless of where you store it. Leaving food exposed not only allows moulds and bacteria to get to work (and they do so even in the refrigerator), but also allows air, heat and light to destroy valuable nutrients. So, for the sake of your health, it is important to invest in suitable containers and to get in the habit of using them.

# storage and covers

Airtight polypropylene (plastic) boxes are essential. Buy several sizes and shapes, remembering that square and rectangular boxes make more efficient use of space than round ones. Equally useful are foil and cling film (plastic wrap), for wrapping things tightly or covering bowls. Polythene bags are invaluable for sandwiches and anything that needs gathering together in a flexible container. Glass storage jars may look attractive, but are not airtight, nor do they protect the contents from light. They are suitable only for non-perishables such as dried pasta and pulses.

### 1  ALUMINIUM FOIL
Foil is used not only to protect food and pans during cooking, but also to exclude air during storage. Being flexible, it can be wrapped tightly round any awkwardly shaped items, such as a cooked chicken. Foil also keeps sandwiches fresh and prevents loose or chunky fillings from escaping. Unlike cling film (plastic wrap) it does not cause cheese to sweat. Buy the heaviest grade possible – though cheaper, thin foil tears easily so what you save in money you waste in damaged foil.

### 2  CLING FILM/PLASTIC WRAP
Use cling film for tightly wrapping food or for covering bowls. Ordinary cling film should never be used in direct contact with very fatty foods, such as butter, high fat cheeses (e.g. Cheddar or Parmesan) or food in an oily medium (e.g. tuna in oil), as harmful substances in the cling film can migrate into the food. When covering bowls for use in a microwave, do not let cling film come in direct contact with the food unless the words 'Safe for use in the microwave' are printed on the packaging.

### 3  ALUMINIUM FOIL DISHES
Made from heavyweight aluminium foil, these are versatile containers in which to freeze, transport or reheat food. A flexible rim folds over a flat cardboard lid, which rests on the flattened edge. Though the foil containers are reusable, the perishable lids limit their useful life.

### 4  FOIL BAG
Strong and flexible, this polythene-lined foil bag is ideal for freezing liquids such as soup.

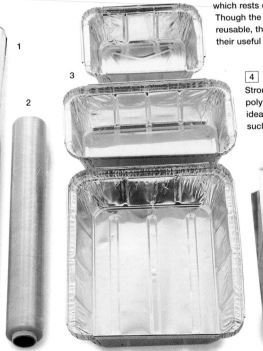

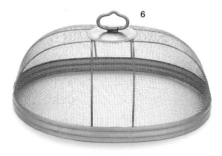

### 5 CHEESE DOME

Cheese needs a cool temperature and circulating air during storage. This attractive glass dome keeps cheese fresh and moist while it is at room temperature. The wooden base has a channel round the edge to keep the dome in place.

### MESH COVERS

6 In pre-refrigeration days, an oval wire-mesh cover was used to protect meat from dust and flies. It allowed air to circulate round the meat, keeping it fresher than a close-fitting wrapping. Nowadays you might use it for refrigerated meat that you are allowing to come to room temperature before barbecuing.

7 This square nylon food umbrella can be used as temporary protection for any food that will fit under it. It can be folded flat when not in use.

### 9 GARLIC POT

Garlic bulbs need access to air to prevent mould, and protection from light to stop premature sprouting. This pot provides both.

### 11 BUTTER DISH

A deep container is useful for protecting a block of butter while not in the fridge. This porcelain butter dish is good-looking enough to be brought to the table.

### 8 CONDIMENT JARS

These attractive jars are made of glazed stoneware and are traditionally used for potted goose and pork. Though not airtight, they do exclude light. They are best used for anything submerged in a protective liquid – such as olives in oil, or pickles in brine – and for dripping and lard. Straight sides, a wide neck and an easily removable lid make them easy to fill and reach into.

### 10 PRESERVING JAR

Certain foods will keep for months if they are vacuum packed in a sterilised container and submerged in a medium suitable for keeping bacteria at bay – acid, brine or oil, for example. This classic glass preserving jar fits the bill. It can be sterilised in the oven and has a rubber gasket and wire clip to seal the lid. The neck is wide enough for easy filling.

### 12 STAINLESS STEEL CONTAINER

This airtight container has a well-fitting lid and is useful for storing cakes, biscuits or home-made muesli. It is smart enough to keep on the work surface.

### 14 HERB KEEPER

Love fresh herbs, but hate it when they droop or turn slimy? To keep leafy herbs spriggy and fragrant they need to be kept lightly damp and well sealed in the fridge. Flimsy packs can get crushed but this tall, capacious acrylic screw-top container holds them upright and fresh for up to three weeks. At 25 cm/10 inches high it is best stored on the fridge door shelf.

13

14

15

### 13 STORAGE JARS

Acrylic, brushed stainless steel, glass or china, whatever your preferred choice of storage jar most of us like a matching set all lined up neatly as a feature on a shelf. Glass or clear acrylic means you can instantly identify the contents – beans, sugar, flours etc – but light can affect the quality of these dry goods so you need to make sure you use them frequently. Steel canisters with air tight seals are best for coffee and tea.

### 15 OIL AND VINEGAR BOTTLES

Hot and cold dishes, salads and BBQs can be enlivened with light drizzles of extra virgin olive oil or sweet-sour vinegar. Trickling from an unstoppered bottle can run the risk of swamping a dish, unless of course you are chef and can master the art of controlling the flow with a well positioned thumb. Decanting oils and vinegars into these bottles fitted with angled stoppers makes the process more controllable.

### 16 ANYLOCK BAGS

If you find sealing polythene food bags too fiddly with a wire tie or plastic clip that doesn't quite shut tight, you should find this sealing rod system an easier option. Fold over the top of a food bag once it is filled and then slide across a plastic sealing rod. The bags are strong enough to be washed (even in a dishwasher) and reused. They are also are microwaveable if the rods are first removed.

16

### 17 FOOD BOXES

Plastic, freezable food storage containers mean keen chefs can save stocks, soups and stews to use for another time. Square shapes that fit tightly together are easier and more efficient to store than rounds or ovals because they don't leave awkward spaces in between. They have a surprisingly large volume for their size. A selection of different coloured lids also makes it easier to identify the contents.

17

### 18 SALT PIG

Keeping a traditional-style ceramic pot for cooking salt next to the stove makes it easier to add pinches or small fistfuls to boiling water or bubbling stews. The wide oval mouth allows for easy access without having to look for the salt shaker.

18

19

20

### 19 HONEY POT

Drizzling honey can be a messy business and it can be tricky to regulate the flow. A wooden honey dipper with concentric rings scoops up clear honey and then releases it in a steady thin stream over toast or whatever else needs to be drizzled. The ceramic beehive design jar nicely graces breakfast and tea tables.

### 20 KITCHEN STRING HOLDER

This is one of the nicest little kitchen utensils we came across – an alderwood acorn-shaped wooden container in which you store a ball of kitchen string. No more rummaging around in a drawer. Great for cooks and gardeners alike, it would also grace a home office desk. A really special classic present – we all want one.

21

### 21 BREADBIN

You may wonder why it is worth having a bread bin when a lot of bread comes bagged, and wouldn't the fridge do? Not unless you want your bread to dry out in the cold. The best place to store bread is in a lidded bin at room temperature. This long sleek shiny bin can also be used for storing muffins, sliced toaster loaves and your favourite crusty special loaf for up to two or more days.

# sources

The following list will help you find many of the items featured in this book. Wherever possible we have given manufacturers so you can contact them to find stockists in your area (see 'manufacturers and distributors', page 330). If the manufacturers are unknown, we have given retail outlets from which the items can be bought (see page 331). A number of items were obtained from the American retailer Sur La Table, which has two retail outlets and a mail order service: www.surlatable.com

**Page**

**16–17** 1 bread knife, 2 cook's knife, 3 utility knife, 4 tomato/sandwich knife, 5 paring knife and 6 vegetable knife by Zwilling J.A.Henckels

**18–19** 1 ham/smoked salmon slicer by Sabatier; 2 freezer knife by Gustav Emil Ern; 3 filleting knife and 4 boning knife by Zwilling J.A.Henckels; 5 'universal' cheese knife and 6 Parmesan knife from David Mellor; 7 grapefruit knife by Rösle; 8 oyster knife by Wüsthof Trident;  9 carving knife and fork by Le Creuset

**20–1** 1–7 Japanese knives by Japanese Knife Co.; 8 cleaver by Global; 9 and 10 Japanese knives by Yoshikin

**22–3** 1 fabric roll from Divertimenti; 2 magnetic knife rack by Richardson Steel; 3 knife block by Victorinox; 4 magnetic knife block by Richardson Steel

**24–5** 1 V–shaped sharpener by Taylor's Eye Witness; 2 Mino whetstone from David Mellor; 3 sharpening steel by Global; 4 water–wheel sharpener by Global; 5 Duo twin sharpener by Zwilling J.A.Henckels (Dexam International)

**26–7** 1 wooden chopping board from David Mellor, polyethylene chopping board from Divertimenti; 2 endgrain chopping board from David Mellor; 3 flexible boards from Steamer Trading; 4 dual chopping board from Joseph Joseph

**36–7** 1 mezzaluna and 3 hachoir from David Mellor; 2 black mandolin by Matfer; 4 swivel peeler and 5 Lancashire peeler from David Mellor; 6 Y-shaped peeler by Good Grips; 7 peeler with potato eye gouger and 8 dual peeler by Rösle; Kyocera ceramic peeler from the Japanese Knife Co.; 10 soft fruit peeler by Zyliss; 11 mango slicer by Good Grips

**38–9** 1 cannelle knife by Rösle, 2 citrus zester from  David Mellor; 3 metal bean slicer by Porkert; 4 plastic bean slicer by Krisk; 5 pizza wheel by Rösle; 6 cheese plane by Wüsthof

Trident; 7 fish tweezers from Divertimenti; 8 fish scaler from Dexam International; 9 hard-boiled egg slicer from Kitchens; 10 chip cutter from Cook's Online; 11 meat slicer from Professional Cookware

**48–9** 1 kitchen shears from Pages; 2 kitchen scissors from David Mellor; 3 poultry shears from Kitchens; 4 apple corer and 5 courgette corers by Pedrini; 6 melon baller from Fenwicks; 7 pineapple corer/slicer by Vacu Products; 8 cherry pitter from Lakeland

**50–1** 1 bamboo skewers from Fenwicks; 2 kebab skewers, 3 potato baking spike and 4 small round skewers from Dexam International; 5 blue can opener from Lakeland; 6 chrome can opener by Pedrini; 7 'universal' opener from Lakeland; 8 bottle opener from David Mellor; 9 waiter's friend by Laguiole; 10 winged corkscrew by Pedrini; 11 screwpull corkscrew and 12 lever-based corkscrew by Screwpull® Le Creuset

**56–7** 1 citrus grater by Sveico; 2 porcelain grater from Divertimenti; 3 card grater from Steamer Trading; 4 box grater by Sveico; 5 nutmeg grater from Pages; 6 rotary grater from Lakeland; 7 Microplane® graters from Gill Wing and Lakeland

**64–5** 1 metal pepper and salt mills from Divertimenti; 2 wooden pepper and salt mills by William Bounds; 3 nutmeg mill by William Bounds; 4 Crushgrind® spice mill by T&G Woodware; electric salt and pepper mill by Peugeot; 6 upside-down spice mill by T&G Woodware

**66–7** 1 meat grinder by Porkert; 2 electric food mincing system by Cuisinart; 3 Wondermincer from Divertimenti

**68–9** 1 hand–cranked perspex coffee mill from Habitat; 1 electric coffee mill by Krups; 4 Burr grinder by Cuisinart

**70–1** 1 metal pestle and mortar and 2 ceramic pestle and mortar from Kitchens; 3 Japanese pestle and mortar from author's collection; 4 marble pestle and mortar from Divertimenti; 5 olive wood pestle and mortar from Steamer Trading; 6 granite pestle and mortar from David Mellor

**74–5** 1 tomato press from Habitat; 2 food mill and 8 potato ricer from Divertimenti; 3 garlic press by Bodum; 4 meat mallet/tenderiser and 7 potato masher by Good Grips; 5 meat mallet/tenderiser from Dexam International; 6 vegetable press from author's collection

**80–1** 1 hinged nutcracker from Divertimenti and David Mellor; 2 ratchet nutcrackers from Kitchens; 3 lobster/crab crackers from David Mellor; 4 lobster pick from Divertimenti

**82–3** 1 wooden reamer from David Mellor; 2 citrus press from Divertimenti; 3 glass lemon squeezer from David Mellor; 4 chrome citrus press from Divertimenti

**86–7** 1 basic glass bowl by Bodum; 2 Duralex 9-piece set from Lakeland; 3 stainless steel bowls by Rösle; 4 copper bowl from David Mellor; 5 ceramic bowl by Mason Cash; 6 melamine bowls by Rosti; 7 batter bowl from Cuisipro

**88–9** 1 straight–edged spoon, 2 beech spoon and 3 boxwood spoon from David Mellor; 4 long-handled wooden spoon from Pages; 5 black plastic spoon from David Mellor; 6 silicone scraper spoon from Gill Wing; 7 ice cream scoop by Zyliss; 8 scoop from David Mellor; 9 metal mixing spoon from David Mellor; 10 wire mixing spoon by Rösle

**92–3** 1 salad dressing ladle and 2 portioning ladle by Rösle; 3 soup ladle from David Mellor; 4 Chinese wok ladle by Typhoon; 5 rubber spatula and 6 plastic spatula from Divertimenti; 7 wooden spatula from David Mellor; 8 coloured plastic spatula by Le Creuset; 9 silicone spatula from Gill Wing

**96–7** 1 balloon whisk, 2 egg whisk, 3 twirl whisk, 4 spiral whisk, 5 jug whisk, 6 flat whisk and 7 saucepan whisk by Rösle; 8 ball-ended whisk and 9 rotary whisk from David Mellor; 10 aerolatte milk frother from Divertimenti

**108–9** 1 standing mixer by KitchenAid; 2 food processor by Magimix; 3 stick blender by Bamix

**110–11** 4 Le Duo juicer by Magimix; 5 blender by Waring; 6 multipurpose kitchen machine by Bosch; 7 ice cream maker by Magimix; 8 hand-held mixer by Dualit; 9 breadmaker by Panasonic

**120–1** 1 and 2 bowl–shaped sieves by Rösle; 3 chinois sieve and pestle from Pages; 4 nylon sieve from Fenwicks; 5 double mesh sieves from Lakeland

**122–3** 7 flour and sugar dredgers by George East; 6 drum sieve by T&G Woodware; 3 flour sifter by Ekco

**124–5** 1 cheesecloth from Lakeland; 2 collapsible colander by Normann Copenhagen; 3 stainless steel colander by Rösle; 4 long-handled colander from David Mellor; 5 enamel colander from Dexam International; sink strainer by Good Grips

**126–7** 1 pan drainer from Divertimenti; 2 perforated spoon from Divertimenti; 3 wire scoop, 4 tea strainer and 5 conical

strainer by Rösle; 6 vegetable scoop by Mermaid; 7 perforated skimmer from David Mellor; 8 wire skimmer from Pages; 9 noodle/pasta scoop from Divertimenti; 10 wire shaker by SEFAMA; 11 salad spinner by Guzzini

**140–1** 1–4 saucepans by All-Clad

**142–3** 1 stainless steel saucepan by Cuisinox; 2 non-stick aluminium saucepan by Berndes; 3 tri–ply pan by Le Creuset; 4 anodised aluminium milk pan by Meyer; 5 titanium pan with removable handle by SKK; 6 infused anodised saucepan by Calphalon; 7 trivet/pot stand and 8 heat diffuser from David Mellor

**144–5** 1 stockpot with pasta insert by Pentole; 2 pressure cooker by Kuhn Rikon; 3 double boiler/casserole by Pentole; 4 copper saucepan from Divertimenti; 5 preserving pan from Divertimenti; 6 slant-sided aluminium saucepan by Mermaid; 7 bain marie from Lakeland; 8 slant-sided anodised aluminium saucepan by Calphalon; 9 butter warmer by Rösle

**148–9** 1 polenta pan from Sur La Table; 2 zabaglione pan and 3 sugar boiler by Mauviel; 4 cheese fondue pot by Emile Henry; 5 fondue pot from David Mellor; 6 cataplana from Divertimenti; 7 saucier by All-Clad; 8 electric chocolate fondue maker by Russell Hobbs

**154–5** 1 3-piece steamer by Cuisinox; 2 bamboo steamers by Typhoon; 3 couscousier from Divertimenti; 4 'universal' steamer insert by Cuisinox; 5 electric steamer by Tefal; 6 rice steamer from Debenhams; 7 steaming trivet from Lakeland; 8 Christmas pudding steamer and 9 fold-out steamer by Lakeland

**156–7** 10 asparagus steamer and 11 fish kettle/poacher from David Mellor; 12 egg poacher from Lakeland

**164–5** 1 drip-filter coffee maker by Krups; 2 cappuccino creamer from Divertimenti; 3 traditional espresso maker by Pezzetti; 4 plunge-filter coffee maker from Steamer Trading; 5 Baby Gaggia coffee machine by Gaggia; 6 Nespresso coffee machine by Magimix; 7 bean-to-cup coffee machine by Jura

**166–7** 1 whistling kettle by Alessi; 2 traditional kettle by Le Creuset; 3 China teapot/tea press from Lakeland; 4 glass teapot by Bodum; 5 cordless kettle by Dualit; 6 Japanese teapot and 7 ball tea infuser from David Mellor

**170–1** 1 pot roaster and 2 braising pan by All-Clad; 3 Brittany pot and 4 enamelled Dutch oven by Le Creuset; 5 cast iron

Dutch oven and 6 brushed stainless steel casserole by Hackman; 7 non-stick casserole by SKK; 8 enamelled cast iron cookware by Lafont

**172–3** 9 Tri-ply stainless steel casserole and 10 doufeu by Le Crueset; 11 baby remoska from Lakeland; 12 mussel pot from David Mellor

**178–79** 1 bean pot/fait-tout by Emile Henry; 2 marmite and 4 round terracotta pot by Gres et Poteries de Digoin; 3 oval terrine by Emile Henry; 5 ceramic stew pot by Emile Henry; 6 earthenware potato baker by Gres et Poteries de Digoin; 7 tierra negra from Scot Columbus; 8 Tontopf pot from Lakeland

**180–1** tagine by Le Crueset; 10 puchero from Saborear; 11 cazuela from Sayell Foods

**190–1** 1 ridged square frying pan from David Mellor; 2 wok by Typhoon; 3 stainless steel sauté pan by Pentole; 4 round frying pan from David Mellor; 5 deep sauté pan by Cristel; 6 steel omelette pan by Rösle; 7 hard-anodised aluminium chef's pan by Meyer; 8 frying pan by Swiss Diamond; frying pan by All-Clad; 10 splatter screen by Ekco; 11 hard-anodised aluminium stir-fry pan by Meyer

**194–5** 1 crêpe/pancake pan and 2 oval pan by Matfer; 3 fajita pan by Calphalon; 4 small blini pan by Matfer; 5 blini/fried egg pan from David Mellor; 6 karhai (Indian wok) from William Levene; 7 paella pan by Meyer; 8 chestnut pan from Divertimenti; 9 Danish cake pan by Lodge

**202–3** 1 chip pan from Divertimenti; 2 tempura pan from Habitat; 3 potato nest fryers by Wirax; 4 electric deep-fat fryer by Magimix

**208–9** 1 blow torch by Kitchen Craft; 2 toaster by Rowlett; 3 salamander from David Mellor

**210–11** 1 reversible grill by Lodge; 9 ridged stove-top grill from David Mellor; 3 waffle iron by SEFAMA; 4 flat stove-top grill by Typhoon; 5 flat griddle from David Mellor; 6 circular wire rack from Sur La Table; 7 electric waffle pan by Cuisinart

**218–19** 1 disposable barbecue from Woolworths; 2 pedestal barbecue by SAEY; 3 hibachi barbecue from John Lewis; 4 oval portable barbecue by Lodge; 5 kettle barbecue by Weber-Stephen Products; 6 long-handled fork, turner and tongs by Good Grips, basting brush from Divertimenti; 7 wire holders from Dexam International

**224–5** 1 fish lifter from Divertimenti; 2 wok turner by Meyer; 3 fish turner by Rösle; 4 spring-action tongs from Lakeland; 5 scissor-action tongs from Divertimenti; 6 angled turner by Rösle; 7 non-stick turner from David Mellor; 8 bamboo rice paddle and fork by Typhoon; 9 turning fork by Rösle; 10 flexi turner and spatula from David Mellor; 11 paella skimmer from Saborear

**228–9** 1 enamelled self-basting roaster, 3 anodised aluminium roasting pan, 4 anodised aluminium roasting tray and 10 double oven gloves all from Lakeland; 2 lifting forks from George East; 5 stainless steel mini roasting pan from Lakeland; 6 bulb baster by Ekco; 7 oven plate from Cookrite; 8 professional quality roasting pan from Divertimenti; 9 V-shaped roasting rack from David Mellor; 11 silicone oven mitt from Lakeland

**230–1** 12 trussing needle from Pages; 13 vertical roaster and 15 porcelain fat separator from David Mellor; gravy separator by Good Grips

**242–3** 1 rectangular ceramic gratin dishes and 2 oval ceramic gratin dishes by Emile Henry; 3 porcelain soufflé dishes by Apilco; 4 enamelled cast iron egg dish and 5 enamelled cast iron baking dish by Le Creuset; 6 porcelain ramekins, 7 porcelain oval gratin dishes and 8 porcelain chocolate pots by Apilco; 9 cast iron rectangular terrine by Le Creuset; 10 aluminium pudding basins from Pages; 11 glazed earthenware basins by Mason Cash; 12 non-stick steel meat loaf pan from Sur La Table

**252–3** 1 silicone baking mould by De Buyer; 2 joined small tins from Pages; 3 foil and paper cups from Divertimenti; 4 English bun tray and 5 Yorkshire pudding tray by Kaiser; 6 popover/muffin tray from Sur La Table; 7 cooling racks from Steamer Trading

**254–5** 8 traybake tin from Lakeland; 9 square cake tin by Mermaid; 10 madeleine tray from Pages; 11 angel food cake tin from author's collection; 12 springform tin by Kaiser; 13 deep, round cake tins by Tathams Tinware; 14 Swiss roll tin by Le Creuset; 15 shallow cake tin by Kaiser

**262–3** 1 deep fluted tart tins and 2 shallow fluted tart tins by Le Creuset; 3 non-stick sponge tart tin by Kaiser; 4 tarte tatin tin by Mauviel; 5 rectangular tranche tray from David Mellor; 6 ceramic crinkle–cut pie dish from David Mellor; 7 ceramic tart-pizza dish from Divertimenti; 8 silicone tart tin by de Buyer

**264–5** 9 deep pie dish by Mason Cash; 10 pie bird by ICTC; 11 shallow pie dish from Lakeland; 12 pie plates from Sur La Table; 13 non-stick pie plate with insert from Lakeland; 14 aluminium baking sheet from David Mellor, blackened steel baking sheet by Bourgeat

**270–1** 1 dough scraper and 11 baking beans from Lakeland; 2 pastry wheel, 3 lattice cutter and 4 flexible palette knife from Pages; 5 pastry blender from Lakeland; 6 natural bristle pastry brushes by Kaiser; 7 marble pastry board, 8 crinkle pastry cutters and 10 double–ringed doughnut cutter all from David Mellor; 9 rolled edged pastry cutters from Pages

**272–3** 12 wooden pastry brush and 14 pastry cutters from David Mellor; 13 silicone pastry brushes from Absolute Form; 15 mini rolling pin from David Mellor, stainless steel rolling pin from Divertimenti and silicone-coated rolling pin from Steamer Trading

**278–9** 1 non-stick bread tins from Lakeland; 2 non-stick French bread tin from Dexam International; 3 brioche tin by Matfer; 4 silicone loaf tin from Lakeland; 5 extendable loaf tin from David Mellor

**284–5** 1 perforated pizza pan by George East; 2 pizza stone from Lakeland; 3 pizza peel/paddle from Dexam International; 4 wooden rollers, 5 pasta cutting wheels and 8 ravioli cutter from author's collection; 6 pasta machine and 7 ravioli tray by Imperia

**294–5** 1 ring moulds by Bradford Metal Spinning Co; 2 giant ice cube tray by Lékué Articulos Menaje; 3 fish mould from David Mellor; 4 bombe mould from David Mellor; 5 dariole moulds from author's collection; 6 Charlotte mould by Le Creuset; 7 heart mould from David Mellor; 8 large jelly/blancmange mould and small jelly/blancmange mould from Pages

**300–1** 1 burger press, 2 tortilla press and 5 falafel press from author's collection; 3 turnover press and 6 burger press from Lakeland; 4 shortbread mould from David Mellor; 7 rosti/food presentation rings from David Mellor; 8 food ring press by Mermaid; 9 forcing bags by Staines Catering Equipment; 10 biscuit press from Lakeland; 11 icing syringe and 12 forcing/icing nozzles by George East

**306–7** 1 balance scales from Divertimenti; 2 spring scales by Typhoon; 3 jug scales, 4 nutritional value electronic scales, 5 block digital scales and 6 infrared scales all by Salter 7 and

8 plastic measuring jugs by Stewart; 9 Pyrex measuring jug by Ekco; 10 dry measuring beaker by George East; 11 cocktail shaker by Rösle; angled measuring jug by Good Grips; 13 European measuring cups from author's collection; 14 British measuring spoons from Lakeland; 15 American measuring cups from Sur La Table; 16 flat-bottomed measuring spoons, 18 odd size measuring spoons and 19 small amounts measuring spoons from author's own collection

**312–13** 1 spirit oven thermometer by Brannan; 2 candy/fat and 3 meat thermometer from Lakeland; 4 spring–loaded oven thermometer by Kuhn Rikon; 5 fridge/freezer thermometer and 6 digital probe thermometer from Pages; 7 water/chocolate thermometer by Matfer; 8 sugar/jam thermo-meter and 10 clockwork timer from Lakeland; 9 microwave thermometer by George East; 12 electronic timer and 13 clockwork timer by Salter

**314–15** 1 jam jars and 4 disks from Lakeland; 2 wide neck funnel and 3 strainer from John Lewis

**323–4** 1 aluminium foil, 2 cling film, 3 aluminium foil dishes and 4 foil bag from Lakeland; 5 cheese dome from Divertimenti; 6 wire–mesh cover by Wirax; 7 nylon food umbrella from Lakeland; 8 condiment jars and 9 garlic pot by Renault; 10 preserving jar from Lakeland; 11 butter dish by ICTC; 12 stainless steel container by Rösle

**324–5** 13 plastic storage jars from Habitat and stainless steel jars from Conran Shopfood; 14 herb keeper from Lakeland; 15 oil and vinegar bottles from Habitat; 16 anylock bags, 17 storage boxes and 18 salt pig from Lakeland; 19 honey pot and 20 kitchen string holder from David Mellor; 21 bread bin by Herstal

# manufacturers and distributors

This list should be used with the 'sources' list to track down particular items featured in the book. Contact manufacturers or distributors for details of your nearest stockist.

**Absolut Form**
www.absolutform.co.uk

**Aerolatte**
www.aerolatte.com

**Alessi S.p.A**
www.alessi.com

**All-Clad Metalcrafters Inc**
www.allclad.com

**Apilco**
www.apilco.com

**Bamix**
www.bamix-blender.co.uk
www.bamix-usa.com

**Berndes**
www.berndes.com
UK importer: www.ictc.co.uk

**Bodum**
www.bodum.com
www.bodum.co.uk

**Bosche**
www.bosche.com
www.bosche.co.uk

**Bourgeat**
www.borgeat.com

**S.Brannon & Sons Ltd**
www.brannonshop.co.uk

**Braun**
www.braun.com

**Calphalon Corporation**
www.calphalon.com
www.calphalon.co.uk

**Cookrite**
www.cookrite.com

**Cristel**
www.cristel.com

**Cuisinart**
www.cuisinart.com
www.cuisinart.co.uk

**Cuisinox**
www.cuisinox.com

**Cuisipro**
www.cuisipro.com

**Dexam International**
www.dexam.co.uk

**Dualit Ltd**
www.dualit.com

**De Buyer**
www.chomette.co.uk

**Ecko Housewares Co.**
www.ecko.com

**Emile Henry**
www.emilehenry.com

**Eva Solo**
www.evasolo.dk
UK importer: www.ictc.co.uk

**Gaggia**
www.gaggia.uk.com

**George East (Housewares) Plc**
www.george-east.com

**Gilberts**
www.gilberts-foodequipment.com

**Global**
www.globalknives.uk.com
UK importer:
www.grunwerg.co.uk

**Good Grips**
www.oxo.com

**Gres et Poteries de Digoin**
www.poterie-digoin-gres.com

**Gustav Emil Ern**
UK importer:
www.gilberts-foodequipment.co.uk

**Guzzini**
www.guzzini.co.uk

**Hackman**
www.hackman.fi

**Henckels**
(see Zwilling J. A. Henckels)

**Herstal**
www.herstal.dk
UK importer:
www.absolutform.co.uk

**Imperia Trading**
www.imperia.com

**ITCT**
www.ictc.co.uk

**Japanese Knife Company**
www.
japaneseknifecompany.com

**Joseph Joseph**
www.josephjoseph.com

**Jura**
www.jura.com

**W.F Kaiser & Co. GmbH**
UK importer ICTC:
www.ictc.co.uk

**Kenwood Ltd**
www.kenwood.com
www.kenwood.co.uk

**KitchenAid**
www.kitchenaid.com

**Kitchen Craft**
www.kitchencraft.co.uk

**Krups**
www.krups.com
www.krups.co.uk

**Kuhn Rikon UK Ltd**
www.kuhnrikon.co.uk

**Lékué**
www.lekueusa.com

**Laguiole**
www.laguiole.com
UK importer:
www.wineware.co.uk

**Le Creuset UK Ltd**
www.lecreuset.co.uk

**Lodge Manufacturing Company**
www.lodgemfg.com

**Lafont**
UK importer: www.jwpltd.co.uk

**Magimix**
www.magimix.com

**Mason Cash & Co. Ltd**
www.tggreen.co.uk

**Matfer**
www.matfer.com

**Mauviel**
UK importer: www.ictc.co.uk

**Mermaid**
www.mermaidbakeware.co.uk

**Metalurgica**
www.portugaloffer.com

**Meyer**
www.meyergroup.co.uk

**Microplane**
www.us.microplane.com

**Moulinex**
www.moulinex.com
www.moulinex.co.uk

**Normann Copenhagen**
www.
normann-copenhagen.com

**Panasonic**
www.panasonic.co.uk

**Pedrini**
www.pedrini.com

**Pentole**
www.pentoleagnelli.com

**Peugeot**
www.peugeotmills.co.uk

**Porkert**
www.kitchencraft.co.uk

**Renault**
www.ictc.co.uk

**Richardson Sheffield**
www.richardson-sheffield.co.uk

**Russell Hobbs**
www.russell-hobbs.com

**Rösle**
www.rosle.com
UK importers:
www.inthehaus.co.uk

**Rowlett**
www.rowlettrutland.co.uk

**Sabatier**
www.sabatier.com

**Saborear**
www.saborear.co.uk

**SAEY**
www.saey.com

**Salter**
www.salterhousewares.com

**SEFAMA**
www.vega-sefama.com

**Scot Columbus**
www.scotcolumbus.co.uk
www.tierranegra.co.uk

# uk retailers

SKK
www.chomette.co.uk

Soehnle Waagen AG
www.soehnle.com

The Stewart Company
www.stewart–solutions.co.uk

Sveico
www.sveico.se

Swiss Diamond
www.swissdiamond.com

T&G Woodware
www.tg-woodware.com

Tathams Tinware
www.tathams.co.uk

Taylor's EyeWitness
www.taylors-eye-witness.co.uk

Tefal
www.tefal.com
www.tefal.co.uk

Typhoon Products
www.typhooneurope.com

Vacu Products
www.vacuvin.nl

Victorinox
www.swissarmy.com

Waring
www.waringproducts.com

Weber-Stephen Products
(UK) Ltd
www.weber.com

William Bounds
www.wmboundsltd.com

William Levene
www.williamlevene.com

Wirax
www.wirax.co.za

Wüsthoff Trident
www.wuesthof.de

Yoshikin
www.yoshikin.co.jp

Zwilling J. A. Henckels
www.zwilling.com

Zyliss
www.zyliss.com

This is a selection of good retail outlets. The list is organised by region for ease of use, but note that many outlets offer mail order. As well as specialist shops, it is also worth trying the cookshops within department stores such as Debenhams, Fenwicks, Habitat, Conran Shop, Heals, IKEA, John Lewis, Liberty and Selfridges, some of which have branches nationwide. Lakeland is listed under Northern England but has shops throughout Britain – see entry.

LONDON AND SOUTH EAST

**Anything Left-Handed**
18 Avenue Road, Belmont,
Surrey SM2 6JD
Tel 020 8770 3722
www.anythingleft-handed.co.uk
*Knives, ladles, lifters, turners, zesters and peelers for the left-handed.*

**Aria**
295–296 Upper Street,
London N1 2TU
Tel 020 7704 1999
www.ariashop.co.uk
*An emporium for Alessi fans, carrying the full range of pans, kettles, coffee machines and other iconic items.*

**The COOKSshop @ Eynsham Emporium**
32 Mill Street, Eynsham,
Oxfordshire OX29 4JS
Tel 01865 731717
www.eynsham-emporium.co.uk
*A wide selection of high quality kitchenware. The owner is more than happy to order anything that she doesn't stock in the shop.*

**The Conran Shop**
Michelin House, 81 Fulham Road,
London SW3 6RD
Tel 020 7589 7401
55 Marylebone High Street,
London W1M 3AE
Tel 020 7723 2223
www.conran.co.uk
*Selected housewares, kitchen tools and cookware.*

**Classic Cookware**
4 Causeway Side, High Street, Haslemere,
Surrey GU27 2 JZ
Tel 01428 641415
*Popular cookshop with wide range of stock.*

**La Cuisinière,**
81–83 Northcote Road,
London SW11 6PJ
Tel 020 7223 4487
*Recommended cookshop.*

**David Mellor**
4 Sloane Square,
London SW1W 8EE
Tel 020 7730 4259
www.davidmellordesign.co.uk
*Professional kitchen tools, cookware and tableware. Mail order available.*

**Divertimenti**
227–229 Brompton Road,
London SW3 2EP
Tel 020 7581 8065
33-34 Marylebone High Street, London W1U 4PT
Tel 020 7935 0689
www.divertimenti.co.uk
*Superb range of kitchen tools, cookware, housewares and tableware.*

**Fairfax Cookshop**
1 Regency Parade
Finchley Road,
London NW3 5EQ
Tel 020 7722 7646
www.fairfaxcookshop.com
*Specialises in coffee, coffee equipment and kitchenware.*

**Kitchen Kapers**
55 Peascod Street, Windsor,
Berkshire SL4 1DE
Tel 01753 621002
www.kitchenkapers.co.uk
*A veritable Aladdin's cave, packed to the gunwales with stuff. Staff are knowledgeable and helpful. Branches in Farnham, Basingstoke, Camberley and Woking.*

**Gill Wing**
190 Upper Street,
London N1 1RQ
Tel 020 7226 5392
*Comprehensive range of kitchen tools,
cookware and bakeware.*

**Hob**
5 Brunswick Centre,
London WC1N 1AY
Tel 020 7837 8843
www.hobstore.co.uk

**Japanese Knife Company**
The Abbey Road Motorist Centre,
131–179 Belsize Road,
London NW6 4AQ
Tel 0870 240 2248
www.
japaneseknifecompany.com
*Excellent selection of Japanese knives.*

**Kooks Unlimited**
2–4 Eton Street, Richmond,
Surrey TW9 1EE
Tel 020 8332 3030
www.kooksunlimited.com
*Professional kitchen tools, cookware, cake
decorating equipment, oven-to-tableware.*

**The Kitchen Range**
162 High St, Beckenham,
BR3 1EW
Tel 020 86636323
*Recommended kitchen shop with branch
in West Wickham.*
Tel 020 87770224

**Mistral Catering Equipment,**
52 Stoke Newington High Street,
London N16 7PB.
Tel 020 7241 5070
www.mistraluk.net

**Nasons**
46–47 The High Street, Canterbury,
Kent CT1 2SB
Tel 01227 456755
www.nasons.co.uk
*Excellent range of all kinds of kitchen tools
and cookware.
Mail order available.*

**Outdoor Chef**
Alexander Rose Ltd, Alexander Road,
Burgess Hill, Sussex RH15 9LE

Tel 01444 258928
www.alexander-rose.co.uk
www.outdoorchef.net
*Gas-fired kettle barbecues with specialist
cooking systems for pizza, paella, etc.
Good range of tools and accessories. Mail
order available.*

**Pages**
121 Shaftsbury Ave,
London WC2H 8AD
Tel 0845 3734017
www.pagescatering.co.uk
*Professional kitchen tools, cookware,
catering equipment and tableware. Mail
order available.*

**Professional Cookware**
Bluewater
Lower Rose Gallery, Bluewater,
Kent DA9 9SH
Tel 01322 624324
www.cookware.co.uk
*Large number of cook shops nationwide
and comprehensive online service.*

**Sayell Foods**
71 Fanshaw Street,
London N1 6LA
Tel 020 7256 1080
www.sayellfoods.co.uk
*Specialises in Spanish food and cookware.*

**Steamer Trading**
High Street, Lewes,
East Sussex BN7 2LN
Tel 01273 487230
www.steamertrading.co.uk
*Excellent, extensive range of cookware,
tableware and kitchen tools. Currently one
of thirteen shops throughout South East
England, including Brighton, Guildford,
Dorking, St. Albans, Westerham,
Canterbury, Alfriston and Battle.*

**Whisk**
1a Devonshire Road, Chiswick,
London W4 2EU
Telephone 020 8995 8990
www.whiskcooking.co.uk
*Great selection of top quality items and
very helpful, knowledgeable staff. Also
shop in Ealing, London.*

SOUTH WEST

**Kitchens (Catering Utensils)**
4–5 Quiet Street,
Bath BA1 2JS
Tel 01225 330524
167 Whiteladies Road,
Bristol BS8 2SQ
Tel 0117 973 9614
*Comprehensive range of professional
kitchen tools, cookware and catering
equipment.*

**Owen & Simpson**
Antelope Walk, Dorchester,
Dorset DT1 1BE
Tel 01305 250050
cookshop@hotmail.com
*Long-established shop with a
comprehensive range of quality tools.*

**Richmond Cookshop**
Unit 10, Wessex Trade Centre,
Ringwood Road, Poole,
Dorset BH12 3PQ.
Tel 01202 749428
www.richmondcookshop.co.uk
*Wide range of kitchenware and an online
service.*

**Salamander**
57 High Street, Wimborne,
Dorset BH21 1HS
Tel 01202 840144
www.salamander.com

EAST ANGLIA

**Elizabeth David Cookshop**
22 Fitzroy Street,
Cambridge CB1 1EW
Tel 01223 321579
www.lecrueset.co.uk
*Cookware, kitchen tools and more.*

**Head Cook and Bottlewasher**
8 Church Street, North Walsham,
Norfolk NR28 9DA
Tel 01692 405984
www.headcook.co.uk
*Extensive range of cookware and kitchen
tools with an online service.*

**Marchants Cookware**
78-79 St John's Street, Bury St Edmunds,
Suffolk IP33 1SQ
Tel 01284 705636
www.marchantscookware.co.uk

*An Aladdin's cave of professional kitchen tools and cookware, run by cooks for cooks. Mail order available.*

## Williams and Griffin
152 High Street, Colchester,
Essex CO1 1PN
Tel 01206 571212
www.williegee.com
*Professional equipment for the home cook.*

MIDLANDS

## Abraxas Cookshop
Heart of the Shires Shopping Village,
nr Brockhall, Weedon,
Northamptonshire NN7 4LB
Tel 01327 342335
www.abraxascookshop.com
*Excellent range of professional kitchen tools and cookware, based in a converted farm complex.*

## Ceci Paolo
The New Cook's Emporium,
21 High Street, Ledbury,
Herefordshire HR8 1DS
Tel 01531 632976
*Very good selection of quality products and books. Also runs cookery classes.*

## Cheltenham Kitchener
4 Queen's Circus, Cheltenham,
Gloucestershire GL50 1RX
Tel 01242 235688
*Professional kitchen tools, cookware and catering equipment. Mail order available.*

## David Mellor Country Shop
The Round Building, Hathersage,
Hope Valley, Sheffield S32 1BA
Tel 01433 650220
*See entry under London and South East.*

## Elizabeth David Cookshop
51 Mill Lane, Solihull,
West Midlands B91 3AT
Tel 0121 709 2302
www.lecrueset.co.uk
*Wide selection of cookware and tools.*

## Kirklands The Cookshop
North Walls, Stafford,
Staffordshire ST16 3AD
Tel 01785 259960
www.kirklands.co.uk
*Professional tools and cookware for the home cook. Also a branch in Stoke.*

## The Original Cookware Company
8 Silver Walk, St Martin's Square,
Leicester LE1 5EW
Tel 0116 251 2842
www.originalcookware.co.uk
*Professional tools and cookware for the home cook.*

## Robert Welch Studio Shop
Lower High Street,
Chipping Campden,
Gloucestershire GL55 6DY
Tel 01386 840522
19 Old Square, Warwick CV34 4RU
Tel 01926 400422
www.welch.co.uk
*Ironware, glassware and cookware. Mail order available.*

NORTHERN ENGLAND

## Barkers
198–202 High Street, Northallerton,
North Yorkshire DL7 8LP
Tel 01609 772303
www.barkers-northallerton.co.uk
*Department store with very large selection of items for the kitchen.*

## Lakeland Ltd
Alexandra Buildings, Windermere,
Cumbria LA23 1BQ
Tel 015394 88100
www.lakelandlimited.co.uk
*Outstanding mail order company selling an enormous range of kitchen tools, cookware, tableware and housewares. Currently have 34 shops throughout the country.*

## Peter Maturi and Sons
84–86 Vicar Lane,
Leeds LS1 7JH
Tel 0113 245 3887
www.maturionline.co.uk
*Professional kitchen tools and cookware with good range of knives.*

SCOTLAND

## The Cook's Shop
46–48 High Street, Banchory,
Grampian AB31 5SR
Tel 01330 825511
www.cookware-online.co.uk
*A specialist shop for the enthusiastic cook.*

## Studio One Cookshop
71 Morningside Road,
Edinburgh EH10 4AY
Tel 0131 447 0452
*Professional kitchen tools and cookware for the home cook.*

WALES

## Kitchens (Catering Utensils)
14 High Street, Cardiff CF10 1AX
Tel 02920 229814
*See entry under South West.*

## Peppercorns
5 King Street, Llandeilo,
Carmarthenshire SA19 6BA
Tel 01558 822410
www.peppercorn.net
*Professional kitchen tools and cookware.*

IRELAND

## Brown, Thomas and Co.
88–95 Grafton Street, Dublin 2
Tel 353 (0)1 605 6666
www.brownthomas.com
*Department store with kitchen tools and cookware section.*

## Captain Cook's Homestore at Moores
9–11 Church Street, Coleraine,
Londonderry
Tel 028 7034 4444
*American-style cookshop selling a wide range of professional kitchenware for the home cook. Also branches at Ballymena, Lisburn, Portadown, Portrush.*

## La Cucina
63 High Street, Holywood,
County Down BT18 9AQ
Tel 028 9042 2118
*Professional kitchen tools and cookware for the home cook.*

## Kitchen Complements
Chatham House, Chatham Street,
Dublin 2
Tel 353 (0)1 677 0734
www.kitchencomplements.ie
*Well-presented cook shop with online service*

# us retailers

### NORTHEAST

**A Cook's Wares**
www.cookswares.com

**ABC Carpet & Home**
www.abchome.com

**Bridge Kitchenware**
www.bridgekitchenware.com

**Broadway Panhandler**
www.broadwaypanhandler.com

**Fante's**
www.fantes.com

**Gracious Home**
www.gracioushome.com

**Kitchen, Etc.**
www.kitchenetc.com

**Korin Japanese Trading Corp.**
www.korin.com

### SOUTHEAST

**Campbell's Gourmet Cottage**
www.gourmetcottage.com

**Complements to the Chef**
www.complementstothechef.com

**Metropolitan Kitchen**
www.metrokitchen.com

**Rolling Pin Kitchen Emporium**
www.rollingpin.com

### MIDWEST

**Kitchen Glamor**
www.kitchenglamor.com

**The Kitchen Port**
www.kitchenport.com

**Kitchen Tools and Skills**
www.kitchentoolsandskills.com

**Kitchen Window**
www.kitchenwindow.com

**Pickles, Peppers, Pots & Pans**
www.p4Online.com

### SOUTHWEST

**Chefstore**
www.chefstore.com

**Cooking**
www.cooking.com

**Dorothy McNett's Place**
www.happycookers.com

**Homechef**
www.homechef.com

**Kitchen Classics**
www.kitchen-classics.com

**Peppercorn**
www.peppercorn.com

**Sur la Table (also in Northwest)**
www.surlatable.com

### NORTHWEST

**Kitchen Kaboodle**
www.kitchenkaboodle.com

**Reed & Cross**
www.reedcross.com

### NATIONAL CHAINSTORES

**Bed, Bath & Beyond**
www.bedbathandbeyond.com

**Crate & Barrel**
www.crateandbarrel.com

**Dean & Deluca**
www.deandeluca.com

**Dillards**
www.dillards.com

**Kitchen Collection**
www.kitchencollection.com

**Linen 'n Things**
www.Lnthings.com

**Williams-Sonoma**
www.williams-sonama.com

### SELECTED WEBSITES FOR ONLINE SHOPPING

www.amazon.co.uk

www.armorica.co.uk

www.blueshoots.com

www.boswellsofoxford.co.uk

www.chefscatalog.com

www.chefresource.com

www.cheftools.com

www.cutleryandmore.com

www.cooking.com

www.cookingcompany.com

www.cooks-knives.co.uk

www.cookshops.com

www.cookware-online.co.uk

www.cooksparaphernalia.co.uk

www.cookingtreasures.com

www.cookware.co.uk

www.cucinadirect.com

www.decuisine.co.uk

www.gourmetcook.co.uk

www.gourmetwarehouse.com

www.grandgourmet.com

www.kitchenshoppe.com

www.kitchenemporium.com

ww.kitchenware.co.uk

www.kitchkof.com

www.lakeland.co.uk

www.marthabymail.com

www.pots-and-pans.co.uk

www.cookware.co.uk

www.richmondcookshop.co.uk

www.salamandercookshop.com

# index of recipes and chefs

# author's acknowledgements

Producing this book was a highly complex project and many people were involved in making it happen. I would like to thank Jacqui Small for publishing this new expanded edition, and managing editors Kate John and Judith Hannam for steering the project through what were, at times, choppy waters.

Particular thanks go to food writer friends Nicola Graimes, Roz Denny and Susan Campbell: Nicola for the mammoth task of sourcing tools and cookware, Roz for writing new techniques and captions, and Susan for kindly allowing me to use information from her own book *The Cook's Companion*.

I remain deeply indebted to the late Robert Welch for his help and support with the first version of the book.

My appreciation and thanks also to the many chefs and food writers who kindly contributed recipes; to Janet James for designing such a beautiful book; to Alice Hart and Victoria Allen for inspired styling of food and props; and to David Munns and Mark Williams for the photography.

# publisher's acknowledgements

With thanks and appreciation to the chefs and writers who contributed recipes and to the retailers, Habitat, Conran Shop, Divertimenti, David Mellor, Steamer Trading, Sayell Foods, Lakeland and Gill Wing for lending numerous items for photography as well as for their help and advice. Thanks also to The Japanese Knife Company, Richardson Steel, Dexam International, All-clad Metalcrafters, Global, Rösle, Professional Cookware, Wine Cellar (laguiole), Peugeot, Oxo Good Grips, T. & G. Woodware, Cuisinart, Magimix, Dualit, Panasonic, Mermaid, Waring, Le Crueset, Fairfax Engineering (Calphalon, Jura), Tefal, Lafont, Gaggia, Salton Europe (Russell Hobbs), Scot Columbus (tierra negra), Saborear, Meyer, Cookrite, Rowlett, Kitchen Craft, Chomette (SKK), Herstal (Absolut Form), Salter, Gilberts Catering Company

In particular we would like to thank the following for contributing recipes to this book:

Darina Allen: raspberry and cassis preserve, © Darina Allen 2007

Monisha Bharadwaj: saibhaji, dilled vegetables, from *India's Vegetarian Cooking – A Regional Guide*, Kyle Cathie © Monisha Bharadwaj 2006

Garlton Blackiston: roast leg of spring lamb, studded with garlic and rosemary, © Garlton Blackiston 2007

Raymond Blanc: scallop and shiitake stir-fry, from *Blanc Vite*, Headline, © Raymond Blanc 1998

Sam and Sam Clark: falafel, from *Moro the Cookbook*, Ebury Press © Sam and Sam Clark 2001

Alain Ducasse: chicken stock, pumpkin and girolle soup, from *Ducasse Flavours of France, Artisan*, © Alain Ducasse 1998

Jill Dupliex: risotto with red wine and sausages, © Jill Dupliex 2000

Bobby Flay: black bean mango salsa, © Bobby Flay 2007

Paul Gayler: cannellini bean soup with fontina gremolata, from *A Passion for Cheese*, Kyle Cathie, © Paul Gayler 2007; pizza with wild mushrooms and fontina, from *World Breads*, Jacqui Small © Paul Gayler 2006; rubs, from *Steak*, Jacqui Small © Paul Gayler 2006

Nicola Graimes: apple and carrot juice; orchard fruit juice; banana and cardamom smoothie; double lemon muffins; mocha brownies; strawberries and cream smoothie, © Nicola Graimes 2007

Peter Gordon: slightly smoky grilled quails, from *Cooking at Home with Peter Gordon*, Hodder & Stoughton, © Peter Gordon 1999

Bill Granger: easy lime delicious, © William Granger 2007

Sam Hart : paella, © Sam Hart 2007

Marcella Hazan: ricotta and mint tortelloni, from *Marcella Cucina*, Macmillan, © Marcella Hazan 1997

Ken Hom: Hong Kong-style broccoli and baby corn, © Ken Ham 2000

Mark Hix: chicken with vegetables in a pot, © Mark Hix 2007

Stephen Jackson: brioche, © Stephen Jackson 2007

Madhur Jaffrey: chicken in red pepper sauce, from *Madhur Jaffrey's Quick and Easy Cookery Course*, BBC Books, © Madhur Jaffrey 1997

Emi Kazuko: modern tuna nigiri, from *New Sushi*, Jacqui Small, © Emi Kazuko 2006; ramen with pork and vegetables, © Emi Kazuko 2000

Christine Manfield: passion fruit curd, © Christine Manfield 2007

Jamie Oliver: pork and crackling, from *The Naked Chef*, Michael Joseph, © Jamie Oliver 1999

Sri Owen: spring rolls, © Sri Owen 2007

Roger Pizey: bakewell tart, from *Small Cakes*, Jacqui Small, © Roger Pizey 2007

Wolfgang Puck: barbecue seafood skewers, © Wolfgang Puck 1993

Claudia Roden: chicken tagine with preserved lemons, from *Tamarind & Saffron*, Penguin Books, © Claudia Roden 1999

Ruth Rogers and Rose Gray: grilled squid with chillies, from *The River Café Cookbook*, Ebury, © Ruth Rogers and Rose Gray 1995

Michel Roux: pot-roast chicken with beer and mushrooms, © Michel Roux 2007

Chris and James Tanner: vanilla soufflé with chocolate sauce, white chocolate and chilli ice cream, from *For Chocolate Lovers*, Jacqui Small, © James and Chris Tanner 2006

Eric Treuille and Ursula Ferrigno: Swedish dill bread, from *Bread*, Dorling Kindersley, © Eric Treuille and Ursula Ferrigno 1998

Charlie Trotter: academia nut-crusted chicken breasts with lemon grass-coconut emulsion, © Charlie Trotter 2000

Mich Turner: lemon and lime roulade, from *Fantastic Party Cakes*, Jacqui Small, © Mich Turner 2007; moist carrot cake, from *Spectacular Cakes*, Jacqui Small, © Mich Turner 2005

Das Sreedharan: coconut vegetable stew, © Das Sreedharan 2000

Alice Waters: fresh shell bean gratin, from *Chez Panisse Vegetables*, HarperCollins, © Alice Waters 1996. Reprinted by permission of HarperCollins Publishers, Inc.

Anne Willan: summer squash salad, from *Burgundy*, Weidenfeld and Nicholson, © Anne Willan 2000

Paula Wolfert: Tunisian couscous with greens, red pepper and garlic, from *Mediterrean Cooking* (revised edition) HarperPerennial © Paula Wolfert 1994

Aldo Zilli: mussels diablo, from *Fish Cook*, Jacqui Small, © Aldo Zilli 2006